Wiley Study Guide for 2015 Level I CFA Exam

Volume 4: Corporate Finance, Portfolio Management & Equity

Thousands of candidates from more than 100 countries have relied on these Study Guides to pass the CFA® Exam. Covering every Learning Outcome Statement (LOS) on the exam, these review materials are an invaluable tool for anyone who wants a deep-dive review of all the concepts, formulas and topics required to pass.

Originally published by Elan Guides, this study material was produced by CFA® Charterholders, CFA® Institute members, and investment professionals. In 2014 John Wiley & Sons, Inc. purchased the rights to Elan Guides content, and now this material is part of the Wiley Efficient Learning suite of exam review products. For more information, contact us at info@efficientlearning.com.

Wiley Study Guide for 2015 Level I CFA Exam

Volume 4: Corporate Finance, Portfolio Management & Equity

WILEY

Contents

LESSON 1: CAPITAL BUDGETING

Capital budgeting is the process that companies use for making long-term investment decisions (e.g., acquiring new machinery, replacing current machinery, launching new products, and spending on research and development). Capital budgeting is very important because:

- A significant amount of capital is usually tied up in long-term projects. The success of these investments has a significant influence on the future prospects of the company.
- The principles of capital budgeting can also be used in making other operating decisions (e.g., investments in working capital and acquisitions of other companies).
- The valuation principles used in capital budgeting are also applied in security analysis and portfolio management.
- Sound capital budgeting decisions maximize shareholder wealth.

LOS 35a: Describe the capital budgeting process, including the typical steps of the process, and distinguish among the various categories of capital projects.
Vol 4, pp 6–7

The steps typically involved in the capital budgeting process are as follows:

1. Generating ideas: Generating good investment ideas is the most important step in the process. These ideas can be generated from any part of the organization or even from sources outside the company.

2. Analyzing individual proposals: This step involves collecting information to forecast the cash flows of a particular project as accurately as possible. Cash flows are then used to evaluate the feasibility of the project.

3. Planning the capital budget: Projects that are undertaken should fit into the company's overall strategy. Further considerations include the timing of the project's cash flows and availability of company resources.

4. Monitoring and post-auditing: In this step, actual performance is compared to forecasts and the reasons behind any differences are sought. Post-auditing helps monitor the forecasts to improve their accuracy going forward *and* to improve operations to make them more efficient. Concrete ideas for future investments may also abound from this step.

Capital budgeting projects can usually be classified into the following categories:

1. Replacement projects: These projects help in maintaining the normal course of business and do not usually require very thorough analysis. For example, if a piece of equipment becomes obsolete, the decision whether to replace it usually does not require detailed analysis. Replacement decisions that involve replacing existing equipment with more efficient equipment, or with newer technology, usually require more detailed analysis.

2. Expansion projects: These are projects that increase the size of the business. Expansion decisions require more careful consideration compared to simple replacement projects because there are more uncertainties involved.

3. New products and services: Venturing into new products and services brings added uncertainties to the firm's overall operations. These decisions require extremely detailed analysis along with the participation of a lot more people in the decision making process.

4. Regulatory, safety, and environmental projects: These projects are sometimes made mandatory by a governmental agency or some external party. They might not generate any revenues themselves, but may accompany other revenue-generating projects undertaken by the company. Sometimes however, the cost of these obligatory projects is so high that the company may be better off shutting down operations altogether or just closing the part of the business that is related to the project.

5. Other projects: Some projects cannot be analyzed through capital budgeting techniques. They could be pet projects of senior management and so needless or so risky that they are difficult to evaluate and justify using the typical assessment methods. An example of such a decision is the acquisition of a new private jet by the CEO of a company.

LOS 35b: Describe the basic principles of capital budgeting, including cash flow estimation. Vol 4, pp 8–10

Let's go over some important capital budgeting concepts before moving on to the basic principles of capital budgeting.

Sunk costs are those costs that cannot be recovered once they have been incurred. Capital budgeting ignores sunk costs because it is based only on current and future cash flows. An example of a sunk cost is the market research costs incurred by the company to evaluate whether a new product should be launched.

Opportunity cost is the value of the next best alternative that is *foregone* in making the decision to pursue a particular project. For example, if we invest $1 million in a piece of equipment, the opportunity cost of investing in that piece of equipment is the amount that $1 million would have earned in its next most profitable use. Opportunity costs should be *included* in project costs.

An incremental cash flow is the additional cash flow realized as a result of a decision. Incremental cash flow equals cash flow with a decision minus the cash flow without the decision.

An externality is the effect of an investment decision on things other than the investment itself. Externalities can be positive or negative and, if possible, externalities should be considered in investment decision-making. An example of a negative externality is *cannibalization* as a new product reduces sales of existing products of the company.

A conventional cash flow stream is a cash flow stream that consists of an initial outflow followed by a series of inflows. The sign of the cash flows changes only once. For a nonconventional cash flow stream however, the initial outflow is not followed by inflows only, but the direction of the flows change from positive to negative again. There is more than one sign change in a nonconventional cash flow stream.

The basic principles (assumptions) of capital budgeting are:

1. **Decisions are based on actual cash flows:** Only incremental cash flows are relevant to the capital budgeting process, while sunk costs are completely ignored. Analysts must also attempt to incorporate the effects of both positive and negative externalities into their analysis.

2. **Timing of cash flows is crucial:** Analysts try to predict exactly when cash flows will occur, as cash flows received earlier in the life of the project are worth more than cash flows received later.

3. **Cash flows are based on opportunity costs:** Projects are evaluated on the incremental cash flows they bring in, over and above the amount they would generate in their next best alternative use (opportunity cost).

4. **Cash flows are analyzed on an after-tax basis:** The impact of taxes on cash flows is always considered before making decisions.

5. **Financing costs are ignored from calculations of operating cash flows:** Financing costs are reflected in the required rate of return from an investment project, so cash flows are not adjusted for these costs. If financing costs were also included in the calculation of net cash flows, analysts would be counting them twice. Therefore, they focus on forecasting operating cash flows and capture costs of capital in the discount rate.

6. **Accounting net income is not used as cash flows for capital budgeting** because accounting net income is subject to noncash charges (e.g., depreciation) and financing charges (e.g., interest expense).

LOS 35c: Explain how the evaluation and selection of capital projects is affected by mutually exclusive projects, project sequencing, and capital rationing. Vol 4, pp 10–11

1. **Independent versus mutually exclusive projects.** Independent projects are those whose cash flows are unrelated. Mutually exclusive projects compete directly with each other for acceptance. If Project A and B are mutually exclusive, the firm may only accept one of them, not both.

2. **Project sequencing.** Many projects can only be undertaken in a certain order, so investing in one project creates the opportunity to invest in other projects in the future. For example, a company might invest in a project today and then invest in a second project after three years if the first project is successful and the economic scenario has not been adversely affected. However, if the initial project does not do so well, or if the economic environment is no longer favorable, the company will not invest in the second project.

3. *Unlimited funds versus capital rationing.* When the company has no constraints on the amount of capital it can raise, it will invest in all profitable projects to maximize shareholder wealth. The need for capital rationing arises when the company has limited funds to invest. If the capital required to invest in all profitable projects exceeds the resources available to the company, it must allocate funds to only the most lucrative projects to ensure that shareholder wealth is maximized.

LOS 35d: Calculate and interpret the results using each of the following methods to evaluate a single capital project: net present value (NPV), internal rate of return (IRR), payback period, discounted payback period, and profitability index (PI). **Vol 4, pp 10–18**

The two most popular measures used to evaluate a single capital project are net present value (NPV) and internal rate of return (IRR).

Net Present Value (NPV)

For a project with one investment outflow, which occurs at the *beginning* of the project, the net present value is the present value of the future after-tax cash flows minus the investment outlay. NPV measures the amount in monetary units that a project is expected to add to shareholder wealth.

$$NPV = \sum_{t=1}^{n} \frac{CF_t}{(1+r)^t} - Outlay$$

where
CF_t = after-tax cash flow at time, t.
r = required rate of return for the investment. This is the firm's cost of capital adjusted for the risk inherent in the project.
Outlay = investment cash outflow at t = 0.

Decision Rules for NPV

- A project should be undertaken if its NPV is greater than zero. Positive NPV projects increase shareholder wealth.
- Projects with a negative NPV decrease shareholder wealth and should not be undertaken.
- A project with an NPV of zero has no impact on shareholder wealth.

Example 1-1: Calculating NPV

Calculate the NPV of a capital project with an initial investment of $30 million. The project generates after-tax cash flows of $10 million at the end of Year 1, $14 million at the end of Year 2, and $18 million at the end of Year 3. The required rate of return is 10%.

Solution

$$NPV = -\$30m + \frac{\$10m}{(1.10)^1} + \frac{\$14m}{(1.10)^2} + \frac{\$18m}{(1.10)^3}$$

$$NPV = -\$30m + \$9.09m + \$11.57m + \$13.52m$$

$$NPV = \$4.184 \text{ million}$$

TI BAII Plus® calculator keystrokes:

Keystrokes	Explanation	Display
[CF][2nd][CE|C]	Clear CF Memory registers	CF0 = 0.0000
30 [+/−][ENTER]	Initial Cash Outlay	CF0 = −30.0000
[↓] 10 [ENTER]	Period 1 cash flow	C01 = 10.0000
[↓] [↓] 14 [ENTER]	Period 2 cash flow	C02 = 14.0000
[↓] [↓] 18 [ENTER]	Period 3 cash flow	C03 = 18.0000
[NPV] 10 [ENTER]	10% discount rate	I = 10
[↓] [CPT]	Calculate NPV	NPV = 4.184

The NPV rule for independent projects recommends investing in a project if the NPV is greater than zero. This project generates a positive NPV of $4.184 million so it should be undertaken.

Internal Rate of Return (IRR)

For an investment project with only one investment outlay that is made at inception, IRR is the discount rate that makes the sum of present values of the future after-tax cash flows equal to the initial investment outlay. Alternatively, IRR is the discount rate that equates the sum of the present values of all after-tax cash flows for a project (inflows and outflows) to zero. Therefore, IRR is the discount rate at which NPV equals zero.

$$\sum_{t=1}^{n} \frac{CF_t}{(1+IRR)^t} = Outlay \qquad \sum_{t=1}^{n} \frac{CF_t}{(1+IRR)^t} - Outlay = 0$$

- A company should invest in a project if its IRR is *greater* than the required rate of return. When the IRR is greater than the required return, NPV is positive.
- A company should not invest in a project if its IRR is *less* than the required rate of return. When the IRR is lower than the required return, NPV is negative.

Example 1-2: Calculating IRR

Calculate the IRR of a capital project with an initial cost of $30 million. The project generates positive after-tax cash flows of $10 million at the end of Year 1, $14 million at the end of Year 2, and $18 million at the end of Year 3. Determine whether the project should be undertaken given that the required rate of return is 10%.

Solution

$$0 = -\$30m + \frac{\$10m}{(1+IRR)^1} + \frac{\$14m}{(1+IRR)^2} + \frac{\$18m}{(1+IRR)^3}$$

IRR = **17.02%**

TI BAII Plus® calculator keystrokes:

Keystrokes	Explanation	Display
[CF][2nd][CE|C]	Clear CF Memory registers	CF0 = 0.0000
30 [+/−][ENTER]	Initial Cash Outlay	CF0 = −30.0000
[↓] 10 [ENTER]	Period 1 cash flow	C01 = 10.0000
[↓] [↓] 14 [ENTER]	Period 2 cash flow	C02 = 14.0000
[↓] [↓] 18 [ENTER]	Period 3 cash flow	C03 = 18.0000
[IRR] [CPT]	Calculate IRR	**IRR = 17.02%**

Decision: The project should be undertaken because its IRR (17.02%) is greater than the required return (10%).

Payback Period

Note that if two projects have the same payback period and identical cash flows after the payback period, the project for which cash flows within the payback period occur earlier would be preferred, as it would have a higher NPV.

A project's payback period equals the time it takes for the initial investment for the project to be recovered through after-tax cash flows from the project. All other things being equal, the best investment is the one with the shortest payback period.

Example 1-3: Calculation of Payback Period

Calculate the payback period for a project that has the following cash flows:

Year	0	1	2	3	4	5
	$	$	$	$	$	$
Cash flow	−1,000	250	300	300	400	500

Solution

First we calculate cumulative cash flows received till the end of each year:

Year	0	1	2	3	4	5
	$	$	$	$	$	$
Cumulative cash flow	−1,000	−750	−450	−150	250	750

The payback for this investment occurs somewhere between the Year 3 and Year 4, where the sign of the cumulative cash flows changes from negative to positive. As of the end of Year 3, the project still needs to recover $150 of the initial outlay. This amount is recovered from the $400 earned over Year 4. The payback period for this investment equals 3 full years plus a fraction of the fourth year. This fraction equals $150 (the amount still not recovered at the end of Year 3) divided by $400 (total amount earned during Year 4). Therefore, the payback period equals 3.375 years.

> The Professional model of the TI calculator allows you to calculate the payback period and discounted payback period directly. When NPV is displayed on the screen, repeatedly press the down arrow [↓] key until PB (payback) is displayed and then press CPT (compute).
>
> Also note that if net annual cash flows are equal, the payback period can be easily calculated by dividing project cost by the annual cash flow.

Advantages

- It is simple to calculate and explain.
- It can also be used as an indicator of *liquidity*. A project with a shorter payback period may be more liquid than one that has a longer payback period.

Drawbacks

- It ignores the risk of the project. Cash flows are *not* discounted at the project's required rate of return.
- It ignores cash flows that occur after the payback period is reached.
- It is not a measure of profitability so it cannot be used in isolation to evaluate capital investment projects. The payback period should be used along with the NPV or IRR to ensure that decisions reflect the overall profitability of the project being considered.

Discounted Payback Period

The discounted payback period equals the number of years it takes for cumulative *discounted* cash flows from the project to equal the project's initial investment outlay. A project's discounted payback period will always be *greater* than its payback period because the payback period does not discount the cash flows.

Example 1-4: Calculating the Discounted Payback Period

Assuming a discount rate of 10%, calculate the discounted payback period for a project that has the following cash flows:

Year	0 $	1 $	2 $	3 $	4 $	5 $
Cash flow	−1,000	250	300	300	400	500
Cumulative cash flow	−1,000	−750	−450	−150	250	750
Discounted cash flows	−1,000	227.27	247.93	225.39	273.21	310.46
Cumulative discounted cash flows	−1,000	−772.73	−524.80	−299.41	−26.20	284.26

Solution

$$\text{Discounted payback period} = 4 \text{ full years} + \frac{26.20}{310.46} = \textbf{4.08 years}$$

Advantage

- It accounts for the time value of money and risks associated with the project's cash flows.

Drawback

- It ignores cash flows that occur after the payback period is reached. Therefore, it does not consider the overall profitability of the project.

Average Accounting Rate of Return (AAR)

The AAR is the ratio of the project's average net income to its average book value.

$$AAR = \frac{\text{Average net income}}{\text{Average book value}}$$

Example 1-5: Calculating the Average Accounting Rate of Return

ABC Company invests $150,000 in a piece of equipment that is depreciated straight line over a 5-year period and has zero salvage value. Depreciation expense and net income for the 5 years are given in the table below. Calculate the AAR of the project.

Year	1 $	2 $	3 $	4 $	5 $
Depreciation	30,000	30,000	30,000	30,000	30,000
Net income	25,000	27,000	28,000	26,000	26,500

Solution

For the 5-year period, the **average net income** equals:

$$(25,000 + 27,000 + 28,000 + 26,000 + 26,500)/5 = \$26,500$$

The initial book value of the investment is $150,000. The book value declines (as it is depreciated) by $30,000 every year until it equals zero at the end of 5 years. The **average book value** of the asset equals the average of the beginning-of-project and the end-of-project book values:

$$(150,000 + 0)/2 = \$75,000$$

$$\text{AAR} = \frac{\text{Average net income}}{\text{Average book value}} = \frac{\$26,500}{\$75,000} = \mathbf{35.33\%}$$

Advantage
- It is easy to understand and easy to calculate.

Drawbacks
- It is based on accounting numbers and not cash flows. Accounting numbers are more susceptible to manipulation than cash flows.
- It does not account for time value of money.
- It does not differentiate between profitable and unprofitable investments accurately as there are no benchmarks for acceptable AARs.

Profitability Index

The profitability index (PI) of an investment equals the present value (PV) of a project's future cash flows divided by the initial investment.

$$\text{PI} = \frac{\text{PV of future cash flows}}{\text{Initial investment}} = 1 + \frac{\text{NPV}}{\text{Initial investment}}$$

The PI equals the *ratio* of discounted future cash flows to the initial investment. NPV equals the *difference* between discounted future cash flows and the initial investment. The PI indicates the value we receive in exchange for one unit of currency invested. It is also known as the "benefit-cost" ratio.

Decision Rules for PI

- A company should invest in a project if its PI is *greater* than 1. The PI is greater than 1 when NPV is positive.
- A company should not invest in a project if its PI is *less* than 1. The PI is less than 1 when NPV is negative.

Example 1-6: Calculating the Profitability Index

Calculate the profitability index of a capital project with an initial cost of $30 million. The project generates after-tax cash flows of $10 million at the end of Year 1, $14 million at the end of Year 2, and $18 million at the end of Year 3. The required rate of return is 10%.

Solution

$$\text{PV of future cash flows} = \frac{\$10m}{(1.10)^1} + \frac{\$14m}{(1.10)^2} + \frac{\$18m}{(1.10)^3} = \textbf{\$34.18m}$$

Initial cost = **$30m**

$$PI = \frac{\text{PV of future cash flows}}{\text{Initial investment}} = \frac{\$34.18m}{\$30m} = \textbf{1.14}$$

The project's PI is greater than 1 so the company should invest in the project.

LOS 35e: Explain the NPV profile, compare the NPV and IRR methods when evaluating independent and mutually exclusive projects, and describe the problems associated with each of the evaluation methods. Vol 4, pp 18–24

NPV Profiles

An NPV profile is a graphical illustration of a project's NPV at different discount rates. NPV profiles are downward sloping because as the cost of capital increases, the NPV of an investment falls.

Let's consider two projects, Project A and Project B. The cash flow streams for both projects are given below. For both projects, the required rate of return equals 7%.

Year	0	1	2	3	NPV	IRR
Project A	−$350,000	$425,000	$0	$0	**$47,196**	**21.43%**
Project B	−$350,000	$16,000	$16,000	$466,000	**$59,323**	**12.96%**

The NPVs of the projects at the various discount rates are listed in Table 1.

Table 1-1: Project NPVs

Discount Rate	NPV-Project A	NPV-Project B
%	$	$
0.000	75,000	148,000
5.000	54,762	82,299
7.000	47,196	59,323
8.715	**40,930**	**40,930**
10.000	36,364	27,881
12.960	26,239	0
20.000	4,167	−55,880
21.43	0	−65,712
25.000	−10,000	−88,368

The NPV profiles for the projects are illustrated in Figure 1-1. Discount rates are plotted on the x-axis and NPVs are plotted on the y-axis.

Figure 1-1: NPV Profiles

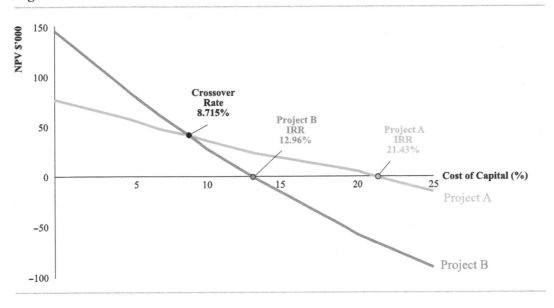

Analysis of the NPV Profiles

- The NPVs of the projects are equal at a cost of capital of 8.715%. This rate, where the NPVs of the two projects are the same and their NPV profiles intersect, is called the **crossover rate**.
- At discount rates above 8.715% (to the right of the crossover point), the NPV of Project A is greater than the NPV of Project B.
- At discount rates below 8.715% (to the left of the crossover rate), the NPV of Project B is greater than Project A.
- The NPV of Project A at a discount rate of 7% (the company's required rate of return) equals $47,196. The NPV of Project B at 7% equals $59,323.
- A project's IRR equals the discount rate at which its NPV equals 0. This means that a project's IRR is the point where its NPV profile *intersects the x-axis*. Therefore, the IRR of Project A equals 21.43% and that of Project B equals 12.96%.

> The crossover rate can be calculated by subtracting the cash flows of one project from the other and then calculating the IRR of the differences.

- Project B has higher total cash flows over its entire life. This is why it has a higher NPV at a discount rate of 0%. ($148,000 versus $75,000)
- More of Project B's cash flows come later in its life. This is the reason why the NPV profile for Project B falls faster as the cost of capital increases. At a cost of capital above 8.715%, the effect of Project B's total cash flows being higher is more than offset by the effect of its cash flows coming later.

NPV and IRR Applied to Independent Projects

If Project A and Project B were independent projects and the cost of capital were 7%, the company would accept both projects as they both have positive NPVs and their IRRs exceed the cost of capital (7%).

NPV and IRR Applied to Mutually Exclusive Projects

If the projects are mutually exclusive, the company can only choose one of them. Project A has a higher IRR (21.43% vs. 12.96%), but Project B has a higher NPV ($59,323 vs. $47,196). The conflict in recommendations is due to the *different pattern of cash flows*. Project A receives a lump sum amount of $425,000 in the first year while Project B receives equal cash flows in the first two years and then a lump sum amount of $466,000 in the third year.

When NPV and IRR rank two mutually exclusive projects differently, the *project with the higher NPV must be chosen*. NPV is a better criterion because of its more realistic reinvestment rate assumption.

IRR assumes that interim cash flows received during the project are reinvested at the IRR. This assumption is sometimes rather inappropriate, especially for projects with high IRRs. NPV on the other hand, makes a more realistic assumption that interim cash flows are reinvested at the required rate of return.

Aside from cash flow timing differences, NPV and IRR may also give conflicting project rankings because of *differences in project size*.

Consider two mutually exclusive projects, Project C and Project D, whose cash flows are given below. For both projects, the required rate of return equals 5%. The NPVs and IRRs of the projects are also included in the table below.

Project Cash Flows

Year	0	1	2	3	4	5	NPV	IRR
Project C	−1,000	500	500	500	500	500	$1,164.7	41.04%
Project D	−100,000	32,000	32,000	32,000	32,000	32,000	$38,543.3	18.03%

Note that while the NPV is theoretically the best method (as it is a direct measure of the expected increase in shareholder wealth) it has a shortcoming in that it does not account for differences in project size.

Project C has a higher IRR (41% vs. 18%) but Project D has a higher NPV ($38,543 vs. $1,165). Once again, NPV is the *better* criterion for making the investment decision. NPV represents the absolute increase in shareholder wealth attributable to a particular project. In this case, Project D should be chosen.

A project has a nonconventional cash flow pattern when the initial outflow is not followed by inflows only. The direction of cash flows changes from positive to negative over the project's life (i.e., there is *more than one sign change* in the cash flow stream). Figure 1-2 illustrates the NPV profile of a nonconventional cash flow stream that suffers from the multiple IRR problem. Notice that the NPV profile intersects the x-axis at two different points.

Figure 1-2: NPV Profile for a Project with Multiple IRRs

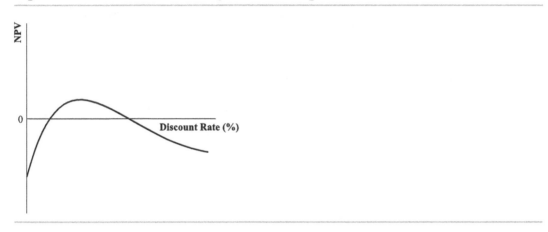

Sometimes cash flow streams have no IRR (i.e., there is no discount rate that results in a zero NPV). Figure 1-3 illustrates the NPV profile of a nonconventional cash flow stream that suffers from the "no IRR" problem. The figure also illustrates that projects with no IRRs may have positive NPVs.

Figure 1-3: NPV Profile for a Project with No IRR

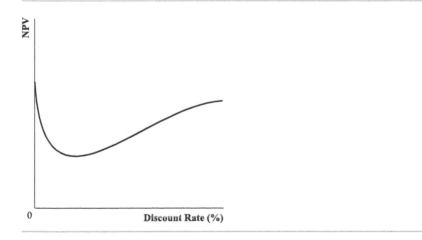

Surveys have studied the relative popularity of various capital budgeting techniques and have found that:

- The payback method is very popular in European countries.
- Larger companies prefer the NPV and IRR methods over the payback method.
- Private corporations use the payback period more often than public companies.
- Companies headed by MBAs have a preference for discounted cash flow techniques.

LOS 35f: Describe expected relations among an investment's NPV, company value, and share price. Vol 4, p 26

If a company invests in a positive NPV project, the expected addition to shareholder wealth should lead to an increase in the stock price. The following example illustrates this.

Example 1-7: NPV and its Effect on Stock Price

Freeman Corp. is planning to invest $50 million in a new project. The present value of the future after-tax cash flows from the project is estimated to be $75 million. This is new information and is independent of other expectations regarding the company. The company has 5 million shares outstanding and the market price of the company's stock is $100.

What should be the effect of the new project on:
1. The value of the company.
2. The company's stock price.

Solution

NPV of the new project
= $75 million − $50 million = $25 million

Company value before the new project
= 5 million shares × $100 = $500 million

Company value after the new project
= $500 million + $25 million = $525 million

Price/share after the new project
= $525 million/5 million shares = $105

1. The new project will have a positive effect of $25 million on the value of the company (shareholder wealth).

2. The stock price should increase to $105. The positive NPV of the new project should have a positive direct impact on its stock price.

However, the effect of a project's NPV on share prices is not as simple as shown in Example 1-7. The value of a company is determined by valuing its existing investments and adding the expected NPV of its future investments. The impact of the decision to undertake a particular project on a company's stock price will depend on how the actual profitability of the investment differs from the expected profitability of a company's investments. Expected profitability is usually already factored into current market prices.

If the profitability of a positive NPV project that the company is about to undertake is below expectations, stock prices may fall. On the other hand, certain capital projects undertaken by the company may signal that there are other potentially lucrative projects to follow. Taking on a project that brings with it the expectation of even greater future profits from subsequent opportunities may increase stock prices beyond the actual addition to the company value from said project alone.

Capital budgeting processes tell us two things about company management:

- The extent to which management pursues the goal of shareholder wealth maximization.
- Management's effectiveness in pursuit of this goal.

PRESTON RIDGE CAMPUS

READING 36: COST OF CAPITAL

Cost of capital refers to the rate of return that the suppliers or providers of capital require to contribute their capital to the firm. We can also think of the cost of capital as the opportunity cost of funds for the providers of capital. Unless the return offered by a company meets or exceeds the rate that could be earned elsewhere from an investment of similar risk, a potential supplier of capital will not provide capital to the company.

LESSON 1: COST OF CAPITAL

LOS 36a: Calculate and interpret the weighted average cost of capital (WACC) of a company. Vol 4, pp 36–37

To raise capital, a company can either issue equity or debt (some instruments may have features of both debt and equity). An instrument that is used to obtain financing is called a component, and each component has a different required rate of return, which is known as the component cost of capital. The weighted average of the costs of the various components used by the company to finance its operations is known as the weighted average cost of capital (WACC) or the marginal cost of capital (MCC). The WACC is the expected rate of return that investors demand for financing an average risk investment of the company. A company's WACC is calculated using the following formula (See Example 1-1):

$$WACC = (w_d)(r_d)(1-t) + (w_p)(r_p) + (w_e)(r_e)$$

Where:
w_d = Proportion of debt that the company uses when it raises new funds
r_d = Before-tax marginal cost of debt
t = Company's marginal tax rate
w_p = Proportion of preferred stock that the company uses when it raises new funds
r_p = Marginal cost of preferred stock
w_e = Proportion of equity that the company uses when it raises new funds
r_e = Marginal cost of equity

Example 1- 1: Calculating WACC

Axen Company's capital structure is composed of 40% debt, 5% preferred stock, and 55% common equity. Axen's before-tax cost of debt is 7%, cost of preferred equity is 8%, and cost of common equity is 10%. The company's marginal tax rate is 30%. Calculate Axen's WACC.

Solution

$$WACC = (w_d)(r_d)(1-t) + (w_p)(r_p) + (w_e)(r_e)$$

$$WACC = (0.4)(0.07)(1-0.3) + (0.05)(0.08) + (0.55)(0.10) = \mathbf{7.86\%}$$

LOS 36b: Describe how taxes affect the cost of capital from different capital sources. **Vol 4, pp 37–38**

Let's assume that a company pays $50,000 in interest for a given year. The $50,000 is an expense that the company is allowed to recognize for tax purposes to reduce taxable income. Interest expense reduces the company's profits before tax by $50,000, and assuming a 30% tax rate, reduces profits after tax by only $35,000. This is because interest expense provides a tax shield of $15,000. This tax shield is calculated as interest expense multiplied by the tax rate ($50,000 × 30% = 15,000).

Adjusting for the interest tax shield, the real after-tax cost of debt for the company is not really $50,000, but only $35,000. Tax savings are only realized on payments to holders of debt instruments. Payments to preferred and common stock holders are not expensed on the income statement and do not result in tax savings. Notice that only the cost of debt is adjusted for tax savings in the WACC formula.

LOS 36c: Explain alternative methods of calculating the weights used in the WACC, including the use of the company's target capital structure. **Vol 4, pp 38–40**

In determining the cost of capital (WACC) for a project, we would ideally want to use the weights of the various components in proportion to their employment in financing the new project. If we assume that the company has a target capital structure and will raise capital in line with its target structure, we should use the target capital structure in calculating WACC.

The target capital structure is the capital structure that the company aims to maintain. The weights used in the calculation of the WACC are the proportions of debt, preferred stock, and equity that the firm hopes to achieve and maintain in its capital structure over time. A simple way to transform a debt-to-equity ratio (D/E) into a weight is to simply divide the ratio by (1 + D/E):

$$\frac{D/E}{1+D/E} = \frac{D}{D+E} = w_d$$
$$w_d + w_e = 1$$

If information about the target capital structure is not easily available, we can use the weights in the company's current capital structure. The weights of the various components should be based on *market values*.

Another option is to examine trends in the company's capital structure over time or statements by management regarding the company's capital structure policy to estimate the target capital structure.

An analyst may also use the average weights of comparable companies' capital structures as the target capital structure for the company. See Examples 1-2 and 1-3.

Example 1-2: Calculating Capital Structure Weights

The market values of a company's sources of capital are as follows:

Bonds outstanding $10 million
Preferred stock $2 million
Common stock $38 million
Total capital   **$50 million**

Based on the firm's existing capital structure, what weights should be used to determine the company's WACC?

Solution

Weight of debt = w_d = $10 million/$50 million = 20%
Weight of preferred stock = w_p = $2 million/$50 million = 4%
Weight of common stock = w_e = $38 million/$50 million = 76%

Always check that the weights add up to 1: $w_d + w_e + w_p = 0.2 + 0.04 + 0.76 = 1$

Example 1-3: Estimating Proportions of Capital

The market value of Becker Inc.'s debt is $25 million and the market value of its equity is $35 million.
1. What is the weight of debt and equity in the company's current capital structure?
2. If the company announces that a debt-to-equity ratio of 0.6 reflects its target capital structure, what weights should be assigned to debt and equity in calculating the company's WACC?

Solution

1. Using the current capital structure:

   Weight of debt = w_d = $25 million / ($25 million + $35 million) = 0.417
   Weight of equity = w_e = $35 million / ($25 million + $35 million) = 0.583

2. The weight of debt in the target capital structure is calculated by dividing the target D/E ratio by (1 + D/E):

$$w_d = \frac{D}{D+E} = \frac{D/E}{1+D/E}$$

$$w_d = 0.6/(1+0.6)$$

$$w_d = 0.375$$

$$w_e = 1 - w_d$$

$$w_e = 1 - 0.375 = 0.625$$

A company's marginal cost of capital (MCC) *increases* as it raises additional capital. This is because most firms must pay a higher cost to obtain increasing amounts of capital. For example, the more a company borrows, the *greater* the risk that it will be unable to repay its lenders, and therefore, the *higher* the return required by investors.

The profitability of a company's investment opportunities *decreases* as the company makes additional investments. The company prioritizes investments in projects with the highest IRRs. As more resources are invested in the most rewarding projects, remaining opportunities offer lower and lower IRRs. This fact is represented by an investment opportunity schedule (IOS) that is downward-sloping.

The **optimal capital budget** occurs at the point where the marginal cost of capital intersects the investment opportunity schedule (see Figure 1-1).

Figure 1-1: Optimal Investment Decision

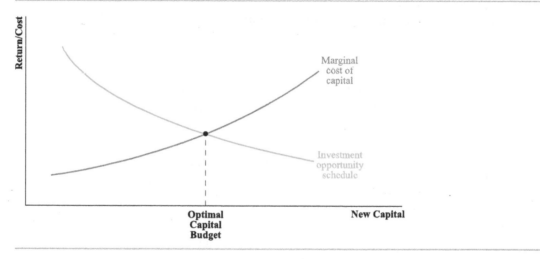

- The company should raise capital (at the given MCC) and undertake all projects (to earn the given IRR) to the left of the intersection point because these projects enhance shareholder wealth given the cost of financing them.

- To raise capital in excess of the optimal capital budget (to the right of the intersection point) the firm will be required to incur a cost of capital that is greater than the return on available investments. Undertaking these projects, given the MCC, will erode the firm's value.

LOS 36e: Explain the marginal cost of capital's role in determining the net present value of a project. Vol 4, p 41

The WACC is the discount rate that reflects the average risk of the company. When we choose WACC as the discount rate to evaluate a particular project, we assume that:

- The project under consideration is an average risk project.
- The project will have a constant capital structure (which equals the company's target capital structure) throughout its life.

The cost of capital for a particular project should reflect the risk inherent in that particular project, which will not necessarily be the same as the risk of the company's average project. If the risk of the project under consideration is above or below the average risk of the company's current portfolio of projects, an adjustment is made to the WACC. Specifically:

- If a project has *greater* risk than the firm's existing projects, the WACC is adjusted *upward*.
- If the project has *less* risk than the firm's exiting projects, the WACC is adjusted *downward*.

The WACC or MCC adjusted for the project's level of risk plays an important role in capital budgeting because it is used to calculate the project's NPV.

LESSON 2: COSTS OF THE DIFFERENT SOURCES OF CAPITAL

LOS 36f: Calculate and interpret the cost of debt capital using the yield-to-maturity approach and the debt-rating approach. Vol 4, pp 42–44

The cost of fixed rate capital is the cost of debt financing when a company issues a bond or takes a bank loan. We will discuss two approaches to estimate the before-tax cost of debt (r_d).

1. Yield-to-Maturity Approach

The bond's yield to maturity (YTM) is a measure of the return on the bond assuming that it is purchased at the current market price and held till maturity. It is the yield that equates the present value of bond's expected future cash flows to its current market price. See Example 2-1.

$$P_0 = \left[\sum_{t=1}^{n} \frac{PMT}{\left(1 + \frac{r_d}{2}\right)^t} \right] + \frac{FV}{\left(1 + \frac{r_d}{2}\right)^n}$$

This equation assumes that we are considering a semiannual-pay coupon bond so the interim cash flows are discounted at $r_d/2$.

where:
P_0 = Current market price of the bond.
PMT_t = Interest payment in period t.
r_d = Yield to maturity on BEY basis.
n = Number of periods remaining to maturity.
FV = Par or maturity value of the bond.

Example 2-1: Calculating the Cost of Debt Using the YTM Approach

Fordova Inc. issues a semiannual-pay bond to finance a new project. The bond has a 10-year term, a par value of $1,000, and offers a 6% coupon rate. Assuming that the bond is issued at $1,010.30 and that the tax rate for the company is 40%, calculate the before-tax and after-tax cost of debt.

Solution

Present value = $1,010.30
Future value = Par = $1,000
Periodic payment = 6%/2 × 1,000 = $30
Number of discounting periods = 10 × 2 = 20

$$P_0 = \left[\sum_{t=1}^{20} \frac{\$30}{\left(1 + \frac{r_d}{2}\right)^t} \right] + \frac{1{,}000}{\left(1 + \frac{r_d}{2}\right)^n}$$

Or using our calculator:

N = 20; PV = −$1,010.30; FV = $1,000; PMT = $30; CPT I/Y; I/Y = 2.931

The yield to maturity on the bond equals 2.931 × 2 = 5.862%. This is the before-tax cost of debt (r_d).

After-tax cost of debt = $r_d (1 − t)$ = 5.862 (1 − 0.4) = 3.52%

The semiannual yield is multiplied by 2 to calculate the bond's YTM on a BEY basis.

2. Debt-Rating Approach

When a reliable current market price for the company's debt is not available, the before-tax cost of debt can be estimated using the yield on similarly rated bonds that also have similar terms to maturity as the company's existing debt. See Example 2-2.

Example 2-2: Debt-Rating Approach

Alextar Inc. has a capital structure that includes AAA-rated bonds with 10 years to maturity. The yield to maturity on a comparable AAA-rated bond with a similar term to maturity is 6%. Using a tax rate of 40%, calculate Alextar's after-tax cost of debt.

Solution

Alextar's after-tax cost of debt = $r_d (1 − t)$ = 0.06(1 − 0.4) = 3.6%

When using the debt-rating approach, adjustments might have to be made to the before-tax cost of debt of the comparable company. The relative seniority and security of different issues affect ratings and yields, and these factors should be considered when selecting a comparable bond and using its before-tax cost of debt as a proxy for the cost of debt of the company being studied.

Issues in Estimating Cost of Debt

- **Fixed-rate versus floating-rate debt:** The cost of floating-rate debt is reset periodically based on a reference rate (usually LIBOR) and is therefore, more difficult to estimate than the cost of fixed-rate debt. For floating-rate bonds, analysts may use the current term structure of interest rates and term structure theory to estimate the cost of debt.

- **Debt with option-like features:** If currently outstanding bonds contain embedded options, an analyst can only use the yield to maturity on these bonds to estimate the cost of debt if she expects similar bonds (with embedded options) to be issued going forward. If however, option-like features are expected to be removed from future debt issues, she should adjust the yield to maturity on existing bonds for their option features, and use the adjusted rate as the company's cost of debt.

- **Nonrated debt:** If a company does not have any debt outstanding (to be rated) or yields on existing debt are not available (due to lack of relevant current prices), an analyst may not be able to use the YTM or the debt-rating approach to estimate the company's cost of debt.

- **Leases:** If a company uses leases as a source of finance, the cost of these leases should be included in its cost of capital.

LOS 36g: Calculate and interpret the cost of noncallable, nonconvertible preferred stock. Vol 4, pp 45–46

A company promises to pay dividends at a specified rate to its preferred stock holders. When preferred stock is noncallable and nonconvertible, has no maturity date, and pays dividends at a fixed rate, the value of the preferred stock can be calculated using the perpetuity formula.

$$V_p = D_p / r_p$$

where:
V_p = Current value (price) of preferred stock.
D_p = Preferred stock dividend per share.
r_p = Cost of preferred stock.

Rearranging this equation gives us the formula to calculate the cost of preferred stock (see Example 2-3):

$$r_p = D_p / V_p$$

Example 2-3: Determining the Cost of Preferred Stock

Shirley Inc. has outstanding preferred stock on which it pays a dividend of $10 per share. If the current price of Shirley's preference shares is $100 per share, what is its cost of preferred stock?

Solution

$$r_p = \frac{\$10}{\$100} = 10\%$$

LOS 36h: Calculate and interpret the cost of equity capital using the capital asset pricing model approach, the dividend discount model approach, and the bond yield plus risk-premium approach. Vol 4, pp 46–52

The cost of equity is the rate of return required by the holders of a company's common stock. Estimating the cost of equity is difficult due to the uncertainty of future cash flows that common stock holders will receive in terms of their amount and timing.

Three approaches are commonly used to determine the cost of common equity.

1. Capital Asset Pricing Model (CAPM)

The capital asset pricing model (CAPM) states that the expected rate of return from a stock equals the risk-free interest rate plus a premium for bearing risk. See Example 2-4.

> We will learn more about the CAPM in Reading 43.

$$r_e = R_F + \beta_i[E(R_M) - R_F]$$

where
$[E(R_M) - R_F]$ = Equity risk premium.
R_M = Expected return on the market.
β_i = Beta of stock. Beta measures the sensitivity of the stock's returns to changes in market returns.
R_F = Risk-free rate.
r_e = Expected return on stock (cost of equity)

Example 2-4: Using CAPM to Estimate the Cost of Equity

Becker Inc.'s equity beta is 1.3. The risk-free rate is 6% and the equity risk premium stands at 10%. What is Becker's cost of equity using the CAPM approach?

Solution

$$r_e = R_F + \beta_i[E(R_M) - R_F]$$
$$r_e = 0.06 + 1.3\,(0.10) = 0.19 \text{ or } 19\%$$

The equity market risk premium, $(R_M - R_F)$ can be estimated using a **survey approach** where the average of the forecasts of financial experts is adjusted for the specific stock's systematic (nondiversifiable) risk. We will learn about systematic and unsystematic risks in the Portfolio Management section.

2. Dividend Discount Model Approach

The dividend discount model asserts that the value of a stock equals the present value of its expected future dividends. We will use the constant-growth dividend discount model, (also known as a Gordon growth model) in which dividends grow at a constant rate, to determine the cost of equity. While this model is studied in greater detail in Reading 50, at this stage we just need to know the following equation, which is used to calculate the price of a stock assuming a constant growth rate in dividends:

$$P_0 = \frac{D_1}{r_e - g}$$

where:
P_0 = current market value of the security.
D_1 = next year's dividend.
r_e = required rate of return on common equity.
g = the firm's expected constant growth rate of dividends.

Rearranging the above equation gives us a formula to calculate the required return on equity:

$$r_e = \frac{D_1}{P_0} + g$$

The growth rate, g, is a very important variable in this model. There are two ways to determine the growth rate. See Example 2-5.

1. Use the forecasted growth rate from a published source or vendor.

2. Calculate a company's sustainable growth rate using the following formula:

$$g = \left(1 - \frac{D}{EPS}\right) \times (ROE)$$

Where $(1 - (D/EPS))$ = Earnings retention rate

We will discuss the calculation of the retention rate in Equity section.

Example 2-5: Dividend Discount Model Approach

Diamond Inc. has an earnings retention rate of 60% and a return on equity of 20%. Its next year's dividend is forecasted to be $2 per share and the current stock price is $40. What is the company's cost of equity?

Solution

$$g = (\text{Earnings retention rate}) \times (\text{ROE}) = 60\% \times 20\% = 12\%$$

$$\text{Cost of equity} = r_e = \frac{D_1}{P_0} + g$$

$$r_e = \frac{2}{40} + 0.12 = 17\%$$

3. Bond Yield Plus Risk Premium Approach

The bond yield plus risk premium approach is based on the assumption that the cost of capital for riskier cash flows is higher than that of less risky cash flows. Therefore, we calculate the return on equity by adding a risk premium to the before-tax cost of debt. See Example 2-6.

$$r_e = r_d + \text{risk premium}$$

Example 2-6: Cost of Equity Using the Bond Yield Plus Risk Premium Approach

The yield to maturity on Graf Inc.'s long-term debt is 9%. The risk premium is estimated to be 6%. Calculate Graf's cost of equity.

Solution

$$r_e = r_d + \text{risk premium}$$

$$r_e = 9\% + 6\% = 15\%$$

Each of the three approaches to determine a company's cost of equity usually gives a different value. Analysts must use their judgment to decide which model is appropriate to compute a particular company's cost of equity.

LESSON 3: TOPICS IN COST OF CAPITAL ESTIMATION

LOS 36i: Calculate and interpret the beta and cost of capital for a project. Vol 4, pp 52–58

An analyst must estimate a stock's beta when using the CAPM approach to estimate a company's cost of equity. Beta can be calculated by regressing the company's stock's returns against market returns over a given period. The results of the regression will be in the following format:

$$R_i = a + bR_{mt}$$

where:

a = Estimate of the intercept.

b = Estimated slope of the regression (Beta).

R_i = The company's stock's returns.

R_{mt} = Market returns over the given period.

Beta estimates are sensitive to many factors and the following issues should be considered when determining beta:

- Beta estimates are based on historical returns and are therefore sensitive to the length of the estimation period.
- Smaller standard errors are found when betas are estimated using small return intervals (such as daily returns).
- Betas are sensitive to the choice of the market index against which stock returns are regressed.
- Betas are believed to revert toward 1 over time, which implies that the risk of an individual project or firm equals market risk over the long run. Due to "mean reversion," smoothing techniques may be required to adjust calculated betas.
- Small-cap stocks generally have greater risks and returns compared to large-cap stocks. Some experts argue that the betas of small companies should be adjusted upward to reflect greater risk.

While it is fairly simple to use regression to estimate betas for publicly listed companies, (given the ease of access to stock and market return data) determining betas for nonlisted companies or individual projects is quite difficult.

A company or project's beta is exposed to the following systematic (nondiversifiable) risks:

- Business risk comprises of sales risk and operating risk. Sales risk refers to the unpredictability of revenues and operating risk refers to the company's operating cost structure.
- Financial risk refers to the uncertainty of profits and cash flows because of the use of fixed-cost financing sources such as debt and leases. The greater the use of debt financing, the greater the financial risk of the firm.

Analysts use the pure-play method to estimate the beta of a particular project or of a company that is not publicly traded. This method requires adjusting a comparable publicly-listed company's beta for differences in financial leverage.

- First we find a comparable company that faces similar business risks as the company or project under study and estimate the equity beta of that company. Betas vary with the level of financial risk in a company. Highly leveraged companies have higher financial risk, which is reflected in their high equity betas.

- To remove all elements of financial risk from the comparable's beta we "unlever" the beta. This unlevered beta reflects only the business risk of the comparable and is known as *asset beta*.

- Finally, we adjust the unlevered beta of the comparable for the level of financial risk (leverage) in the project or company under study.

We use the following formula to estimate the asset beta for the comparable publicly traded firm:

Reflects only business risk of the comparable company. Therefore it is used as a proxy for business risk of the project being studied.

Reflects business and financial risk of comparable company.

$$\beta_{ASSET} = \beta_{EQUITY}\left[\dfrac{1}{1+\left((1-t)\dfrac{D}{E}\right)}\right]$$

where:

D/E = Debt-to-equity ratio of the comparable company.

t = Marginal tax rate of the comparable company.

To adjust the asset beta of the comparable for the capital structure (financial risk) of the project or company being evaluated, we use the following formula (see Example 3-1):

Reflects business and financial risk of the project.

Reflects business risk of project.

$$\beta_{PROJECT} = \beta_{ASSET}\left[1+\left((1-t)\dfrac{D}{E}\right)\right]$$

where:

D/E = Debt-to-equity ratio of the subject company.

t = Marginal tax rate of the subject company.

Example 3-1: Calculation of a Project's Beta and WACC

Rukaiya Inc. is considering an investment in the confectionaries business. Rukaiya has a D/E ratio of 1.5, a before-tax cost of debt of 6%, and a marginal tax rate of 35%. Tastelicious Foods is a publicly traded company that operates only in the confectionaries industry and has a D/E ratio of 2, an equity beta of 0.7, and marginal tax rate of 40%. The risk-free rate is 4.5% and the expected return on the market is 11%. Calculate the appropriate WACC that Rukaiya should use to evaluate the risk of entering the confectionaries business.

Solution

First we calculate Tastelicious Foods' (the reference company's) unlevered (asset) beta, which eliminates the impact of financial risk, and only reflects the business risk of the confectionaries industry.

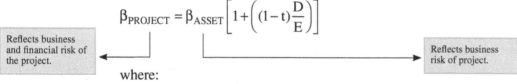

$$\beta_{ASSET} = \beta_{EQUITY}\left[\dfrac{1}{1+\left((1-t)\dfrac{D}{E}\right)}\right]$$

$$\beta_{ASSET} = 0.7\left[\dfrac{1}{1+((1-0.4)2)}\right] = 0.318$$

Then we "relever" the reference company's beta to reflect Rukaiya's financial risk:

$$\beta_{PROJECT} = \beta_{ASSET}\left[1+\left((1-t)\frac{D}{E}\right)\right]$$

$$\beta_{PROJECT} = 0.318\{1+[(1-0.35)1.5]\} = 0.628$$

Finally, we use the project's cost of equity and the component weights to calculate the WACC of Rukaiya's confectionaries project:

$$\text{Cost of equity} = r_e = 4.5\% + 0.628\,(11\% - 4.5\%) = 8.582\%$$

Rukaiya's D/E ratio is given as 1.5. It has 1.5 units of debt for every unit of equity (the denominator of the D/E ratio is 1). The ratio of debt to equity is 1.5 to 1, or 3:2. The weight for debt in the capital structure is therefore 3/(3+2) or 0.6 [(D/D+E)] and that of equity is 2/(3+2) or 0.4 [E/(D+E)].

$$WACC = (w_d)(r_d)(1-t)+(w_p)(r_p)+(w_e)(r_e)$$

$$WACC = 0.6(0.06)(1 - 0.35) + 0.4(0.08582) = 5.77\%$$

LOS 36j: Describe uses of country risk premiums in estimating the cost of equity. Vol 4, pp 58–60

Studies have shown that a stock's beta captures the country risk of a stock accurately only in developed markets. Beta does not effectively capture country risk in developing nations. To deal with this problem, the CAPM equation for stocks in developing countries is modified to add a country spread (also called the country equity premium) to the market risk premium.

$$r_e = R_F + \beta\,[E(R_M) - R_F + CRP]$$

The country risk premium (CRP) is calculated as the product of sovereign yield spread and the ratio of the volatility of the developing country's equity market to the volatility of the sovereign bond market denominated in terms of the currency of a developed country. The sovereign yield spread is the difference between the developing country's government bond yield (denominated in the currency of a developed country) and the yield of a similar maturity bond issued by the developed country.

Country risk premium	=	Sovereign yield spread	×	Annualized standard deviation of equity index
				Annualized standard deviation of sovereign bond market in terms of the developed market currency

The sovereign yield spread captures the general risk of an investment in a particular country. This spread is then adjusted for the volatility of the stock market relative to the bond market. See Example 3-2.

Example 3-2: Using Country Risk Premium to Estimate the Cost of Equity

An analyst wants to calculate the cost of equity for a project in Malaysia. She has the following information:

- The yield on Malaysia's dollar-denominated 10-year government bond is 10%.
- The yield on a 10-year U.S. Treasury bond is 4.2%.
- The annualized standard deviation of Malaysia's stock market is 29%.
- The annualized standard deviation of Malaysia's dollar-denominated 10-year government bond is 20%.
- The project's beta equals 1.1.
- The expected return on the Malaysian equity market is 9%.
- The risk-free rate equals 5%.

Calculate the country risk premium and the cost of equity for this project in Malaysia.

Solution

$$CRP = (0.10 - 0.042)\left(\frac{0.29}{0.20}\right) = 8.41\%$$

$$r_e = R_F + \beta\,[E(R_M) - R_F + CRP]$$

$$r_e = 0.05 + 1.1\,[0.09 - 0.05 + 0.0841] = \mathbf{18.65\%}$$

Malaysia's country risk premium equals 8.41% and the cost of equity for this project equals 18.65%.

LOS 36k: Describe the marginal cost of capital schedule, explain why it may be upward-sloping with respect to additional capital, and calculate and interpret its break-points. **Vol 4, pp 60–63**

> The marginal cost of capital is the cost of the last additional dollar of capital raised by a firm.

A company's marginal cost of capital (MCC) increases as additional capital is raised. This is because of the following reasons:

1. The company may have existing *debt covenants* that restrict it from issuing debt with similar seniority. Subsequent rounds of debt will be subordinated to the senior issue so they will obviously carry more risk, and therefore entail a higher cost.

2. Due to economies of scale in raising a significant amount of a component (debt or equity) of capital in one go, firms may deviate from their target (optimal) capital structure over the short term. These deviations may cause the marginal cost of capital to rise.

The marginal cost of capital schedule shows the WACC at different amounts of total capital. Figure 3-1 illustrates the fact that it is upward sloping. The amount of capital at which the WACC changes is referred to as a break point. A break point is calculated using the following formula (see Example 3-3):

$$\text{Break point} = \frac{\text{Amount of capital at which a component's cost of capital changes}}{\text{Proportion of new capital raised from the component}}$$

Example 3-3: Determining Break Points

Charlton Inc. has a target capital structure of 70% equity and 30% debt. The schedule of costs for components of capital for the company is contained in the table below. Calculate the break points and illustrate the marginal cost of capital schedule for Charlton.

Amount of New Debt ($ millions)	After-Tax Cost of Debt	Amount of New Equity ($ millions)	Cost of Equity
0 to 150	3.90%	0 to 300	6.00%
150 to 300	4.40%	300 to 600	7.80%
300 to 450	4.80%	600 to 900	10.00%

Solution

Charlton Inc. will have a break point each time the cost of a component of capital changes. Specifically, its MCC schedule will have four break points.

Break Point	Calculation	Amount
When debt exceeds $150 million	$150 million/0.3	$500 million
When debt exceeds $300 million	$300 million/0.3	$1,000 million
When equity exceeds $300 million	$300 million/0.7	$428.57 million
When equity exceeds $600 million	$600 million/0.7	$857.14 million

The following table shows the company's WACC at the different levels of total capital:

Capital	Equity (70%)	Cost of Equity	Debt (30%)	After-Tax Cost of Debt	WACC
$100.00	70	6%	30	3.90%	5.37%
$428.57	300	7.80%	128.57	3.90%	6.63%
$500.00	350	7.80%	150	4.40%	6.78%
$857.14	600	10.00%	257.14	4.40%	8.32%
$1,000.00	700	10.00%	300	4.80%	8.44%

Figure 3-1: Marginal Cost of Capital Schedule

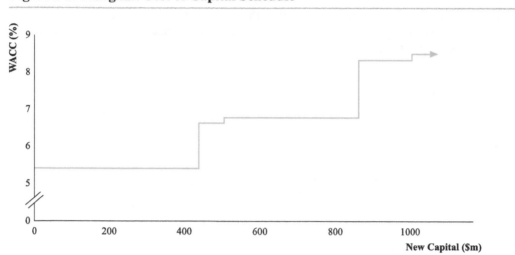

LOS 36l: Explain and demonstrate the correct treatment of flotation costs.
Vol 4, pp 63–65

Flotation costs refer to the fee charged by investment bankers to assist a company in raising new capital. In the case of debt and preferred stock, we do not usually incorporate flotation costs in the estimated cost of capital because the amount of these costs is quite small, often less than 1%. However, for equity issues, flotation costs are usually quite significant.

There are two ways of accounting for flotation costs. The first approach, which is often found in finance textbooks, incorporates flotation costs into the cost of capital. When this approach is applied, the cost of capital is calculated in the following manner (see Example 3-4):

$$r_e = \left[\frac{D_1}{P_0(1-f)} \right] + g$$

where:
f = flotation costs as a percentage of the issue price.

Example 3-4: Accounting for Flotation Costs Directly into the Cost of Equity

Ben Company currently pays a dividend of $1 per share, has a current stock price of $20, and has an expected growth rate of 4%. The company wants to raise equity capital and flotation costs will be 5% of the total issue. Calculate the company's cost of equity:

1. Before it issues new capital.
2. After it issues new capital, including flotation costs in the cost of equity.

Solution

1. Cost of equity before Ben raises new capital:

$$r_e = \frac{D_1}{P_0} + g$$

$$r_e = [\$1(1+0.04)/\$20] + 0.04 = \mathbf{9.2\%}$$

2. Cost of equity after issuance:

$$r_e = \left[\frac{D_1}{P_0(1-f)}\right] + g$$

$$r_e = [\$1(1+0.04)/\$20(1-0.05)] + 0.04 = 9.47\%$$

Ben's cost of equity was 9.2% before it issued new equity. After issuance, when flotation costs are included in cost of equity, the cost rises by 27 basis points to 9.47%.

However, adjusting the cost of capital for flotation costs is incorrect. Flotation costs are a part of the initial cash outlay for a project. Adjusting the cost of capital to account for flotation costs adjusts the present value of *all* future cash flows by a fixed percentage (27 basis points in Example 3-4). This adjustment will not necessarily equal the present value of flotation costs.

Correct Treatment of Flotation Costs

The correct way to account for flotation costs is to adjust the cash flows used in the valuation. We add the estimated dollar amount of flotation costs to the initial cost of the project (see Example 3-5).

Example 3-5: Correct Treatment of Flotation Costs

Alex Company is planning to invest in a project. The following information is provided:
- Initial cash outflow = $75,000.
- Expected future cash flows = $20,000 every year for the next 5 years.
- Alex's before-tax cost of debt = 5%.
- Tax rate = 30%.
- Next year's expected dividend = $1 per share.
- The current price of the stock = $25.
- Expected growth rate = 4%.
- The target capital structure = 70% equity and 30% debt.
- Flotation costs for equity = 4%.

While both approaches to incorporating flotation costs are illustrated, the LOS stresses the correct treatment only

Calculate the NPV of the project after adjusting cash flows to account for flotation costs.

Solution

First, we determine the after-tax cost of debt and equity to calculate the WACC of the project:

Source of Capital	Weight	Formula	After-Tax Cost
Debt	30%	$r_d(1 - \text{tax rate})$	$0.05(1 - 0.3) = 3.5\%$
Equity	70%	$r_e = \dfrac{D_1}{P_0} + g$	$(1/25) + 0.04 = 8\%$

$$\text{WACC} = 0.3\,(3.5\%) + 0.70\,(8\%) = \mathbf{6.65\%}$$

Next, we calculate the dollar amount of flotation costs:

70% of the investment is financed by using equity.
70% of $75,000 = $52,500

$$\text{Dollar amount of flotation costs} = \$52{,}500 \times 4\% = \$2{,}100$$

Finally, we calculate the **NPV** of the project:

Initial cash outflow = Initial outlay for project + Flotation costs = $77,100
Cash inflows = $20,000 for the next 5 years
WACC (discount rate) = 6.65%

$$\text{NPV} = -\$77{,}100 + \frac{\$20{,}000}{(1.0665)^1} + \frac{\$20{,}000}{(1.0665)^2} + \frac{\$20{,}000}{(1.0665)^3} + \frac{\$20{,}000}{(1.0665)^4} + \frac{\$20{,}000}{(1.0665)^5}$$

NPV = $5,678.20

READING 37: MEASURES OF LEVERAGE

LESSON 1: MEASURES OF LEVERAGE

LOS 37a: Define and explain leverage, business risk, sales risk, operating risk, and financial risk, and classify a risk, given a description. **Vol 4, pp 82–100**

LOS 37b: Calculate and interpret the degree of operating leverage, the degree of financial leverage, and the degree of total leverage. **Vol 4, pp 85–100**

LOS 37c: Analyze the effect of financial leverage on a company's net income and return on equity. **Vol 4, pp 94–95**

Leverage refers to a company's use of fixed costs in conducting business. Fixed costs include:
- Operating costs (e.g., rent and depreciation).
- Financial costs (e.g., interest expense).

Fixed costs are referred to as leverage because they support the company's activities and earnings. It is important for analysts to understand a company's use of leverage for the following reasons:

- Leverage increases the volatility of a company's earnings and cash flows, thereby increasing the risk borne by investors in the company.
- The more significant the use of leverage by the company, the more risky it is and therefore, the higher the discount rate that must be used to value the company.
- A company that is highly leveraged risks significant losses during economic downturns.

Leverage is affected by a company's cost structure. Generally companies incur two types of costs.

- Variable costs vary with the level of production and sales (e.g., raw materials costs and sales commissions).

- Fixed costs remain the same irrespective of the level of production and sales (e.g., depreciation and interest expense).

Let's work with two companies, Blue Horizons and Red Electronics to illustrate the effects of leverage on company value. See Tables 1-1 and 1-2.

Table 1-1: Sales and Cost Information

	Blue Horizons ($)	Red Electronics ($)
Number of units produced and sold	200,000	200,000
Sales price per unit	20	20
Variable cost per unit	7	14
Fixed operating cost	1,000,000	200,000
Fixed financing expense	800,000	200,000

For simplicity, we are ignoring the effects of taxes. However, the general conclusions remain the same even if taxes are included in our analysis.

Table 1-2: Calculation of Net Income

	Blue Horizons $	Red Electronics $
Revenue	4,000,000	4,000,000
Operating costs (fixed + variable)	2,400,000	3,000,000
Operating income	1,600,000	1,000,000
Financing expense	800,000	200,000
Net income	**800,000**	**800,000**

Both companies earned a net income of $800,000. However, it is important to observe that Blue Horizons has a higher proportion of fixed costs (higher leverage) in its cost structure, while Red Electronics has a higher proportion of variable costs.

In Table 1-3, we vary the number of units produced and sold by the companies to evaluate the impact of their differing cost structures on net income.

Table 1-3: Net Income in Different Sales Scenarios

	If 150,000 Units are Produced and Sold		If 200,000 Units are Produced and Sold		If 250,000 Units are Produced and Sold	
	Blue Horizons	Red Electronics	Blue Horizons	Red Electronics	Blue Horizons	Red Electronics
Revenue	3,000,000	3,000,000	4,000,000	4,000,000	5,000,000	5,000,000
Operating costs	2,050,000	2,300,000	2,400,000	3,000,000	2,750,000	3,700,000
Operating income	950,000	700,000	1,600,000	1,000,000	2,250,000	1,300,000
Financing expense	800,000	200,000	800,000	200,000	800,000	200,000
Net income	150,000	500,000	800,000	800,000	1,450,000	1,100,000
Percentage change in net income	−81%	−38%			81%	38%

Takeaway: The dominance of fixed costs (both operating and financial) in Blue Horizons' cost structure (higher leverage) results in higher earnings volatility. A 25% fluctuation in sales results in an 81% fluctuation in Blue Horizons' net income, but only a 38% fluctuation in Red Electronics' net income. See Figure 1-1.

Figure 1-1: Net Income for Different Numbers of Units Produced and Sold

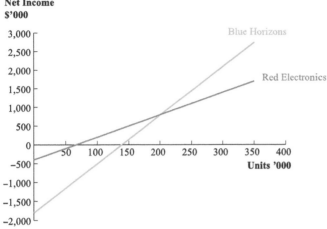

The greater the degree of leverage for a company, the steeper the slope of the line representing net income. For a given change in the number of units produced and sold, the net income of Blue Horizons will change by a greater amount than that of Red Electronics.

Business Risk and Financial Risk

Business Risk

Business risk refers to the risk associated with a company's operating earnings. Operating earnings are risky because total revenues and costs of sales are both uncertain. Therefore, business risk can be broken down into sales risk and operating risk.

> Companies in the same line of business have similar business risk.

Sales risk: The uncertainty associated with total revenue is referred to as sales risk. Revenue is affected by economic conditions, industry dynamics, government regulation, and demographics. See Exhibit 1-1.

Exhibit 1-1: Sales Risk

Blue Horizons expects to produce and sell 200,000 units over the coming year, and the standard deviation of units sold is 10,000 units. Further, assume that the selling price per unit is $20 with a standard deviation of $2.

Green Manufacturers has the same cost structure as Blue Horizons and expects to sell the same number of units at the same price as Blue Horizons. However, its standard deviation of units sold is 20,000 units and its price standard deviation is $4.

> For simplicity, we have assumed that the fixed operating costs are known with certainty and that units sold follow a normal distribution. Figures 1-2 and 1-3 show the distributions of operating income for the two companies.

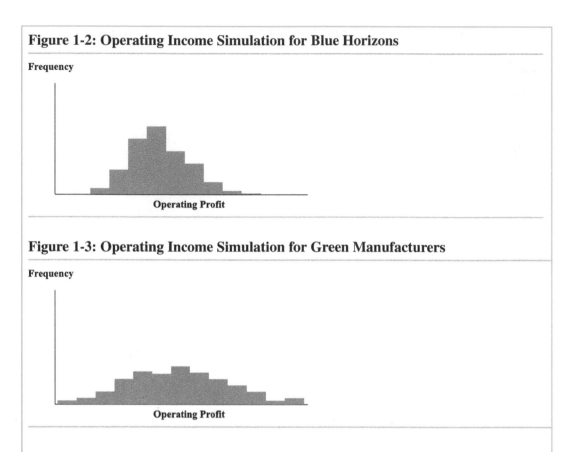

Figure 1-2: Operating Income Simulation for Blue Horizons

Frequency

Operating Profit

Figure 1-3: Operating Income Simulation for Green Manufacturers

Frequency

Operating Profit

Figures 1-2 and 1-3 illustrate how a company's profitability is affected by the variability in price and quantity sold. The higher the standard deviation of price and units sold, the wider the distribution of operating profit. The greater volatility in earnings shows that Green Manufacturers has more sales risk than Blue Horizons.

Operating risk: The risk associated with a company's operating cost structure is referred to as operating risk. As shown earlier, a company that has a greater proportion of fixed costs in its cost structure has greater operating risk.

The cost structure of a company generally depends on the type of industry that it operates in. However, companies within the same industry may vary their cost structures by employing different production methods. A company that has a greater proportion of fixed costs relative to variable costs in its cost structure will find it more difficult to adjust its operating costs to changes in sales and is therefore more risky. In order to examine a company's sensitivity of operating income to changes in unit sales, we use the degree of operating leverage (DOL). DOL is the ratio of the percentage change in operating income to the percentage change in units sold.

> We assume that the company sells everything that it produces in the same period.

$$DOL = \frac{\text{Percentage change in operating income}}{\text{Percentage change in units sold}}$$

Table 1-4 illustrates the effects of a 10% increase in the number of units sold on Blue Horizon's operating income:

Table 1-4: Sensitivity of Operating Income to Unit Sales

	Number of Units Produced and Sold		Percentage Change
	200,000	**220,000**	
Revenues	$4,000,000	$4,400,000	10.00%
Less variable costs	1,400,000	1,540,000	10.00%
Less fixed costs	1,000,000	1,000,000	0.00%
Operating income	$1,600,000	$1,860,000	16.25%

For a 10% increase in revenues, Blue Horizons' operating income increases by 16.25%.

The DOL can also be expressed in terms of its basic elements:

$$DOL = \frac{Q \times (P - V)}{Q \times (P - V) - F}$$

You are not required to derive this formula, but make sure you commit it to memory.

where:

Q = Number of units sold
P = Price per unit
V = Variable operating cost per unit
F = Fixed operating cost
Q × (P – V) = Contribution margin (the amount that units sold contribute to covering fixed costs)
(P – V) = Contribution margin per unit

Looking at the formula for DOL you should realize that if there are no fixed costs, DOL would equal one. This implies that if there are no fixed costs, there would be no operating leverage.

Using the equation above, the DOL for Blue Horizons can be calculated as:

$$DOL \ (at \ 200,000 \ units) = \frac{200,000 \times (20 - 7)}{200,000 \times (20 - 7) - 1,000,000} = 1.625$$

Interpretation: At 200,000 units, a 1% change in units sold will result in a 1.625% change in Blue Horizons' operating income.

Next, let's calculate Blue Horizons' DOL at a sales volume of 400,000 units.

$$DOL \ (at \ 400,000 \ units) = \frac{400,000 \times (20 - 7)}{400,000 \times (20 - 7) - 1,000,000} = 1.238$$

Interpretation: At 400,000 units, a 1% change in units sold will result in a 1.238% change in Blue Horizons' operating income. See Figure 1-4.

Conclusion: DOL is different at different levels of sales. If the company is making operating profits, the sensitivity of operating income to changes in units sold decreases at higher sales volumes (in units).

Figure 1-4: Blue Horizons' DOL for Different Number of Units Produced and Sold

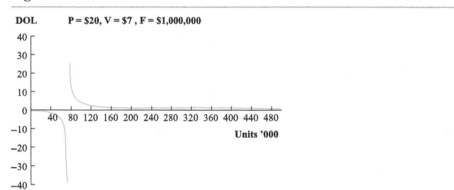

Takeaways:

- DOL is negative when operating income (the denominator in the DOL equation) is negative, and is positive when the company earns operating profits.
- Operating income is most sensitive to changes in sales around the point where the company makes zero operating income.
- DOL is undefined when operating income is zero.

The degree of operating leverage is also affected by a company's cost structure. Let's work with Red Electronics, which has a lower proportion of fixed costs in its cost structure relative to Blue Horizons. The DOL of Red Electronics at 200,000 units is calculated as:

$$\text{DOL (at 200,000 units)} = \frac{200,000 \times (20 - 14)}{200,000 \times (20 - 14) - 200,000} = 1.2$$

At 200,000 units, a 1% change in units sold will change Red Electronics' operating income by 1.2%.

The point to recognize here is that at 200,000 units, Red Electronics has a lower DOL (1.2) than Blue Horizons (1.625), which implies that its operating income is less sensitive to changes in units sold compared to Blue Horizons. The lower the proportion of fixed costs in a company's cost structure, the less sensitive its operating income is to changes in units sold and therefore, the lower the company's operating risk. The degrees of operating leverage are similar for the two companies at higher quantities sold.

Business risk is composed of operating and sales risk, both of which are largely determined by the industry in which the company operates. It is important to note however, that a company has more control over operating risk than sales risk. This is because it cannot control the number of units it will sell and the price per unit (sales risk), but it does choose the production method it wants to employ (which determines operating risk).

Industries that require a significant initial investment, but less expenditure to make and distribute the product (e.g., pharmaceuticals) have a higher proportion of fixed costs and therefore higher operating leverage. On the other hand, companies that have a significant portion of variable costs in cost of goods sold (e.g., retailers) have relatively low operating leverage.

Most companies produce more than one product, which makes it difficult to obtain a breakdown of costs. In such cases, we can regress the company's operating income (the dependent variable) against changes in sales (the independent variable) over time to estimate the degree of operating leverage. When comparing two companies, the one with a greater slope of the least-square regression would have higher operating leverage.

Financial Risk

Financial risk refers to the risk associated with how a company chooses to finance its operations. If a company chooses to issue debt or acquire assets on long-term leases, it is obligated to make regular payments when due. Failure to perform on these obligations can lead to legal action against the company, so by taking on these fixed obligations the company increases its financial risk. On the other hand, if it uses its retained earnings or issues shares (common equity) to finance operations, the company does not incur fixed obligations. Therefore, the higher the amount of fixed financial costs taken on by a company, the greater its financial risk.

Financial risk can be measured as the sensitivity of cash flows available to owners to changes in operating income. This measure is known as the degree of financial leverage (DFL).

$$DFL = \frac{\text{Percentage change in net income}}{\text{Percentage change in operating income}}$$

Table 1-5 illustrates the variation in Blue Horizons' net income with different levels of fixed financial costs. We have worked with the base case operating profit scenario (operating profit = $1,600,000) and another scenario where operating profit rises by 20%, to calculate changes in net income.

Table 1-5a: Sensitivity of Net Income to Fixed Financial Costs of $800,000

Fixed Financing Cost = $800,000			Percentage Change
Operating Income	1,600,000	1,920,000	20.00%
Less Interest	800,000	800,000	0.00%
Net Income	800,000	1,120,000	40.00%

Table 1-5b: Sensitivity of Net Income to Fixed Financial Costs of $1,200,000

Fixed Financing Cost = $1,200,000			Percentage Change
Operating Income	1,600,000	1,920,000	20.00%
Less Interest	1,200,000	1,200,000	0.00%
Net Income	**400,000**	**720,000**	**80.00%**

For simplicity we have ignored taxes from this analysis.

Notice that at higher levels of fixed financing costs ($1.2 million versus $800,000) the same percentage change in operating income (20%) leads to a higher percentage change in net income (80% versus 40%). This implication here is that higher fixed financial costs increase the sensitivity of net income to changes in operating income.

The degree of financial leverage (DFL) equation can be simplified into its basic elements as follows:

The factor that adjusts for taxes $(1-t)$ cancels out. The DFL is not affected by taxes.

$$DFL = \frac{[Q(P-V)-F](1-t)}{[Q(P-V)-F-C](1-t)} = \frac{[Q(P-V)-F]}{[Q(P-V)-F-C]}$$

Looking at the formula for DFL you should realize that if there are no interest costs, DFL would equal one. This implies that if there are no interest costs, there would be no financial leverage.

where:
Q = Number of units sold
P = Price per unit
V = Variable operating cost per unit
F = Fixed operating cost
C = Fixed financial cost
t = Tax rate

Blue Horizons' DFL when operating income is $1.6 million and fixed financial costs are $800,000 is calculated as:

$$DFL = \frac{200,000 \times (20-7) - 1,000,000}{200,000 \times (20-7) - 1,000,000 - 800,000} = 2$$

Blue Horizons' DFL when operating income is $1.6 million and fixed financial costs are $1.2 million is calculated as:

$$DFL = \frac{200,000 \times (20-7) - 1,000,000}{200,000 \times (20-7) - 1,000,000 - 1,200,000} = 4$$

These calculations verify that the higher the use of fixed financing sources by a company, the greater the sensitivity of net income to changes in operating income and therefore the higher the financial risk of the company. Also note that the degree of financial leverage is also different at different levels of operating income.

The degree of financial leverage is usually determined by the company's management. While operating costs are similar among companies in the same industry, capital structures may differ to a greater extent.

Generally, companies with relatively high ratios of tangible assets to total assets or those with revenues that have below-average business cycle sensitivity are able to use more financial leverage than companies with relatively low ratios of tangible assets to total assets or those with revenues that have high business cycle sensitivity. This is because stable revenue streams and assets that can be used as collateral make lenders more comfortable in extending credit to a company. See Example 1-1.

Example 1-1: The Leveraging Role of Debt

Alpha Inc.

Expected next year's operating earnings ($)	1,000,000
Interest rate on debt	6%
Income tax rate	35%

Scenario A: Alpha has total assets of $5 million and does not use any debt financing.
Scenario B: Alpha has total assets of $5 million, financed by $2.5 million of shareholders' equity and $2.5 million of debt.

Calculate the company's net income and return on equity for the coming year assuming that operating earnings may vary as much as 50% from expectations.

Scenario A: Total Assets = $5 million Shareholders' Equity = $5 million Debt = Nil	Operating Earnings 50% Lower than Expectations	Expected Operating Earnings	Operating Earnings 50% Higher than Expectations
Earnings before interest and taxes	500,000	1,000,000	1,500,000
Interest expense	–	–	–
Earnings before taxes	500,000	1,000,000	1,500,000
Taxes	175,000	350,000	525,000
Net income	**325,000**	**650,000**	**975,000**
Return on equity	**6.50%**	**13.00%**	**19.50%**

Scenario B: Total Assets = $5 million Shareholders' Equity = $2.5 million Debt = $2.5 million	Operating Earnings 50% Lower than Expectations	Expected Operating Earnings	Operating Earnings 50% Higher than Expectations
Earnings before interest and taxes	500,000	1,000,000	1,500,000
Interest expense	150,000	150,000	150,000
Earnings before taxes	350,000	850,000	1,350,000
Taxes	122,500	297,500	472,500
Net income	**227,500**	**552,500**	**877,500**
Return on equity	**9.10%**	**22.10%**	**35.10%**

Takeaway:

The larger the proportion of debt in a company's capital structure, the greater the sensitivity of net income to changes in operating income, and therefore the greater the company's financial risk. Bear in mind that taking on more debt also magnifies earnings upward, if the company is performing well (illustrated by the higher ROEs in Scenario B).

Total Leverage

DOL looks at the sensitivity of operating income to changes in units sold, while DFL looks at the sensitivity of net income to changes in operating income. The degree of total leverage (DTL) looks at the combined effect of operating and financial leverage (i.e., it measures the sensitivity of net income to changes in units produced and sold).

Table 1-6 demonstrates the effects of a 10% change in revenues on Blue Horizons' operating income and net income. Again, we assume that the company sells all that it produces during the same period.

Table 1-6: Total Leverage of Blue Horizons

	Units Produced and Sold		
	180,000	**200,000**	**220,000**
Revenues	3,600,000	4,000,000	4,400,000
Less variable costs	1,260,000	1,400,000	1,540,000
Less fixed operating costs	1,000,000	1,000,000	1,000,000
Operating income	1,340,000	1,600,000	1,860,000
Less interest	800,000	800,000	800,000
Net income	**540,000**	**800,000**	**1,060,000**
Relative to 200,000 units produced and sold			
Percentage change in units sold	−10.00%		10.00%
Percentage change in operating profit	−16.25%		16.25%
Percentage change in net income	−32.50%		32.50%

DTL is calculated as:

$$DTL = \frac{\text{Percentage change in net income}}{\text{Percentage change in the number of units sold}}$$

$$DTL = DOL \times DFL$$

$$DTL = \frac{Q \times (P - V)}{[Q(P - V) - F - C]}$$

where:
Q = Number of units produced and sold
P = Price per unit
V = Variable operating cost per unit
F = Fixed operating cost
C = Fixed financial cost

The DTL for Blue Horizons can be calculated as:

$$DTL = 1.625 \times 2 = 3.25$$

$$DTL = \frac{200,000 \times (20 - 7)}{200,000 \times (20 - 7) - 1,000,000 - 800,000} = 3.25$$

This implies that a 1% change in the number of units sold will change net income by 3.25%.

Note that DTL is also different at different numbers of units produced and sold. This is because DOL is different at different levels of units produced and sold, while DFL is different at different levels of operating earnings. DTL combines the effects of DOL and DFL.

LOS 37d: Calculate the breakeven quantity of sales and determine the company's net income at various sales levels. **Vol 4, pp 98–100**

LOS 37e: Calculate and interpret the operating breakeven quantity of sales. **Vol 4, pp 98–100**

Breakeven Points and Operating Breakeven Points

A company's breakeven point occurs at the number of units produced and sold at which its net income equals zero. It is the point at which a company's revenues equal its total costs and the company goes from making losses to making profits. Figure 1-5 plots Blue Horizons' revenues and expenses against the number of units produced and sold.

Figure 1-5: Blue Horizons' Breakeven

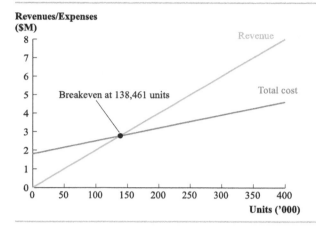

The breakeven point for a company occurs when:

$$PQ = VQ + F + C$$

where:
P = Price per unit
Q = Number of units produced and sold
V = Variable cost per unit
F = Fixed operating costs
C = Fixed financial cost

The breakeven number of units can be calculated as:

$$Q_{BE} = \frac{F + C}{P - V}$$

The breakeven number of units for Blue Horizons and Red Electronics can be calculated as:

Blue Horizons:

$$Q_{BE} = \frac{1,000,000 + 800,000}{20 - 7} = 138,461 \text{ units}$$

Red Electronics:

$$Q_{BE} = \frac{200,000 + 200,000}{20 - 14} = 66,666 \text{ units}$$

Blue Horizons must produce and sell 138,461 units in order to break even, while Red Electronics must only produce and sell 66,666 units to cover its costs. Blue Horizons must sell a higher number of units to break even because it needs to cover a higher amount of fixed costs. However, once Blue Horizons passes its breakeven point, it earns larger profits than Red Electronics. The implication here is that while greater leverage entails higher risk, it also raises the company's potential for profit.

A breakeven point can also be specified in terms of operating profit, in which case it is known as the operating breakeven point. At this point, revenues equal operating costs. The expression for operating breakeven point is given as:

$$PQ_{OBE} = VQ_{OBE} + F$$

$$Q_{OBE} = \frac{F}{P - V}$$

The operating breakeven points for Blue Horizons and Red Electronics are computed as:

Blue Horizons:

$$Q_{OBE} = \frac{1,000,000}{20 - 7} = 76,923 \text{ units}$$

Red Electronics:

$$Q_{OBE} = \frac{200,000}{20 - 14} = 33,333 \text{ units}$$

Blue Horizons also has a higher operating breakeven point compared to Red Electronics.

Note:
The farther unit sales are from the breakeven point for high-leverage companies, the greater the magnifying effect of leverage.

The Risks of Creditors and Owners **Vol 4, pp 100–102**

The risk borne by creditors and owners differs because of the different rights and responsibilities associated with their investment in the company.

Creditor claims on the assets of the company are senior to those of equity holders. In return for lending money to the company, creditors demand timely interest and principal payments. Payments to creditors must be made irrespective of whether the company is profitable. Inability to make these payments may lead to the company having to declare bankruptcy. Returns for creditors are predefined; even if the company does very well, they do not see any of the upside.

On the other hand, owners only have a claim on what is left over after all the financial obligations of the company have been met. In return for the lower priority in claims, equity holders enjoy decision-making power in the company and participate in the upside if the company does well.

Legal codes in most countries provide for companies to file for bankruptcy protection. There are two main types of bankruptcy protection.

- Reorganization (Chapter 11), which provides the company temporary protection from creditors so that it can reorganize its capital structure and emerge from bankruptcy as a going concern.

- Liquidation (Chapter 7), which allows for an orderly settlement of the creditors' claims. In this category of bankruptcy, the original business ceases to exist.

Companies with high operating leverage have less flexibility in making changes to their operating structures, so bankruptcy protection does little to help reduce operating costs. On the other hand, companies with high financial leverage can use Chapter 11 protection to change their capital structure and, once the restructuring is complete, emerge as ongoing concerns.

Under both Chapter 7 and Chapter 11, providers of equity capital generally lose out. On the other hand, debt holders typically receive at least a portion of their capital, but only after the period of bankruptcy protection ends.

READING 38: DIVIDENDS AND SHARE REPURCHASES: BASICS

LESSON 1: DIVIDENDS

There are two ways that a company can distribute cash to its shareholders—dividends and share repurchases. Ordinary dividend payments are different from interest payments in that dividend payments are at the company's discretion (i.e., the company is not legally obligated to pay dividends to its shareholders).

Dividends and share repurchases represent the company's payout over the year. A company's payout is a very important analytical consideration because distributions to shareholders are an important component of total return, particularly when stock price volatility is high.

LOS 38a: Describe regular cash dividends, extra dividends, stock dividends, stock splits, and reverse stock splits, including their expected effect on shareholders' wealth and a company's financial ratios. Vol 4, pp 112–120

Companies can make dividend payments in a number of ways—cash dividends, stock dividends, and stock splits.

Cash Dividends

Regular Cash Dividends

Most companies pay out cash dividends to shareholders on a regular schedule. Typically, cash dividends are paid on a quarterly basis in the United States, on a semiannual basis in Europe and Japan, and on an annual basis in other Asian markets.

Companies strive to maintain or increase their cash dividend payouts. A company's cash dividend payout record sends important messages about the company to investors and potential investors.

- A record of consistent dividends over an extended period of time indicates that the company is consistently profitable.
- A trend of increasing regular dividends over time indicates that the company is doing well and is willing to share profits with shareholders. This suggests that the company's shares are of high investment quality.
- An increase in a company's regular dividend, especially if unexpected, can send a very strong message out to investors and usually has a positive effect on share price.

Dividend Reinvestment Plans (DRPs)

A dividend reinvestment plan (DRP) is a system that allows investors to reinvest all or a portion of cash dividends received from a company in shares of the company. There are three types of DRPs:

- Open market DRPs, in which the company purchases shares (on behalf of plan participants) from the open market.
- New-issue DRPs or scrip dividend schemes, in which the company issues the additional shares instead of repurchasing them.
- Plans where companies are permitted to obtain additional shares through open-market purchases or new issuances.

Advantages to the Company

- The shareholder base is diversified as smaller investors gain easier access to additional shares in the company. Companies usually prefer a broad and diversified shareholder base.
- They may encourage long-term investment in the company by building investor loyalty to the company.
- New issue DRPs allow companies to raise equity capital without incurring floatation costs.

Advantages to Shareholders

Dollar cost averaging is the technique of buying a fixed dollar amount of a particular investment on a regular schedule, regardless of the share price. More shares are purchased when prices are low and fewer shares are bought when prices are high.

- Shareholders can accumulate shares in the company using dollar-cost averaging.
- DRPs are a cost-effective means for small investors to purchase additional shares in the company.
- There are no transaction costs associated with obtaining shares through a DRP.
- Shares offered in a DRP are sometimes issued to shareholders at a discount to the market price.

Disadvantages to Shareholders

For these reasons use of such plans may be especially appropriate in a tax-deferred account (in which investment earnings are not taxed), such as certain types of retirement accounts.

- In jurisdictions where capital gains are taxed, investors must keep record of the cost basis of shares received to accurately compute gains and losses when shares are sold. If the shares are obtained at a price that is higher (lower) than the purchase price of the shares originally held, the investor's average cost basis will increase (decrease).
- Cash dividends are fully taxed in the year they are received (even if reinvested). As a result, an investor who participates in a DRP may have to pay tax on cash that he actually does not receive.
- If new shares are issued at a discount, shareholders that do not participate in the DRP tend to suffer dilution.

Extra or Special (Irregular) Dividends

A special dividend refers to a dividend payment by a company that does not usually pay dividends, or a dividend payment on top of the company's regular dividend. Companies use special dividends to distribute more earnings in strong years and to distribute excess cash to shareholders.

Liquidating Dividends

A dividend payment is known as a liquidating dividend when:

- A company goes out of business and its net assets are distributed to shareholders.
- A company sells off a portion of its business and distributes the proceeds to shareholders.
- A company pays out a dividend that is greater than its retained earnings. Such a payment reduces (impairs) the company's stated capital.

Stock Dividends

A stock dividend or a bonus issue occurs when a company issues additional common shares in the company (instead of cash) to shareholders. Example 1-1 illustrates how stock dividends work.

Example 1-1: Illustration of the Effects of Stock Dividends

ABC Company has 10 million shares outstanding. The stock is currently trading for $25, with an EPS of $1.25 and a P/E multiple of 20.

1. Illustrate the effects of a 5% stock dividend on ABC's EPS, stock price, P/E ratio, and total number of shares outstanding.

2. Illustrate the effects of the stock dividend on the total cost, cost-per-share, and total number of shares held for an investor who holds 1,000 shares in ABC which were purchased for $14 each.

Solution

1. Effects of stock dividend on ABC Company:

	Before Dividend	After Dividend
Shares outstanding	10,000,000	(10,000,000)(1.05) = 10,500,000
Earnings per share	$1.25	($1.25)(10,000,000) / 10,500,000 = $1.19
Total market value	$25,000,000	$25,000,000
Stock price	$25	($25)(10,000,000) / 10,500,000 = $23.81
P/E	$25/$1.25 = 20	$23.81/$1.19 = 20

2. Effects of stock dividend on the investor:

	Before Dividend	After Dividend
Shares owned	1,000	(1,000)(1.05) = 1,050
Total cost	$14,000	$14,000
Cost per share	$14	($14)(1,000) / 1,050 = $13.33
Total value of holding	($25)($1,000) = $25,000	($23.81)(1,050) = $25,000

Observations:

- The investor ends up with more shares, which she did not have to pay for.
- The company issues a dividend without spending any cash.
- The market value of the company does not change in response to a stock dividend.
- The investor's average cost per share falls, but the total cost remains unchanged.

Stock dividends do not affect an investor's proportionate ownership of a company. A stock dividend basically just divides the market value of a firm's equity into smaller pieces, but the percentage of the company owned by each shareholder remains the same, as does the market value of each investor's holding. Stock dividends are generally not taxable.

Advantages of Paying Out Stock Dividends

- With more shares outstanding there is a greater chance of more small shareholders owning the stock, which broadens the company's shareholder base.
- Stock dividends could bring the stock's market price into the "optimal range" (believed to lie somewhere between $20 and $80 for U.S. companies), where investors are attracted to the stock.

Differences Between Stock Dividends and Cash Dividends for the Company

Cash dividends reduce assets (cash) and shareholders' equity (retained earnings). When a company pays out cash dividends, not only do liquidity ratios deteriorate, but leverage ratios (e.g., debt-assets and debt-equity ratios) also worsen. On the other hand, stock dividends do not have any effect on a company's capital structure. Retained earnings fall by the value of stock dividends paid, but there is an offsetting increase in contributed capital so there is no change in shareholders' equity. Therefore, stock dividends have no impact on a company's liquidity and solvency ratios.

Stock Splits

Stock splits are similar to stock dividends in that they increase the total number of shares outstanding and have no economic effect on the company. If a company announces a 3-for-1 stock split, it means that each investor will get an additional 2 shares (to make a total of 3) for each share originally held. Example 1-2 illustrates how stock splits work.

Example 1-2: Effects of a Stock Split

XYZ Company has 25 million shares outstanding. The stock is currently trading for $100, with an EPS of $6 and a P/E multiple of 16.67. XYZ pays an annual dividend of $2 per share and earns net income of $150 million for the year.

1. Illustrate the effects of a 2-for-1 stock split on XYZ's EPS, stock price, P/E ratio, dividend payout ratio, dividend yield, and total number of shares outstanding.

2. Illustrate the effects of the stock split on the total cost, cost-per-share, and total number of shares held for an investor who holds 5,000 shares in XYZ which were purchased for $84 each.

Solution

1. Effects of stock split on XYZ Company:

	Before Split	After Split
Shares outstanding	25,000,000	(25,000,000)(2) = 50,000,000
Earnings per share	$6	($6)(25,000,000) / 50,000,000 = $3
Total market value	$2,500,000,000	$2,500,000,000
Stock price	$100	($100)(25,000,000) / 50,000,000 = $50
P/E	$100/6 = 16.67	$50/$3 = 16.67
Dividend per share	$2	($2)(25,000,000) / 50,000,000 = $1
Dividend payout ratio	($2)(25,000,000) / $150,000,000 = 33%	($1)(50,000,000) / $150,000,000 = 33%
Dividend yield	$2/$100 = 2%	$1/$50 = 2%

> The dividend yield equals dividend per share divided by price per share.

2. Effects of stock split on the investor:

	Before Dividend	After Dividend
Shares owned	5,000	5,000 × 2 = 10,000
Total cost	$420,000	$420,000
Cost per share	$84	$42
Total value of holding	($100)($5,000) = $500,000	($50)(10,000) = $500,000

Observations:

- The investor ends up with more shares, which she did not have to pay for.
- The company issues a dividend without spending any cash.
- The market value of the company does not change in response to a stock split.
- The investor's average cost per share falls, but the total cost remains unchanged.

From Example 1-2, you should also be able to understand that a 2-for-1 stock split has the same effects as a 100% stock dividend. However, there is one important difference between stock splits and stock dividends. A stock dividend results in a transfer of retained earnings to contributed capital, whereas a stock split has no impact on any shareholders' equity accounts.

Companies typically announce stock splits after a period during which the stock price has appreciated significantly to bring it down into a more marketable range. Many investors however, see a stock split announcement as a signal for future stock price appreciation.

A reverse stock split increases the share price and reduces the number of shares outstanding. Similar to stock splits, the aim of a reverse stock split is to bring the stock price into a more marketable range.

> **Cash dividends result in an outflow of cash (decreasing a company's liquidity ratios and increasing its debt-to-assets ratio) and reduce retained earnings and shareholders' equity (increasing the debt-to-equity ratio). On the other hand, stock dividends, stock splits, and reverse stock splits have no impact on a company's liquidity or leverage ratios. They merely result in a change in the number of shares outstanding.**

Example 1-3: Reverse Stock Split

Glitz Corporation's stock is currently trading at $4.50 per share. The company recently announced a 1-for-10 reverse stock split to support its share price.

All other things remaining the same, calculate the expected stock price after the split. Also comment on the effect of a reverse stock split on shareholder wealth and the investors total cost basis.

Solution

Expected stock price after the reverse stock split = $4.50 × 10 = $45 per share

Theoretically, a reverse stock split should not have any impact on shareholder wealth. The market capitalization of the company and the investor's total cost basis should remain the same. However, stock splits and reverse stock splits might sometimes have a positive or a negative effect on share price depending on how the decision is interpreted by investors. For example, a reverse stock split that results in an increase in the share price and allows the company to retain the advantages of being listed on a leading global exchange may result in an increase in the market capitalization of the company.

LOS 38b: Describe dividend payment chronology, including the significance of declaration, holder-of-record, ex-dividend, and payment dates.
Vol 4, pp 120–123

Declaration date: This is the date on which a company announces a particular dividend. The company also announces the holder-of-record date and the payment date on the declaration date.

> **The ex-dividend date is determined by the exchange on which the company's shares are listed.**

Ex-dividend date: The ex-dividend date is the first day that the share trades without the dividend. Any investor who holds the stock on the ex-dividend date or who purchased it the day before the ex-dividend date is entitled to receive the dividend. On the ex-dividend date, the share price is adjusted for the amount of the dividend. For example, if a stock that has announced a $2/share dividend closes at $100 on the trading day before the ex-dividend date, it will open at $98 on the ex-dividend date. The ex-dividend date is also known as the ex-date.

Holder-of-record date: The holder-of-record date is the date at which a shareholder listed in the company's records will be entitled to receive the upcoming dividend. The length of the period between the holder-of-record date and the ex-dividend date depends on the trade settlement cycle of the particular exchange. For example, in the United States, where trades settle 3 days after execution (T+3 settlement), there is a 2-day gap between the ex-dividend date and the holder-of-record date. The holder-of-record date is also known as the owner-of record date, shareholder-of-record date, record date, date of record, or the date of book closure.

> The holder-of-record date is determined by the company itself.

Payment date: The payment date is the date on which the company actually mails out or transfers the dividend payment to shareholders.

> While the time between the ex-date and record date is fixed, the time between other dividend-related dates can vary.

LESSON 2: SHARE REPURCHASES

> Unlike the ex-date and record date, which must fall on a business day, the payment date may fall on a weekday or the weekend.

LOS 38c: Compare share repurchase methods. Vol 4, pp 124–126

A share repurchase occurs when a company buys back its own shares. Shares that are repurchased by the company are known as Treasury shares and once repurchased are not considered for dividends, voting, or calculating earnings per share.

Share Repurchases Versus Cash Dividends

> Unlike stock dividends and stock splits, repurchases entail an outflow of cash from the company. In most developed markets around the world, stock repurchases are becoming more popular as an alternative to cash dividends.

- Just because a company authorizes a share repurchase, it does not necessarily mean that the company is obligated to go through with the purchase. For cash dividends, once a company announces a dividend, it is committed to paying them.
- Cash dividends are distributed to shareholders in proportion to their ownership percentage. However, repurchases generally do not distribute cash in such a manner.

Arguments for Share Repurchases

- They send out a signal to the market that management believes that the company's stock is undervalued, or that management will support the stock price.
- They offer the company flexibility in its cash distributions. A share repurchase does not set the expectation of continued distributions in the future as cash dividends might.
- There is a tax advantage to distributing cash through repurchases in markets where capital gains are taxed at a lower rate than dividends.
- They can be used to limit the increase in the number of shares outstanding when a significant number of employee stock options have been exercised.

Share Repurchase Methods

Buy in the open market: Under this method, the company repurchases shares from the open market. Buying in the open market offers the company flexibility as there is no legal obligation to go through with the entire repurchase once it has been authorized, and the authorization can last for several years. This method is also cost-effective as the company can choose to execute the trades when the price impact is likely to be minimal and when the stock is attractively priced.

Buy back a fixed number of shares at a fixed price: This type of repurchase is known as a fixed price tender offer. The company offers to purchase a fixed number of shares at a fixed price (typically at a premium to the current market price) at a fixed date in the future. If the number of shares offered for sale exceeds the amount of shares that company desires to repurchase, the company will repurchase a pro rata amount from each shareholder who offers her shares for sale. Fixed price tender offers can be accomplished very quickly.

Dutch auction: Instead of specifying a fixed price for all the shares that the company wants to buy back (as is the case in a fixed price tender offer), under a Dutch auction the company specifies a range of acceptable prices. Shareholders who are interested in selling their shares specify their selling price and the amount of shares that they want to sell. The company accepts the lowest bids first and then accepts higher and higher bids until it has repurchased the desired number of shares. Dutch auctions can also be accomplished relatively quickly.

Repurchase by direct negotiation: This occurs when a company negotiates directly with a major shareholder to buy back its shares. This may occur in the following situations:
- A large shareholder wants to sell off its shares and the company wants to prevent the large block of shares from overhanging the market and depressing the share price.
- The company wants to buy out a large shareholder to prevent it from gaining representation on the company's board of directors.

LOS 38d: Calculate and compare the effect of a share repurchase on earnings per share when 1) the repurchase is financed with the company's excess cash and 2) the company uses debt to finance the repurchase. Vol 4, pp 126–129

Share repurchases have an effect on a company's balance sheet and its income statement. If the repurchase is financed with cash, assets (cash) and shareholders' equity decline, and result in an increase in reported debt ratios. On the income statement, repurchases can increase or decrease EPS depending on how and at what cost the repurchase is financed. See Example 2-1.

Share Repurchases Using Excess Cash

Example 2-1: Share Repurchases with Idle Cash

XS Dough Inc. has 20 million shares outstanding and each share is currently worth $20. The company made $40 million in after-tax profits during 2009 and plans to buy back shares worth $2.2 million at the end of the year. The company believes that it will be able to repurchase the shares at a 10% premium to the current market price. Calculate the impact on 2009 EPS if XS Dough manages to buy back the shares at $22 per share.

Solution

Current EPS = $40 million / 20 million shares = $2 per share

After the repurchase:

Net income remains the same ($40 million)
The total number of shares outstanding falls to 20m − 100,000 = 19.9 million.

Therefore, EPS = $40 million / 19.9 million shares = $2.01 per share

Notice that the company's 2009 EPS rises by approximately 0.503% as a result of the repurchase. Further, the increase in EPS would have been more significant had the company managed to buy back the shares at the current market price ($20) rather than at a 10% premium.

Share Repurchases Using Borrowed Funds

See Example 2-2.

Example 2-2: Share Repurchases Using Borrowed Funds

Starsky Inc. plans to repurchase $16 million worth of stock with borrowed funds. The following information is provided:

Repurchase price	$80
Net income after tax	$150 million
EPS before repurchase	$5

1. What is Starsky's EPS assuming that it finances the repurchase by borrowing at an after-tax interest rate of 6.25%?
2. What is Starsky's EPS assuming that it finances the repurchase by borrowing at an after-tax interest rate of 8%?

Solution

1. Number of shares initially outstanding = Net income / EPS = $150 million / $5 = 30 million

    Number of shares repurchased = $16,000,000 / $80 = 200,000

    Number of shares outstanding after repurchase = 30,000,000 − 200,000 = 29,800,000

    EPS after the repurchase is calculated as:

    (Net income after tax − After-tax interest expense) / Shares outstanding after repurchase
    = [150,000,000 − (16,000,000 × 0.0625)] / 29,800,000 = $5

    Notice that Starsky's EPS remains the same after the repurchase if it borrows the funds at 6.25%. This will typically be the case if the company's after-tax cost of borrowing equals its earnings yield.

    Earnings yield = EPS / Stock price = $5/$80 = 6.25%

2. EPS after repurchase is calculated as:

    (Net income after tax − After-tax interest expense) / Shares outstanding after repurchase
    = [150,000,000 − (16,000,000 × 0.08)] / 29,800,000 = $4.99

    When the after-tax cost of borrowing is greater (lower) than the earnings yield, EPS falls (rises) after the repurchase.

Share repurchases may increase, decrease, or have no effect on EPS.

- If the funds used to finance the repurchase are generated internally, a repurchase will increase EPS only if the funds would not have earned the company's cost of capital if they were retained by the company.
- If borrowed funds are used to finance the repurchase, and the after-tax cost of borrowing is greater than the company's earnings yield, EPS will fall.
- If borrowed funds are used to finance the repurchase, and the after-tax cost of borrowing is lower than the company's earnings yield, EPS will rise.

> The total return on a stock is composed of capital gains and dividends.

Bear in mind that it would be incorrect to infer that an increase in EPS indicates an increase in shareholder wealth. The cash used to finance the repurchase could as easily have been distributed as a cash dividend. Any capital gains resulting from an increase in EPS from share repurchases may be offset by a decrease in the stock's dividend yield.

LOS 38e: Calculate the effect of a share repurchase on book value per share. Vol 4, pp 130–131

See Example 2-3.

Example 2-3: The Effect of Share Repurchases on Book Value per Share

The following information relates to two companies that each plan to repurchase $2 million worth of common stock. The only difference between the companies is that Company A has a higher book value of equity and a higher book value per share. Evaluate the impact of the repurchase on the companies' book values per share.

	Company A	Company B
Stock price	$50	$50
Number of shares outstanding	10 million	10 million
Buyback amount	$2 million	$2 million
Book value of equity	$600 million	$200 million

Solution

Book value per share = Book value of equity / Number of shares outstanding

Company A's BV/share = $600m / 10m = $60
Company B's BV/share = $200m / 10m = $20

Both companies repurchase 40,000 shares ($2m/$50) and have 9,960,000 shares outstanding after the repurchase.

After the repurchase:

Company A's BV of equity = $600m – $2m = $598m
Company A's BV/share = $598m / 9.96m = $60.04

Company B's BV of equity = $200m – $2m = $198m
Company B's BV/share = $198m / 9.96m = $19.88

Conclusions:

- When the market price is greater than the book value per share, book value per share will decrease after the repurchase (see change in Company B's BV/share after repurchase).
- When the market price is lower than the book value per share, book value per share will increase after the repurchase (see change in Company A's BV/share after repurchase).

All else being equal, a share repurchase is equivalent to the payment of a cash dividend of an equal amount in terms of its effect on shareholder wealth. Example 2-4 illustrates this.

Example 2-4: Share Repurchase Versus Cash Dividend

Kon Fused Inc. is deciding between distributing $20 million of excess cash to its shareholders through a share repurchase or a special dividend. The company has 10 million shares outstanding and the current market price of its stock is $40. Determine the effects on shareholder wealth under both the distribution methods being considered by the company.

Solution

Cash dividend:

Market value of equity = ($40 × 10 million shares – $20 million) = $380 million

Market price per share after dividend = $380 million / 10 million shares = $38

Once the dividend is distributed ($2 per share) each shareholder gets a $2 dividend and the ex-dividend price of the stock equals $38. Total wealth from the ownership of a single stock equals $40.

Share repurchase:

The company would be able to repurchase 500,000 shares with the $20 million excess cash (at $40/share). The post-repurchase price would remain at $40.

Market value of equity = ($40 × 10 million shares – $20 million) = $380 million

Market price per share after repurchase = $380 million / (10 million shares – 500,000 shares) = $40

If an investor's shares are repurchased, she receives $40 for each share. If she continues to hold the shares, each share is worth $40 in the market.

The takeaway is that the impact on shareholder wealth of distributing cash to shareholders through a share repurchase or a cash dividend is the same. However, the above analysis assumes that:

- Dividends are received as soon as the shares go ex-dividend.
- Tax implications of dividends and repurchases are the same.
- The information content of the two policies does not differ.
- The company can purchase any number of shares at the current market price. If the company must repurchase stock at a premium to the current market price, shareholders whose shares are repurchased benefit, while remaining shareholders suffer a decrease in their wealth.

Concluding Remarks

Many investors believe that on average, share repurchases have a net positive effect on shareholder wealth. Studies have shown that share repurchase announcements have been accompanied by significant positive excess returns around the announcement date, and for the next few years. These findings indicate that management tends to buy back company stock when it is undervalued in the marketplace.

Similarly, unexpected increases in dividends are also frequently associated with positive excess returns.

READING 39: WORKING CAPITAL MANAGEMENT

LESSON 1: WORKING CAPITAL MANAGEMENT

Working capital management deals with short-term aspects of corporate finance activities. Effective working capital management ensures that a company has ready access to funds that are needed for day-to-day expenses and that it invests its assets in the most productive manner at the same time. In this reading we deal with issues associated with managing working capital and look at various methods of evaluating the efficiency of a company's working capital management.

LOS 39a: Describe primary and secondary sources of liquidity and factors that influence a company's liquidity position. **Vol 4, pp 143–145**

Liquidity management refers to the ability of a company to generate cash when required. Sources of liquidity can be classified as:
- Primary sources, which are readily available resources such as cash balances and short-term funds.
- Secondary sources, which provide liquidity at a higher cost than primary sources. They include negotiating debt contracts, liquidating assets, or filing for bankruptcy protection.

Using primary sources of liquidity does not usually result in a change in a company's operations. On the other hand, using secondary sources of liquidity may lead to significant changes in the company's financial structure and operations, and may indicate that the company's financial position is deteriorating.

A drag on liquidity occurs when there is a delay in cash coming into the company. Major drags on liquidity include:
- Uncollected receivables: The longer receivables are outstanding, the greater the risk that they will not be collected at all.
- Obsolete inventory: If inventory remains unsold for a long period, it might indicate that it is no longer usable.
- Tight credit: Adverse economic conditions can make it difficult for companies to arrange short-term financing.

Drags on liquidity can be dealt with by enforcing strict credit and collection policies.

A pull on liquidity occurs when cash leaves the company too quickly. Major pulls on payments include:
- Making payments early instead of waiting until the due date to make them.
- Reduced credit limits as a result of a history of not being able to make payments on time.
- Limits on short-term lines of credit: These can be mandated by the government, market-related, or company-specific.
- Low existing levels of liquidity.

LOS 39b: Compare a company's liquidity measures with those of peer companies. **Vol 4, pp 145–150**

Creditworthiness is the perceived ability of a borrower to satisfy the payment terms on a borrowing in a timely manner. Liquidity contributes to a company's creditworthiness. See Example 1-1.

The following liquidity ratios are used to evaluate a company's liquidity management:

The current ratio is the ratio of current assets to current liabilities.

$$\text{Current ratio} = \frac{\text{Current assets}}{\text{Current liabilities}}$$

- A higher current ratio means that a company is better positioned to meet its short-term obligations.
- A current ratio of less than one indicates negative working capital, which might imply that the company faces a liquidity crisis.

The quick ratio (acid-test ratio) is the ratio of quick assets to current liabilities. Quick assets are those that can be readily converted into cash, and exclude inventory (because it is usually the least liquid of current assets).

$$\text{Quick ratio} = \frac{\text{Cash} + \text{Short term marketable investments} + \text{Receivables}}{\text{Current liabilities}}$$

Higher quick and current ratios indicate greater liquidity. However, in order to gauge whether a given quick or current ratio is good or bad, we must look at the trend in ratios, how they compare with ratios of competitors, and available opportunities to invest in more profitable longer-term investments.

Accounts receivable turnover measures how many times, on average, accounts receivable are created by credit sales and collected over a given period. It is desirable to have an accounts receivable turnover close to the industry average.

$$\text{Accounts receivable turnover} = \frac{\text{Credit sales}}{\text{Average receivables}}$$

The number of days of receivables measures how many days it takes, on average, to collect receivables from customers. It is desirable to have a ratio close to the industry average.

$$\text{Number of days of receivables} = \frac{\text{Accounts receivable}}{\text{Average day's sales on credit}}$$

$$= \frac{\text{Accounts receivable}}{\text{Sales on credit} / 365}$$

- A collection period that is too high might imply that customers are too slow in making payments and too much of the company's capital is tied up in accounts receivable.
- A collection period that is too low might suggest that the company's credit policy is too strict, which might hurt sales.

The number of days of receivables must be evaluated in light of the credit terms offered to customers and the relation between sales and extension of credit.

Inventory turnover (TO) is a measure of how often, inventory is created and sold over a period.

$$\text{Inventory turnover} = \frac{\text{Cost of goods sold}}{\text{Average inventory}}$$

- An inventory TO ratio that is too high might indicate that the company has too little stock on hand at any given point in time, which might hurt sales.
- A low inventory TO ratio might suggest that the company has too much liquidity tied up in inventory, perhaps because the units held are obsolete.

The number of days of inventory tells us the length of the period that inventory remains with the firm before being sold. It is desirable to have this ratio close to industry norms.

$$\text{Number of days of inventory} = \frac{\text{Inventory}}{\text{Average day's cost of goods sold}}$$

$$= \frac{\text{Inventory}}{\text{Cost of goods sold} / 365}$$

Accounts payables turnover measures how many times the company theoretically pays off creditors over a period.

$$\text{Payables turnover} = \frac{\text{Purchases}}{\text{Average trade payables}}$$

- A high payables turnover ratio might indicate that the company is not making full use of available credit facilities.
- A low ratio could suggest that the company has trouble making payments on time.

The number of days of payables measures how long the company takes to pay its suppliers.

$$\text{Number of days of payables} = \frac{\text{Accounts payable}}{\text{Average day's purchases}}$$

$$= \frac{\text{Accounts payable}}{\text{Purchases} / 365}$$

The amount for purchases over the year might not be explicitly stated on the financial statements, but it can be calculated using cost of goods sold (COGS) and beginning and ending inventory balances:

$$\text{Purchases} = \text{Ending inventory} + \text{COGS} - \text{Beginning inventory}$$

Example 1-1: Measuring Liquidity

The following table provides important liquidity ratios of Topaz Inc. along with industry averages. Evaluate the company's liquidity management.

Ratio	2008 Topaz	2008 Industry	2007 Topaz	2007 Industry
Current ratio	1.5	2.2	1	2
Quick ratio	0.8	1	0.5	0.8
Number of days of receivables	40	35	45	30
Number of days of inventory	45	38	48	30
Number of days of payables	36	38	28	36

Solution

The changes in Topaz's ratios over 2008 suggest that its liquidity position has become more comfortable. However, the company still has room to improve, as it is still behind its peers in the industry.

LOS 39c: Evaluate working capital effectiveness of a company based on its operating and cash conversion cycles, and compare the company's effectiveness with that of peer companies. Vol 4, pp 150–151

The operating cycle measures the time needed to convert raw materials into cash from sales.

$$\text{Operating cycle} = \text{Number of days of inventory} + \text{Number of days of receivables}$$

The cash conversion cycle or the net operating cycle is the length of the period from paying suppliers for materials to collecting cash from sales to customers. It can also be calculated as the operating cycle minus the number of days of payables.

$$\text{Net operating cycle} = \text{Number of days of inventory} + \text{Number of days of receivables} - \text{Number of days of payables}$$

Usually, *shorter* cycles are desirable. A conversion cycle that is too long suggests that the company has too much invested in working capital.

For effective management of working capital it is important for a company to accurately forecast cash flows. Forecasts can alert financial managers to potential future cash needs ahead of time, and can provide a standard against which actual performance can be evaluated.

LOS 39d: Describe how different types of cash flows affect a company's net daily cash position. Vol 4, pp 151–153

Most companies prefer keeping a minimum cash balance to run their operations smoothly. Cash may also be needed to cater to unexpected requirements, or to capitalize on lucrative opportunities. Table 1-1 lists the typical elements of a cash flow forecast and classifies them as inflows or outflows. Table 1-2 highlights the important aspects of cash forecasting for different time horizons:

Table 1-1: Examples of Cash Inflows and Outflows[1]

Inflows	Outflows
• Receipts from operations.	• Payables and payroll disbursements.
• Funds transfer from subsidiaries, joint ventures, and third parties.	• Funds transfers to subsidiaries.
• Maturing investments.	• Investments made.
• Debt proceeds (short and long term).	• Debt repayments.
• Other income items (interest, etc.).	• Tax payments.
• Tax refunds.	• Interest and dividend payments.

Table 1-2: Aspects of Cash Forecasting[2]

	Short Term	Medium Term	Long Term
Data Frequency	Daily/weekly for 4–6 weeks	Monthly for one year	Annually for 3–5 years
Format	Receipts and disbursements	Receipts and disbursements	Projected financial statements
Techniques	Simple projections	Projection models and averages	Statistical models
Accuracy	Very high	Moderate	Lowest
Reliability	Very high	Fairly high	Not as high
Uses	Daily cash management	Planning financial transactions	Long-range financial position

Many companies face a predictable surge in demand during a particular time during the year or at a particular stage of the business cycle. For example, firms that manufacture electronic gadgets face a surge in demand for their products over the holiday shopping season. These companies have to ship a significant amount of inventory to retailers in advance, but only receive payments for sales once the season is over. As a result, they have to finance the inventory rollout. Once sales revenues come in, they use their surplus liquidity to pay back borrowed amounts and invest the excess. Predicting sales peaks caused by seasonality is very important if the company must borrow funds to cover its needs.

---

1 - Exhibit 5, Volume 4, CFA Program Curriculum 2014
2 - Exhibit 6, Volume 4, CFA Program Curriculum 2014

- If a company sets aside too much money, it will lose out on investment income (opportunity costs).
- If a company sets aside too little, it will incur higher costs to raise funds quickly.

Investing Short-Term Funds

A company maintains a daily cash position to make sure that it has the necessary funds (the target balance) to carry on its day-to-day activities. Short-term investments represent a temporary store for funds that are not needed for financing daily operations. Typical short-term investments that businesses invest their excess cash in are highly liquid and have low risk. Table 1-3 lists some of the major instruments for short-term investments.

Table 1-3: Short-Term Investment Instruments[3]

Instruments	Typical Maturities	Features	Risks
U.S. Treasury Bills (T-bills)	13, 26, and 52 weeks	• Obligations of U.S. government (guaranteed), issued at a discount • Active secondary market • Lowest rates for traded securities	Virtually no risk
Federal agency securities	5–30 days	• Obligations of U.S. federal agencies (e.g., Fannie Mae, Federal Home Loan Board) issued as interest-bearing • Slightly higher yields than T-bills	Slight liquidity risk; insignificant credit risk
Bank certificates of deposit (CDs)	14–365 days	• Bank obligations, issued interest-bearing in $100,000 increments • "Yankee" CDs offer slightly higher yields	Credit and liquidity risk (depending on bank's credit)
Banker's acceptances (BAs)	30–180 days	• Bank obligations for trade transactions (usually foreign), issued at a discount • Investor protected by underlying company and trade flow itself • Small secondary market	Credit and liquidity risk (depending on bank's credit)
Eurodollar time deposits	1–180 days	• Time deposit with bank off-shore (outside United States, such as Bahamas) • Can be CD or straight time deposit (TD) • Interest-bearing investment • Small secondary market for CDs, but not TDs	Credit risk (depending on bank) Very high liquidity risk for TDs
Bank sweep services	1 day	• Service offered by banks that essentially provides interest on checking account balance (usually over a minimum level) • Large number of sweeps are for overnight	Credit and liquidity risk (depending on bank)

3 - Exhibit 7, Volume 4, CFA Program Curriculum 2014

Instruments	Typical Maturities	Features	Risks
Repurchase agreements (Repos)	1 day+	• Sale of securities with the agreement of the dealer (seller) to buy them back at a future time • Typically over-collateralized at 102% • Often done for very short maturities (< 1 week)	Credit and liquidity risk (depending on dealer)
Commercial paper (CP)	1–270 days	• Unsecured obligations of corporations and financial institutions, issued at discount • Secondary market for large issuers • CP issuers obtain short-term credit ratings	Credit and liquidity risk (depending on credit rating)
Mutual funds and money market mutual funds	Varies	• Money market mutual funds commonly used by smaller businesses • Low yields but high liquidity for money market funds; mutual fund liquidity dependent on underlying securities in fund • Can be linked with bank sweep arrangement	Credit and liquidity risk (depending on fund manager)
Tax-advantaged securities	7, 28, 35, 49, and 90 days	• Preferred stock in many forms, including adjustable rate preferred stocks (ARPs), auction rate preferred stocks (AURPs), and convertible adjustable preferred stocks (CAPs) • Dutch auction often used to set rate • Offer higher yields	Credit and liquidity risk (depending on issuer's credit)

The dividend rate on adjustable-rate preferred stock is reset quarterly in line with market interest rates. These securities offer investors a tax-advantage because a high proportion of the dividend income is exempt from taxes.

When firms need to borrow over the short term, they typically rely on bank overdrafts and commercial paper to meet their needs.

LOS 39e: Calculate and interpret comparable yields on various securities, compare portfolio returns against a standard benchmark, and evaluate a company's short-term investment policy guidelines. Vol 4, pp 153–160

Yields on Short-Term Investments

Since we have already studied various measures of yields in detail in Reading 6, we will not spend much time on them here.

Discount instruments are instruments that are purchased at less than face value, and pay back face value at maturity. See Example 1-2.

Example 1-2: Discount Interest

A discount instrument with a face value of $1,000 pays 5% in interest and has one month remaining till maturity. At what price can the security be purchased today?

Solution

Purchase price = Face value − Discount in dollars

$$= \$1,000 - (5\%)(1/12)(\$1,000)$$

$$= \$1,000 - \$4.167 = \mathbf{\$995.83}$$

The difference between the face value and purchase price ($4.17) is known as **discount interest.**

Interest-bearing securities differ from discounted securities in that the investor pays the face value to purchase the security and receives the face value plus interest at maturity.

Yields on Short-Term Investments

$$\text{Money market yield} = \left(\frac{\text{Face value} - \text{price}}{\text{Price}}\right) \times \left(\frac{360}{\text{Days}}\right) = \text{Holding period yield} \times \left(\frac{360}{\text{Days}}\right)$$

$$\text{Bond equivalent yield} = \left(\frac{\text{Face value} - \text{price}}{\text{Price}}\right) \times \left(\frac{365}{\text{Days}}\right) = \text{Holding period yield} \times \left(\frac{365}{\text{Days}}\right)$$

$$\text{Discount basis yield} = \left(\frac{\text{Face value} - \text{price}}{\text{Face value}}\right) \times \left(\frac{360}{\text{Days}}\right) = \% \text{ discount} \times \left(\frac{360}{\text{Days}}\right)$$

$$\% \text{ Discount} = \frac{\text{Face value} - \text{Price}}{\text{Face value}}$$

Notice that the only difference between the money-market yield and discount-basis yield is the denominator. Money-market yield uses the purchase price, so it calculates the return an investor earns on the actual amount invested, over a 360-day year. Discount-basis yield uses the face value in the denominator and annualizes the yield for 360 days. The bond equivalent yield uses the purchase price in the denominator and uses a 365-day year. Notice that this formula for calculating BEY (for short-term instruments) is different from the one used in Reading 6, where the semiannual yield was multiplied by 2 to determine BEY.

Example 1-3: Money-Market Yields, Discount-Basis Yields, and Bond Equivalent Yields

A 90-day US T-bill with a par value of $1,000 is issued at a discount of 8%. Calculate the money market yield, discount-basis yield, and the bond equivalent yield for this security.

Solution

Purchase price = Face value − Unannualized discount

$$= \$1,000 - (8\%)(90/360)(\$1,000) = \mathbf{\$980}$$

$$\text{Money market yield} = \left(\frac{\text{Face value} - \text{price}}{\text{Price}} \right) \times \left(\frac{360}{\text{Days}} \right) = \left(\frac{\$1,000 - \$980}{\$980} \right) \times \left(\frac{360}{90} \right) = 8.16\%$$

$$\text{Bond equivalent yield} = \left(\frac{\text{Face value} - \text{price}}{\text{Price}} \right) \times \left(\frac{365}{\text{Days}} \right) = \left(\frac{\$1,000 - \$980}{\$980} \right) \times \left(\frac{365}{90} \right) = 8.28\%$$

$$\text{Discount basis yield} = \left(\frac{\text{Face value} - \text{price}}{\text{Face value}} \right) \times \left(\frac{360}{\text{Days}} \right) = \left(\frac{\$1,000 - \$980}{\$1,000} \right) \times \left(\frac{360}{90} \right) = 8.00\%$$

Investment returns are expressed as bond equivalent yields to facilitate comparisons between various investment alternatives. The overall return on a portfolio is calculated as the weighted average of the yields of different assets in the portfolio, where an individual asset's weight is based on the proportion of the portfolio invested in that particular asset.

Investors face several different types of risks, such as credit risk, market risk, liquidity risk, foreign exchange risk, and so on. The key attributes of these risks (i.e., the conditions that lead to them) and the steps that investors may take to mitigate/eliminate associated losses are listed in Table 1-4.

Table 1-4: Types of Investment Risks and Safety Measures[4]

Type of Risk	Key Attributes	Safety Measures
Credit (or default)	• Issuer may default • Issuer could be adversely affected by economy, market • Little secondary market	• Minimize amount • Keep maturities short • Watch for "questionable" names • Emphasize government securities
Market (or interest rate)	• Price or rate changes may adversely affect return • There is no market to sell the maturity to, or there is only a small secondary market	• Keep maturities short • Keep portfolio diverse in terms of maturity, issuers
Liquidity	• Security is difficult or impossible to (re)sell • Security must be held to maturity and cannot be liquidated until then	• Stick with government securities • Look for good secondary market • Keep maturities short
Foreign exchange	• Adverse general market movement against your currency	• Hedge regularly • Keep most in your currency and domestic market (avoid foreign exchange)

Cash Management Investment Strategies

Short-term investment strategies can be categorized as passive or active.

- A passive strategy involves a limited number of transactions, and is based on very few rules for making daily investments. The focus is simply on reinvesting funds as they mature with little attention paid to yields.
- An active strategy involves constant monitoring to exploit profitable opportunities in a wider array of investments. Active strategies call for more involvement, more thorough study, evaluation, forecasts, and a flexible investment policy.
    - *Matching strategies* involve matching the timing of cash outflows with investment maturities. A matching strategy makes use of similar types of investments as passive strategies.
    - *Mismatching strategies* involve intentionally mismatching the timing of cash outflows with investment maturities. A mismatching strategy is riskier and requires very accurate and reliable cash forecasts. This strategy typically involves the use of liquid instruments and derivatives.
    - *Laddering strategies* involve scheduling the maturities of portfolio investments such that maturities are spread out equally over the term of the ladder.

---

4 - Exhibit 8, Volume 4, CFA Program Curriculum 2014

Cash Management Investment Policy

Companies with short-term investment portfolios should have a formal, written policy that guides the investment decision-making process. Having such a policy protects the company and its investment manager, and effectively communicates key aspects of the portfolio to investment dealers. An investment policy has the following basic structure:

- The *purpose* of the investment policy states reasons for the existence of the portfolio and describes its general attributes, such as the investment strategy to be followed.
- It identifies the *authorities* who supervise the portfolio managers and details the actions that must be undertaken if the policy is not followed.
- It describes the types of investments that should be considered for inclusion in the portfolio. The policy also contains *restrictions* on the maximum proportion of each type of security in the portfolio and specifies the minimum credit rating of portfolio securities.

The investment policy statement should be evaluated on the basis of how well it meets the goals of short-term investments (i.e., its ability to generate competitive returns without exposing the company to undue risks). The returns on short-term investments in different instruments should be expressed as bond equivalent yields so that various investment options can be easily compared.

LOS 39f: Evaluate a company's management of accounts receivable, inventory, and accounts payable over time and compared to peer companies. Vol 4, pp 160–174

Key Elements of the Trade Credit Granting Process

A company's credit policy can have a significant impact on sales. A company may be able to enhance sales by loosening acceptance criteria, and could end up restricting sales if the terms offered to customers are too strict. An effective credit management system must follow a proper strategy that is tailored to the company's needs and reflects its goals.

Companies offer different forms of credit terms to customers depending on their financial strength, the nature of their relationship with the company, and the type of credit terms offered by competitors. Some of the forms of terms of credit (excluding cash) include:
- Ordinary terms
- Cash before delivery (CBD)
- Cash on delivery (COD)
- Bill-to-bill
- Monthly billing

Credit managers typically use **credit scoring models** to evaluate customers' credit worthiness. These models consider factors such as availability of ready cash, type of organization (i.e., corporation, sole proprietorship, etc.), and how quickly payments are made to suppliers. The benefit of using credit scoring models is that they allow companies to make decisions quickly, and do not require a great deal of paperwork.

Managing Customers' Receipts

A company's cash collection system depends on the types of customers it has and the methods of payment used by them. A good collection system should accelerate payments along with their information content (e.g., customer's name, identification number, etc.). This can best be achieved by establishing an electronic collection network. However, if payments cannot be converted to electronic payments, then companies may use bank lockbox services.

Companies may measure the performance for check deposits by calculating the **float factor**, which gives the average number of days it takes deposited checks to clear.

| A lockbox system simplifies a company's collection and processing of accounts receivables. Under this system, customers mail their payments to a post office box from where they are collected and processed by the company's bank and deposited into its account. This saves the time for payments to be first processed by the company's accounting system, hence, speeding up cash collection. |

Float factor = Average daily float / Average daily deposit

Float = Amount of money that is in transit between payments made by the customers and funds that can be used by the company

Average daily deposit = Total amount of check deposited / Number of days

Although this measure only tells us the time it takes for checks to clear (and not how long it takes to receive those checks, deposit them, and then have them cleared), it is still very useful as it can be calculated easily for any depository account.

Evaluating Management of Accounts Receivable

An aging schedule classifies accounts receivable according to the length of time that they have been outstanding. Table 1-5 provides an example of an aging schedule. It shows the accounts receivable of ABC Company at the end of the first quarter of 2008.

Table 1-5: ABC's Accounts Receivable Aging Schedule

	January 2008	February 2008	March 2008
Current (1–30 days old)	$15,000	$13,000	$10,000
1–30 days past due	$6,000	$5,000	$9,000
31–60 days past due	$5,000	$4,000	$5,000
61–90 days past due	$3,000	$3,000	$4,000
More than 90 days past due	$2,000	$2,000	$2,000
TOTAL	$31,000	$27,000	$30,000

In Table 1-6, ABC's aging schedule is presented in terms of percentages. This makes it easier to identify changes in the aging schedule over the period. Notice the change in March's aging—a lower proportion of total receivables is in the form of current receivables (33.3%), and a higher proportion of receivables is past due (66.7%). Accounts receivable have not been collected and converted to cash as rapidly in March as they were in January and February.

Table 1-6: ABC's Weighted Average Collection Period

	January 2008	February 2008	March 2008
Current (1–30 days old)	48.4%	48.1%	33.3%
1–30 days past due	19.4%	18.5%	30%
31–60 days past due	16.1%	14.8%	16.7%
61–90 days past due	9.7%	11.1%	13.3%
More than 90 days past due	6.5%	7.4%	6.7%

We can better evaluate the firm's ability to collect its receivables by calculating the weighted average collection period, which measures how long it takes a company to collect cash from its customers irrespective of the changes in sales and the level of sales. Exhibit 1-1 shows the calculation of ABC's weighted average collection period for February 2008 and March 2008.

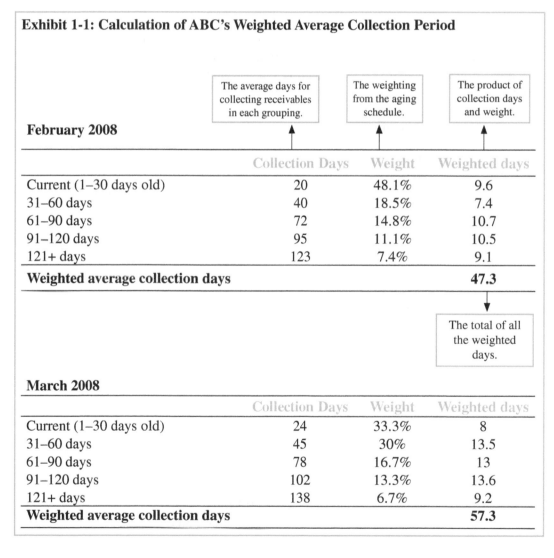

Exhibit 1-1: Calculation of ABC's Weighted Average Collection Period

The average days for collecting receivables in each grouping.

The weighting from the aging schedule.

The product of collection days and weight.

February 2008

	Collection Days	Weight	Weighted days
Current (1–30 days old)	20	48.1%	9.6
31–60 days	40	18.5%	7.4
61–90 days	72	14.8%	10.7
91–120 days	95	11.1%	10.5
121+ days	123	7.4%	9.1
Weighted average collection days			**47.3**

The total of all the weighted days.

March 2008

	Collection Days	Weight	Weighted days
Current (1–30 days old)	24	33.3%	8
31–60 days	45	30%	13.5
61–90 days	78	16.7%	13
91–120 days	102	13.3%	13.6
121+ days	138	6.7%	9.2
Weighted average collection days			**57.3**

The company's weighted average collection period has increased dramatically. An analyst should scrutinize this change and determine whether it is due to an extension of credit terms by the company to promote sales or because major customers are having trouble making payments.

The only drawback of the weighted average collection method is that it requires more information than the number of days of receivables. This information may not be easily available.

Evaluating Inventory Management

The main goal of inventory management is to maintain a level of inventory that ensures smooth delivery of sales without having more than necessary invested in inventory.

- A high level of inventory is undesirable as it inflates storage costs, can result in losses from obsolescence or damage, and can squeeze liquidity from the firm.
- A shortage of inventory, on the other hand, can hurt sales as the company loses out on potential customers.

Companies may have a variety of motives for holding inventory. These include:

- The transactions motive: Inventory is just kept for the planned manufacturing activity.
- The precautionary motive: Inventory is kept to avoid any stock-out losses.
- The speculative motive: Inventory is kept to ensure its availability in the future when prices are expected to increase.

However, companies need to strike a balance in managing their inventory levels (i.e., they need to avoid costs of holding excessive inventory, and at the same time ensure that they hold sufficient stock to avoid hampering sales). Two basic approaches for managing inventory levels are economic order quantity and just-in-time.

- Economic order quantity is the order quantity for inventory that minimizes its total ordering and holding costs. Companies typically use the economic order quantity-reorder point (EOQ-ROP) method, under which the ordering point for inventory is determined on the basis of costs of ordering and carrying inventory, such that total cost associated with inventory is minimized. This method relies on expected demand, which makes it imperative that short-term forecasts are reliable.
- The just-in-time method reduces in-process inventory and associated carrying costs through evaluation of the entire system of delivery of materials and production. Under this method, the reorder point is primarily determined on the basis of historical demand.

We can evaluate a company's inventory management by analyzing the inventory turnover ratio and the number of days of inventory.

$$\text{Inventory turnover} = \frac{\text{Cost of goods sold}}{\text{Average inventory}}$$

$$
\begin{aligned}
\text{Number of days of inventory} &= \frac{\text{Inventory}}{\text{Average days cost of goods sold}} \\[2mm]
&= \frac{\text{Inventory}}{\text{Cost of goods sold} / 365} \\[2mm]
&= \frac{365}{\text{Inventory turnover}}
\end{aligned}
$$

As we have mentioned before, analysts should be careful when interpreting changes in these ratios. Firms in the same industry may have significantly different turnover ratios because of different strategies or product mixes. A decrease in inventory TO for a firm over time could indicate that enough stock is not being sold. On the other hand, a decrease could also indicate that a company wants to reduce the chances of inventory "stock-outs."

Evaluating Management of Accounts Payable

Managing accounts payable is an important part of working capital management, as accounts payable can be a source of working capital for the firm. By paying too early, a company loses out on interest income. If it pays late, the company risks ruining its reputation and relationships with suppliers. Further, penalties and interest charges for late payment can be very significant.

Companies should consider a variety of factors as guidelines for managing their accounts payable effectively. These include:

- Financial organization's centralization: The management of a company's payables is affected by the degree to which its core financial system is centralized or decentralized.
- Number, size, and location of vendors: The sophistication of a company's payables system is affected by its supply chain and how dependent the company is on its trading partners.
- Trade credit and cost of borrowing or alternative cost: The standardization of a company's payables procedures is dependent on the importance of credit to the company and its ability to evaluate trade credit opportunities (e.g., trade discounts).
- Control of disbursement float: The disbursement float (the amount of time between the issuance of a check and its clearance) allows companies to use their funds longer than if they had to fund their checking accounts on the day the checks were mailed.
- Inventory management: Newer management techniques and systems are required to process the increased volume of payments generated through newer inventory control techniques.
- E-commerce and electronic data interchange (EDI): Making payments electronically may be more efficient and cost-effective than making payments through checks. Checks are only more valuable when the value of the disbursement float and interest rates are high.

Evaluating Trade Discounts

A company should review its evaluation of trade discounts periodically. An early payment discount must be availed if the savings from paying suppliers early are greater than the returns that could have been earned by investing the funds instead or greater than the firm's cost of borrowing.

$$\text{Implicit rate} = \text{Cost of trade credit} = \left(1 + \frac{\text{Discount}}{1 - \text{Discount}}\right)^{\left(365 \middle/ \substack{\text{Number of days} \\ \text{beyond discount period}}\right)} - 1$$

Terms of "2/10 net 30" mean that a 2% discount is available if the amount owed is paid within 10 days; otherwise, the full amount is due by the 30TH day. See Example 1-4.

Example 1-4: Evaluating Trade Discounts

Calculate the cost of trade credit if terms are 2/10, net 30 and the account is paid on:

- The 15TH day
- The 25TH day

Solution

$$\text{Cost of trade credit on the 15}^{TH}\text{ day} = \left(1 + \frac{0.02}{1 - 0.02}\right)^{\left(365/5\right)} - 1 = 337.02\%$$

$$\text{Cost of trade credit on the 25}^{TH}\text{ day} = \left(1 + \frac{0.02}{1 - 0.02}\right)^{\left(365/15\right)} - 1 = 63.49\%$$

Cost of credit decreases as the company approaches the net day (the 30TH day).

The cost of trade credit during the discount window is zero percent, so a company should pay toward the end of the discount period if it wants to avail the discount. Once the discount period expires, the cost of credit rises significantly and then declines as the net day nears. If the company's cost of funds or short-term investment rate is less than the calculated rate, it offers a better return than the company's short-term borrowing rate.

We can evaluate a company's management of payables through its number of days of payables.

$$\text{Number of days of payables} = \frac{\text{Accounts payable}}{\text{Average day's purchases}}$$

$$\frac{\text{Accounts payable}}{\text{Purchases} / 365} = \frac{365}{\text{Payables turnover}}$$

This ratio indicates the number of days, on average, that the company takes to pay its suppliers. The number of days must be compared to the credit terms offered to the company; paying sooner than necessary has costs of credit, and paying late might affect relations with suppliers adversely.

LOS 39g: Evaluate the choices of short-term funding available to a company and recommend a financing method. Vol 4, pp 174–180

Short-term financing is available to companies from various bank and nonbank sources. Table 1-7 lists the primary features of bank sources of finance.

Table 1-7: Bank Sources of Short-Term Finance[5]

Source/Type	Users	Rate Base	Compensation	Other
Uncommitted line	Large corporations		None	Mainly in the U.S.; limited liability
Regular line	All sizes	Prime (U.S.) or base rate (other countries)	Commitment Fees	Common everywhere
Overdraft line	All sizes		Commitment Fees	Mainly outside U.S.
Revolving credit agreement	Larger corporations		Commitment fees plus extra fees	Strongest form (primarily in the U.S.)
Collateralized loan	Small, weak borrowers	Base +	Collateral	Common everywhere
Discounted receivables	Large companies	Varies	Extra fees	More overseas, but some in U.S.
Bankers' acceptances	International companies	Spread over commercial paper	None	Small volume
Factoring	Smaller	Prime ++	Service fees	Special industries

- Uncommitted lines of credit: **A bank offers a line of credit to the company for a certain period of time, but reserves the right to refuse to lend. This makes it the weakest and least reliable form of borrowing. Its advantage is that it does not require any compensation other than interest.**

- Committed lines of credit (regular lines of credit): **These are stronger than uncommitted lines of credit as they require a formal commitment from the bank. Further, they are unsecured and are pre-payable without any penalties. Borrowing rates are negotiated, and are usually stated in terms of a money market rate (such as LIBOR) plus a spread to reflect the borrower's credit worthiness. Note that banks also typically charge a fee for a committed line of credit.**

- Revolving credit agreements: **These are the strongest form of short-term borrowing facilities. They are similar to regular lines of credit with respect to borrowing rates, compensation, and being unsecured. However, unlike regular lines of credit, they are in effect for multiple years, and may have optional medium-term loan features.**

Nonbank sources of short-term finance include nonbank finance companies and commercial paper. Table 1-8 lists the features of these sources.

---

5 - Exhibit 15 - Panel A, Volume 4, CFA Program Curriculum 2014

Table 1-8: Nonbank Sources of Short-Term Finance[6]

Source/Type	Users	Rate Base	Compensation	Other
Nonbank finance companies	Small, weak borrowers	Prime + + +	Service fees	Weak credits
Commercial paper	Largest corporations	Money-market sets rate	Back up line of credit, commissions	Lowest rates for short-term funds

Some companies take secured short-term loans, which are known as asset-based loans. These loans are collateralized by current assets of the company (usually receivables and inventory). Companies usually take asset-based loans when they do not have the required credit quality to qualify for bank loans.

Approaches to Short-Term Borrowing

Borrowers should have planned strategies for short-term borrowings. They should:

- Ensure that there is sufficient capacity to handle peak cash needs.
- Maintain sufficient sources of credit to be able to fund ongoing cash requirements.
- Ensure that the rates obtained for these borrowings are cost effective.
- Diversify to have abundant options and not be too reliant on one lender or form of lending.
- Have the ability to manage different maturities in an efficient manner.

Asset-Based Loans

If a company fails to qualify for an unsecured bank loan, it may opt for asset-based loans. These are loans that are collateralized by the company's assets. Assets that are used to secure short-term loans usually include current assets, such as receivables and inventory.

Computing the Costs of Borrowing

Firms must strive to obtain the most cost-effective source of finance. In order to find the best form of short term financing, each of the sources have to be adjusted to a common basis for comparability.

Cost of line of credit (and other sources that require a commitment fee)

$$\text{Line of credit cost} = \frac{\text{Interest} + \text{Commitment fee}}{\text{Loan amount}}$$

Cost of banker's acceptance (and other sources whose costs are stated as "all-inclusive"):

$$\text{Banker's acceptance cost} = \frac{\text{Interest}}{\text{Net proceeds}} = \frac{\text{Interest}}{\text{Loan amount} - \text{Interest}}$$

---

6 - Exhibit 15 - Panel B, Volume 4, CFA Program Curriculum 2014

Cost of commercial paper (and sources with dealer's fees and backup fees, which are quoted as all inclusive)

$$\frac{\text{Interest} + \text{Dealer's comission} + \text{Backup cost}}{\text{Loan amount} - \text{Interest}}$$

Example 1-5: Choosing Between Short-Term Borrowing Alternatives

Evaluate which of the following short-term financing choices should be chosen for having the lowest cost. Assume that $1,000,000 will be borrowed for one month.

1. Drawing on a line of credit at 7% with a 0.5% commitment fee on the full amount. One-twelfth of the commitment fee is allocated to each month.

2. A banker's acceptance at 8%, an all-inclusive rate.

3. Commercial paper at 6% with a dealer's commission of 1/4% and a backup line of cost of 1/2 %.

> This analysis has been simplified by using a factor of 1/12 to determine the effective interest rate and a factor of 12 to annualize the effective interest rate.

Solution

$$\text{Line of credit cost} = \left(\frac{\text{Interest} + \text{Commitment fee}}{\text{Loan amount}}\right) \times 12$$

$$\text{Line of credit cost} = \left(\frac{(0.07 \times 1,000,000 \times 1/12) + (0.005 \times 1,000,000 \times 1/12)}{1,000,000}\right) \times 12$$

Line of credit cost = 7.5%

$$\text{Banker's acceptance cost} = \left(\frac{\text{Interest}}{\text{Loan amount} - \text{Interest}}\right) \times 12$$

$$\text{Banker's acceptance cost} = \left(\frac{(0.08 \times 1,000,000 \times 1/12)}{1,000,000 - (0.08 \times 1,000,000 \times 1/12)}\right) \times 12$$

Banker's acceptance cost = 8.05%

$$\text{Commercial paper cost} = \left(\frac{\text{Interest} + \text{Dealer's comission} + \text{Backup costs}}{\text{Loan amount - Interest}}\right) \times 12$$

$$= \left(\frac{(0.06 \times 1,000,000 \times 1/12) + (0.0025 \times 1,000,000 \times 1/12) + (0.005 \times 1,000,000 \times 1/12)}{1,000,000 - (0.06 \times 1,000,000 \times 1/12)}\right) \times 12$$

Commercial paper cost = 6.78%

Commercial paper offers the lowest cost source of short-term financing in the given scenario.

READING 40: THE CORPORATE GOVERNANCE OF LISTED COMPANIES: A MANUAL FOR INVESTORS

LESSON 1: THE CORPORATE GOVERNANCE OF LISTED COMPANIES: A MANUAL FOR INVESTORS

LOS 40a: Define corporate governance. Vol 4, pp 192–193

Corporate governance is the system of internal controls and procedures through which individual companies are managed. Within an organization, it defines the rights, roles, and duties of the management, board members, and shareowners. Corporate governance aims to minimize and manage conflicts of interest between insiders and shareholders.

Good corporate governance practices seek to ensure that:

- Board members act in the best interests of shareholders. Note that in some jurisdictions, good corporate governance is tied to the interests of a broader stakeholder group (e.g., labor groups, society at large);
- The company acts in a lawful and ethical manner in its dealings with all stakeholders;
- All shareholders have the same right to participate in the governance of the company and receive fair treatment from the board and management;
- The board and its committees are structured to act independently from management and individuals or entities that have control over management, and other nonshareholder groups;
- Appropriate controls and procedures are in place covering management's activities in running the company; and
- The company's governance activities, as well as its operating and financial activities, are consistently reported to shareowners in a fair, accurate, timely, reliable, relevant, complete, and verifiable manner.

LOS 40b: Describe practices related to board and committee independence, experience, compensation, external consultants, and frequency of elections, and determine whether they are supportive of shareowner protection.
Vol 4, pp 198–211

Board members owe a duty to make decisions based on what ultimately is best for the interests of shareholders in the long term. To protect their interests, shareholders and investors should consider whether:

- Board members are independent (i.e., they are not biased or controlled by management).
- Board members report their activities at least annually to shareholders and meet regularly without company management.
- The board chair is also the present CEO or a former CEO of the company. This would give one person too much influence over the company and may impair the ability and willingness of independent board members to exercise fair judgment.
- Independent board members have a lead member if the board chair is not independent.
- Board members are aligned with a supplier, customer, or other parties. Association with these parties may give rise to conflicts of interest.

Compensation and Related-Party Transactions

Investors should look into whether the company engages in outside business relationships with management or board members on behalf of the company. Policies that cover related-party transactions ensure that board members remain independent and discourage them from engaging in the following practices:

- Receiving consultancy fees for work performed on behalf of the company.
- Receiving finders' fees for bringing merger, acquisition, or sales partners to the company's attention.

A company should disclose all material related-party transactions or commercial relationships that it has with board members. Disclosures relating to property or equipment that board members have lent, leased, or provided to the company should also be required.

External Consultants

Board members usually have limited time to dedicate to their board duties and may need specialized advice over some matters. Therefore, board members should be able to hire experienced external consultants to guide them in decision-making (especially with decisions related to mergers, acquisitions, executive compensation, and risk management), without having to take approval from management. Investors should determine whether board members are in fact utilizing the expertise of independent specialized consultants to make decisions in their interests, and ensure that they are being appropriately compensated.

Frequency of Elections

Companies that restrict shareholders from approving or rejecting board members via elections on an annual basis are in effect limiting shareholders' ability to change the board's composition. When reviewing a company's policy for the election of board members, investors should consider whether:

- Shareholders elect members every year, or for staggered multiple-year terms (known as a classified board). An annually elected board provides more flexibility, whereas staggered boards can help protect the company from being taken over.
- The board has filled a vacant position for a remaining term without shareholders' approval.
- Shareholders can vote to remove a board member.
- The board is of the right size given the facts and circumstances of the company.

LOS 40c: Describe board independence and explain the importance of independent board members in corporate governance. **Vol 4, pp 198–200**

Independence, as it relates to board members, refers to the degree to which they are not biased or otherwise controlled by company management. A board that is not predominantly independent may be more likely than independent individuals to make decisions that prioritize the interests of management above those of shareholders. To be considered independent, board members should not have material relationships with:

- Independent board members constitute at least a majority of the board.
- The company or its subsidiaries or members of its group, including former employees and executives and their family members;
- Individuals, groups, or other entities that can exert significant influence on the company's management, such as controlling individuals, controlling families, or governments;
- Executive managers, including their family members;
- Company advisers (including external auditors) and their families; or
- Any entity that has a cross-directorship relationship with the company.

Shareowners also need to understand how other relationships a director may have with the company could compromise his/her independence. They should consider whether a director:

- Has recently had material business relationships with the company; or
- Has represented a company with substantial voting rights in the company in question.

LOS 40d: Identify factors that an analyst should consider when evaluating the qualifications of board members. **Vol 4, pp 200–201**

If board members do not possess the required skills and experience, they would end up relying on management to make decisions. Investors should evaluate the qualifications of board members based on whether they:

- Are able to make informed decisions about the company's future with regard to finance, accounting, business, and law.
- Are able to act with care and competence as a result of relevant understanding of the company's:
    - principal technologies, products, or services,
    - financial position,
    - legal matters,
    - accounting,
    - strategy going forward,
    - risks.
- Have made public statements that provide an indication of their ethical perspectives.
- Have had legal or regulatory problems while serving on the board of another company.
- Have experience serving on other boards, particularly with companies known for having good corporate governance practices.
- Serve on boards for a number of other companies, which constrains the time needed to serve effectively on each board.

- Regularly attend board and committee meetings.
- Have committed to the needs of shareholders.
- Have the background, expertise, and knowledge in specific subjects needed by the board.
- Have served individually on the board for more than 10 years. Such long-term participation may enhance the individual board member's knowledge of the company, but it also may cause the board member to develop a cooperative relationship with management that could impair his/her willingness to act in the best interests of shareholders.

Investors should also consider how many board meetings each board member has attended. Further they should ascertain whether the board conducted self assessments and whether the board provides adequate training for members.

LOS 40f: Explain provisions that should be included in a strong corporate code of ethics. Vol 4, pp 212–214

A company's *code of ethics* is an essential document as it sets standards for ethical conduct based on the principles of integrity, trust, and honesty. It provides guidance for addressing conflicts of interest within and outside the organization.

As part of their analysis of the company's ethical standing, investors should determine whether the company:

- Gives the board access to relevant corporate information in a timely and comprehensive manner.
- Has an ethical code, and whether that code prohibits any practice that would provide advantages to company insiders that are not also offered to shareholders.
- Has an ethical code that the company promotes internally, and requires training for employees on compliance with the code.
- Has designated someone who is responsible for corporate ethics.
- Has an ethical code that provides waivers from its prohibitions to certain levels of management, and the reasons why.
- Has waived any of its code's provisions during recent periods, and why.
- Is in compliance with the corporate governance code of the country that it is located in, or the governance requirements of the stock exchange that it lists its securities on.
- Regularly performs an audit of its ethical/governance policies and procedures to make improvements.

If a company's code of ethics is weak, related-party transactions can be misused to benefit insiders (board members and their associates) at the expense of the company. A weak code of ethics also allows board members (or their family members) and managers to use company assets for personal use. When insiders are able to use company assets for personal reasons, those resources are not available for investment in productive, income-generating activities. To evaluate a company's policies regarding personal use of company assets, investors should determine whether the company:

- Has an ethical code or policies that place limits on insiders' ability to use company assets for personal use.
- Has lent or donated cash or other resources to insiders, their families, or other related parties.
- Has purchased property or other assets for management, board members, or their families.
- Has leased assets to management, board members, or their families, and whether the terms of such contracts are appropriate in light of market conditions.

In evaluating corporate transparency, investors should analyze:

- The amount paid to key executives and the manner in which this compensation is provided to determine whether it is appropriate given the executives' level of responsibilities and performance, and provides appropriate incentives.
- The size, purpose, means of financing, and duration of share repurchase programs and price stabilization programs.

LOS 40e: Describe responsibilities of the audit, compensation, and nominations committees and identify factors an investor should consider when evaluating the quality of each committee. Vol 4, pp 204–210

Audit Committee

The audit committee's main purpose is to ensure that the financial information presented to shareholders by the company is *complete, accurate, reliable, relevant,* and *timely*. It is responsible for hiring external auditors and ensuring that:

- The external auditors' priorities are aligned with the best interests of shareholders.
- The auditor is free from management influence.
- The information included in the financial statements is complete, accurate, reliable, relevant, verifiable, and timely.
- The financial statements are prepared in accordance with generally accepted accounting principles (GAAP) or international accounting standards (IAS) and regulatory disclosure requirements in the company's jurisdiction.
- The audit is conducted in accordance with generally accepted auditing standards (GAAS).

- All conflicts of interest between the external auditor and the company are resolved in favor of shareholders.
- The independent auditors have authority over the audit of the entire group, including foreign subsidiaries and affiliated companies.

Investors should determine whether:

- All the board members that serve on the audit committee are independent.
- The board submits the appointment of the external auditors to a vote of shareholders.
- The audit committee has the authority to approve or reject other proposed nonaudit engagements with the external audit firm.
- The company has procedures and provisions to ensure that the internal auditor reports directly to the audit committee in the case of concerns regarding the accuracy or integrity of the financial reports or accounting practices. Similarly, the audit committee should have unimpeded access to the internal auditor.
- There were any discussions between the committee and the external auditors resulting in a change in the financial reports as a result of questionable interpretations of accounting rules, fraud, or other accounting problems, and whether the company has fired its external auditors as a result of such issues.
- The committee controls the audit budget.
- The company has signed any agreement with the auditor limiting the auditor's liability in the event of negligence, breach of duty, or breach of trust.
- The committee undergoes or is required to undergo periodic training to stay educated about current financial issues.

Remuneration Committee

The remuneration committee should ensure that the various forms of compensation offered to executives encourage them to behave in a manner that enhances the company's long-term performance and profitability. The committee can further these goals by:

- Including only independent board members on the committee.
- Linking executive compensation to the long-term profitability of the company and long-term increases in share value relative to competitors and other comparable companies.
- Eliminating any potential conflicts of interests between the compensation committee and the company by, for instance, using only independent compensation consultants who report solely to the committee.
- Communicating regularly with the company's shareholders about compensation philosophy and how it complements the company's strategic goals.
- Establishing clear mechanisms in compensation packages for recouping incentive pay from management if the money was earned through fraud.
- Developing clear explanations of compensation philosophy and policies that are periodically communicated to shareholders.
- Making sure that compensation committee members understand all components of executive pay packages and are aware of what final payments may be made to executives in both best-case and worst-case scenarios.

Investors should determine whether the committee adequately represents shareholders' interests. In particular, they should determine whether:

- The compensation packages offered to senior management are appropriate.
- The committee adequately articulates its compensation philosophy, policies, and procedures to shareholders.
- Executive compensation is linked to the long-term profitability of the company and long-term increases in share value relative to competitors and comparable companies.
- Compensation packages contain clear mechanisms for recouping incentive pay from management if it was earned through fraud or other activities deemed detrimental to the company's sustainable performance or viability.
- The compensation committee members understand all components of executive pay packages and are aware of what final payment may be made to executives in best-case and worst-case scenario.
- Members of the committee regularly attend meetings during the year.
- The company has provided detailed information to shareholders relating to the compensation paid during the past year to its five highest-paid executives and its board members.
- The terms and conditions of options granted to management and employees are disclosed and whether they are reasonable.
- The company intends to issue newly registered shares to fulfill its share-based remuneration obligations, or whether it intends to settle these options with shares repurchased in the open market.
- The company and the board are required to receive shareholder approval for any share-based remuneration plans.
- The board receives variable remuneration instruments, such as stock options or restricted stock, and whether such awards adequately align the interests of the board with those of shareholders.
- Senior executives from other companies that have cross-directorship links with the company are members of the committee.
- Whether potential conflicts of interest exist between the compensation committee and the company.

Nominations Committee

The nominations committee is responsible for:

- Recruiting new board members with appropriate qualities and experience in light of the company's business needs.
- Regularly examining the performance, independence, skills, and expertise of existing board members to determine whether they meet the current and future needs of the company and the board.
- Creating nominations policies and procedures.
- Preparing for the succession of executive management and the board.

To ensure that a company prioritizes shareholder interests, investors should review the following relating to the nominations committee:

- Company reports over several years to assess whether the nominations committee has recruited board members who act in shareholders' best interests.
- The composition, background, and areas of expertise of existing board members, and whether new nominees complement the board's current portfolio of talents.
- How the committee finds potential new board members. Among the considerations is whether the committee engages in a search for candidates, such as by using an executive search firm, or whether its members rely upon the advice of management or other board members.
- The attendance records of board members at regular and special meetings.
- Whether the company has a succession plan for executive management in the event of unforeseen circumstances, such as the sudden incapacitation of the chief operating and finance officers.
- The report of the committee, including any discussion of its actions and decisions during the previous year.

Other Board Committees

It is important for investors to determine whether the board curtails the activities of other committees that are responsible for overseeing matters related to corporate governance, mergers, and acquisitions or risk management. Because these committees are not covered by national corporate governance codes, they are likely to have members who are also a part of company management. Therefore, these committees may not be as independent as the auditing, nominations, and remuneration committees. Whether other committees have independent members or not is an important criteria in assessing whether they represent shareholders' interests.

Board Communication with Shareowners

Although a corporate board does not usually have the time or resources to meet with all shareowners, it should establish ways for shareowners to communicate their concerns to the board in a way that helps the board understand legitimate shareowner concerns. A board should ensure that it does not breach its fiduciary duty by acting in the interests of a few shareowners at the expense of others.

Management Communication with Shareowners

The management of a company does not usually have the time or the resources to meet with all the shareowners. However, it is also expected to make reasonable efforts to listen to shareowners who hold a significant stake in the company or represent important stakehoders so they it can properly address legitimate shareowner concerns. Further, management should refrain from giving important information to only a select group of shareowners.

Shareowners should:

- Encourage companies to provide frequent and meaningful communications about strategy and long-term vision, including transparent financial reporting that reflects the company's progress toward its strategic goals.
- Encourage the inclusion of statements concerning long-term corporate strategy in all company communications.

LOS 40g: Evaluate, from a shareowner's perspective, company policies related to voting rules, shareowner sponsored proposals, common stock classes, and takeover defenses. Vol 4, pp 220–228

Voting Rules

Ownership Structure and Voting Rights

Investors should determine whether a company has different classes of common shares that separate voting rights from their economic value. If the majority of voting rights is given to one class of holders, management and the board might focus on the interests of the class that holds most of the voting power. When assessing the ownership structure of a company, investors should consider whether:

- There are different classes of shares and how voting rights differ between them.
- The company has safeguards in its articles of organization or by-laws that protect the interests of shareholders with inferior voting rights.
- The company was recently privatized by a government and whether the selling government has retained voting rights that could veto certain decisions of management and the board.
- The super-voting rights granted to certain classes of shareholders have impaired the company's ability to raise equity capital in the future. The company might be left with no choice but to raise debt capital, which would increase the firm's financial risk (leverage).

Proxy Voting

To be able to vote proxies is a fundamental right of any shareholder. If a company makes it difficult for shareholders to vote their common shares, it effectively limits their ability to express their views and influence the direction taken by the company. In order to evaluate whether a particular company permits proxy voting, investors should consider whether it:

- Requires shareholders' presence at the annual general meeting for them to vote.
- Coordinates the timing of its annual general meeting with other companies in its region to ensure that all of them hold their meetings on the same day but in different locations. This prevents shareholders from attending all meetings, and, therefore, from exercising their voting rights.
- Permits proxy voting by means of paper ballot, electronic voting, proxy voting services, or by some other remote mechanism.

- Is permitted under its national governance code to use share blocking, whereby it prevents investors who wish to exercise their voting rights from trading their shares during a period prior to the annual general meeting.
- Gives shareholders enough time between the release of the proxy and the actual annual meeting to thoughtfully review any voting decisions and vote their shares.

Confidential Voting and Vote Tabulation

Investors should determine whether shareholders are able to cast votes in a confidential manner. In determining whether a particular company allows them to vote anonymously, investors should consider whether:

- The company uses a third-party entity to count shareowner votes;
- The company or its third-party agent retains voting records;
- The company provides "timely disclosure" of annual meeting voting results;
- The vote is subject to an audit to ensure accuracy;
- Shareholders are permitted to vote only if they are present.

Cumulative Voting

Cumulative voting enables shareholders to cast the cumulative number of votes allotted to their shares in favor of one or a limited number of board nominees. This structure effectively improves the chances that shareholder interests will be represented on the board.

Investors should consider whether the company has a significant minority shareholder group that might be able to use cumulative voting to elect board members that represent its specific interests at the expense of interests of shareholders.

Voting for Other Corporate Changes

Shareholders should determine whether they have the right to approve changes to the company's corporate structure that may change their relationship with the company. Certain corporate structures have the ability to affect the value and ownership percentages associated with the company's securities. Shareholders should evaluate their ability to effect changes to a company's:

- Articles of organization,
- By-laws,
- Governance structures,
- Voting rights and mechanisms,
- Poison pills,
- Change-in-control provisions, and
- Board membership.

In reviewing issues that require their approval, investors should determine whether they:

- Will have an opportunity to vote on the sale of their company.
- Will have the right to vote on certain aspects of executive compensation.
- Have the right to vote against directors.
- Have the right to approve a new anti-takeover measure, and whether such measures are subject to periodic review by shareholders.

- Have the ability to periodically reconsider and re-vote on rules that require supermajority voting to revise the company's by-laws, articles of organization, or other governance documents.
- May attempt to use their ownership of a limited number of shares to force a vote on special interests that are unrelated to the company's operations.

Investors should also review issues such as:

- Share buy-back programs, particularly if their purpose is to fund share-based compensation grants,
- Amendments to corporate charters and by-laws,
- Issuance of new capital.

Shareowner Proposals

Shareowner-Sponsored Board Nominations

Investors should determine the circumstances under which shareholders can nominate individuals for election to the board. The ability to nominate one or more individuals to the board can prevent erosion in shareholder value. To evaluate whether shareholders can propose nominees to the board, investors should determine:

- Under what circumstances can shareholders nominate board members,
- How the company handles contested board elections.

Shareowner-Sponsored Resolutions

Investors should evaluate shareholders' ability to submit resolutions for consideration at the company's annual general meeting by determining whether:

- The company requires a simple majority, a two-thirds majority, or some other supermajority vote to pass a shareholder resolution.
- Initiatives proposed by shareholders will benefit the long-term interests of all shareholders, not just the interests of those tabling the proposals.
- Any "advance notice provision" exists in the jurisdiction that would require a shareowner to give notice of a proposal a certain amount of time before an annual meeting.

Advisory or Binding Shareowner Proposals

Investors should determine if the board and management are actually required to implement proposals approved by shareholders by considering whether:

- The company has implemented or ignored shareholder approved proposals in the past.
- The company requires a supermajority vote to approve changes to its by-laws and articles of organization.
- Regulatory agencies have had to pressure the company to act on the terms of approved shareholder initiatives.

Other Shareholder Rights Issues

Shareowner Legal Rights

Investors should determine whether the corporate governance code and the jurisdiction of the country in which the company is located allow shareholders to take legal action to protect their ownership rights. Investors should determine whether:

- Local legal statutes permit shareholders to initiate legal actions against management or board members on behalf of the company.
- The regulator has taken action in other cases to enforce shareholder rights or to prevent the denial of their rights.
- Shareholders are permitted to take legal action to enforce fraud charges against management or the board.

Takeover Defenses

Shareholders should scrutinize existing or proposed takeover defenses so that they can evaluate their impact on share value in a normal market environment and in the event of a takeover bid. These defenses hurt a potential acquirer's ability to succeed in a corporate takeover, and might prevent takeovers that could actually benefit shareholders. When reviewing a company's anti-takeover measures, investors should:

- Inquire whether shareholder approval is required before implementation of such anti-takeover measures.
- Find out whether the company has received any formal acquisition interest in the past.
- Consider the possibility that management will use the company's cash and available credit lines to pay a hostile bidder to forego a takeover.
- Consider whether changes of control issues are likely to invite pressure on the seller to change the terms of a proposed acquisition or merger.
- Consider whether change-in-control provisions will trigger large severance packages and other payments to company executives.
- Understand whether the company is involved in any cross-shareholding arrangements with other companies that may function as a defense against hostile takeover bids from unwanted third parties.

READING 41: PORTFOLIO MANAGEMENT: AN OVERVIEW

LESSON 1: PORTFOLIO MANAGEMENT: AN OVERVIEW

LOS 41a: Describe the portfolio approach to investing. Vol 4, pp 235–244

Instead of evaluating each investment in isolation, investment managers should take a portfolio perspective when evaluating an investment. Taking a portfolio perspective means evaluating each investment on the basis of its contribution to the characteristics of the portfolio as a whole.

Reasons for Taking the Portfolio Perspective

Taking the portfolio perspective offers diversification benefits. By not putting all their eggs in one basket (overinvesting in a single security or asset class), individuals can diversify away some of the risk in their investments.

> In a later reading, we will learn that portfolio standard deviation tends to be lower than the average standard deviation of its components due to the less than perfectly positive correlation between the returns on its components.

- Portfolios of securities may offer equivalent expected returns with lower volatility of returns (lower risk) compared to individual securities.
- A simple measure of the value of diversification is the diversification ratio. It is the ratio of the standard deviation of an equal-weighted portfolio to the standard deviation of a randomly selected component of the portfolio. The lower the diversification ratio, the greater the risk reduction benefits of diversification, and the greater the portfolio effect.
- The composition of the portfolio (weight of each security held in the portfolio) is an important determinant of the overall level of risk inherent in the portfolio. By varying the weights of the individual securities, investors can arrive at a portfolio that offers the same return as an equally weighted portfolio, but with a lower standard deviation (risk).

Despite the obvious benefits of subscribing to the portfolio perspective when making investments, it is important to note that portfolios do not necessarily provide downside protection. The correlation between the various components of the portfolio can change over time in a manner unfavorable to investors and reduce diversification benefits. For example, in the recent market turmoil (late 2007 to early 2009) all major market indices fell in unison.

LOS 41b: Describe types of investors and distinctive characteristics and needs of each. Vol 4, pp 244–250

LOS 41c: Describe defined contribution and defined benefit pension plans. Vol 4, pp 244–245

Individual Investors

> An important thing to note about a defined-contribution plan is that the employee accepts the investment risk in the portfolio.

Individual investors can have a variety of reason for investing (e.g., providing for children's college education, saving for retirement, or starting a business). Most individuals accumulate wealth to provide for their needs during retirement through defined-contribution pension plans, where they contribute a part of their wages to the plan while working.

The investment needs of individuals depend on their broader financial circumstances. Younger investors tend to be more aggressive and look for capital gains, while older investors look to generate a stable income stream to meet retirement needs. See Table 1-1.

Institutional Investors

Defined-benefit pension plans: In a defined-benefit (DB) plan, the employer has an obligation to pay a certain amount to its employees every year once they retire. DB plans are long-term investors and aim to match cash flows from plan assets with the timing of future pension payments (liabilities).

Endowments and foundations: A university endowment is established to provide financial support to the university and its students. A charitable foundation invests the donations that it receives in order to fund grants that are in line with its objectives. Typically, endowments and foundations aim to maintain the inflation-adjusted capital value of their funds, while generating the necessary income to meet their objectives. They are generally established with the intent of having a perpetual useful life and must balance short-term spending needs with long-term capital preservation requirements.

Banks: A bank typically aims to earn a return on its reserves that is greater than the interest that it pays to depositors. In addition to being low risk, a bank's investments must be relatively liquid so that they can be easily sold if depositors need to withdraw funds. In the United States, there are legal restrictions on banks owning equity investments.

Insurance companies: An insurance company writes an insurance policy in return for a premium. These premiums must be invested in a manner that allows the company to meet insurance claims when they arise. Insurance companies are also relatively conservative with their investments as they need to satisfy claims when due. Life insurance companies typically have a longer time horizon than nonlife insurance companies, as they are expected to have to make payments after a longer period.

Investment companies: Investment companies and mutual funds are discussed in detail later in the reading under LOS 41d.

Sovereign wealth funds: A sovereign wealth fund (SWF) is a government-owned investment fund. SWFs are usually established to invest revenues from finite revenue sources (e.g., oil) to benefit future generations of citizens or to manage a country's foreign exchange reserves.

Table 1-1: Summary of Investment Needs by Client Type[1]

Client	Time Horizon	Risk Tolerance	Income Needs	Liquidity Needs
Individual investors	Varies by individual	Varies by individual	Varies by individual	Varies by individual
Defined-benefit pension plans	Typically long term	Typically quite high	High for mature funds; low for growing funds	Typically quite low
Endowments and foundations	Very long term	Typically high	To meet spending commitments	Typically quite low
Banks	Short term	Quite low	To pay interest on deposits and operations expenses	High to meet repayment of deposits

(Table continued on next page...)

1 - Exhibit 14, Volume 4, CFA Program Curriculum 2014

Table 1-1: (*continued*)

Client	Time Horizon	Risk Tolerance	Income Needs	Liquidity Needs
Insurance companies	Short term for property and casualty; long term for life insurance companies	Typically quite low	Typically low	High to meet claims
Investment companies	Varies by fund	Varies by fund	Varies by fund	High to meet redemptions

LOS 41d: Describe the steps in the portfolio management process.
Vol 4, pp 250–254

The portfolio management process involves the following steps:

- Planning
  - Understanding the client's needs.
  - Preparing the investment policy statement (IPS).
- Execution
  - Determining the asset allocation.
  - Analyzing securities.
  - Constructing the portfolio.
- Feedback
  - Monitoring and rebalancing the portfolio.
  - Measuring and reporting performance.

Planning

The planning step involves understanding the client's needs and constraints and developing an investment policy statement (IPS). The IPS is a written document that describes the objectives and constraints of the investor. It may also include a benchmark against which the portfolio manager's performance can be evaluated. An IPS should be reviewed and updated regularly, especially if there has been a drastic change in the client's circumstances.

Execution

Asset allocation: The asset allocation of a portfolio refers to the distribution of investable funds between various asset classes (e.g., equities, fixed-income securities, alternative investments, etc.). Analysts form economic and capital market expectations and allocate funds across asset classes based on how each class is expected to perform in the forecasted scenario. Although decisions regarding which individual securities are chosen do have an effect on portfolio performance, differences in asset allocation explain most of the differences between returns on portfolios.

Security analysis: Analysts use their knowledge of various companies and the industry to identify investments that offer the most attractive risk return characteristics from within each asset class.

Portfolio construction: After determining the target asset allocation and conducting security analysis, the portfolio manager will construct the portfolio in line with the objectives outlined in the IPS. The portfolio must be well diversified and the risk inherent in the portfolio must be in line with the client's risk tolerance level as specified in the IPS.

Once the portfolio manager has decided which securities to purchase and in what amount, she will pass instructions to a trader, who will execute the transactions.

Feedback

Portfolio monitoring and rebalancing: The portfolio must be regularly monitored. Changes in fundamental factors and client circumstances may require changes in the portfolio's composition. Rebalancing may be required when changes in security prices cause a significant change in weights of assets in the portfolio.

Performance measurement and reporting: This step involves measuring the performance of the portfolio relative to the benchmark stated in the IPS and reporting portfolio performance to the client.

LOS 41d: Describe mutual funds and compare them with other investment products. Vol 4, pp 254–261

Pooled Investments

Pooled investments are investments in securities issued by entities that represent ownership in the underlying assets held by those entities. These include:
- Mutual funds and exchange traded funds, in which investors can participate with a relatively small initial investment
- Hedge funds and private equity funds, which may require a minimum investment of U.S. $1 million or more.

Mutual Funds

Mutual funds pool money from several investors and invest these funds in a portfolio of securities. Individuals and institutions invest in mutual funds to obtain diversification benefits and to avail the investment management services of qualified managers. Each investor has a pro-rata share in the income and value of the fund.

The value of a mutual fund is referred to as "net asset value" (NAV), which is calculated on a daily basis based on the closing price of the underlying securities. There are two types of mutual funds:

- *Open-end funds* accept new investment funds and issue new shares at a value equal to the fund's net asset value per share at the time of investment. These funds also allow investors to redeem their investment in the fund at the prevailing net asset value per share.

- *Closed-end funds* accept no new investment money into fund. Shares in the fund are traded in the secondary market so new investors invest in the fund by purchasing shares in the market, and investors liquidate their holdings by selling the shares in the market. Unlike open-end funds, shares of closed-end funds can trade at a discount or premium to the net asset value per share, depending on the demand and supply of shares in the market.

The structure of open-end funds makes it easy for them to grow in size, but it does pose the following problems:
- The portfolio manager needs to manage cash inflows and outflows.
- An inflow of new investment requires the manager to find new investments.
- Funds need to keep cash for redemptions.

Closed-end funds do not face these problems, but as mentioned earlier, they cannot accept new investments.

Mutual funds may also be classified into:

- *Load funds* that charge a percentage fee for investing in the fund and/or for redemptions from the fund on top of an annual fee.
- *No-load funds* that only charge an annual fee based on a percentage of the fund's NAV.

Types of Mutual Funds

- *Money-market funds:* These invest in high-quality, short-term debt instruments. Money-market mutual funds can be divided into tax-free and taxable funds.

- *Bond funds:* These invest in individual bonds and sometimes preference shares as well. Unlike money-market mutual funds, they usually invest in longer term instruments.

- *Stock funds:* These invest in equities and equity indices. Stock mutual funds can be actively or passively managed. Active portfolio management aims to outperform a benchmark portfolio or index by tilting the individual weights of stocks in the portfolio away from their weights in the benchmark. On the other hand, passive management (followed by index funds) aims to track the performance of a benchmark portfolio by attaching the same weights to individual stocks as prescribed by the benchmark.

   Active management entails higher management fees to compensate managers for the research conducted to select mispriced securities. Further, it results in a higher turnover of portfolio securities, which leads to greater capital gains tax liabilities and transaction costs relative to index funds.

- *Hybrid or balanced funds:* These invest in both bonds and equities.

Other Investment Products

Exchange Traded Funds (ETFs)

Exchange traded funds (ETFs) issue shares in a portfolio of securities and are designed to track the performance of a specified index. An ETF purchases a large number of shares in the same proportion as the index it tracks and issues shares in the ETF to investors who want to track the same index.

ETFs combine features of closed-end and open-end mutual funds. They are similar to closed-end funds in that they are traded in the secondary market. However, like open-end funds, their prices stay close to the NAV per share.

ETFs differ from index mutual funds in the following ways:

- Investors in index mutual funds purchase shares directly from the fund, while investors in an ETF purchase shares from other investors (just like buying or selling shares of stock). Investors are allowed to short ETF shares and even purchase them on margin.
- ETFs have lower costs, but unlike index mutual funds, investors do incur brokerage costs when trading ETFs.
- ETFs are constantly traded throughout the business day. Each trade occurs at the prevailing market price at that time. All purchases and redemptions for a mutual fund for a given day occur at the end of a trading day, at the same price.
- ETFs pay out dividends, while index mutual funds usually reinvest dividends.
- The minimum required investment is usually smaller for an ETF.
- ETFs are generally considered to have a tax advantage over index mutual funds.

Separately Managed Accounts (SMAs)

A separately managed account (also called a managed account, wrap account, or individually managed account) is a fund management service for wealthy investors. The portfolio manager manages the account exclusively for the benefit of the client and aims to meet the needs of the client in relation to investment objectives, risk tolerance, and tax situation. The client may also receive personalized investment advice in return for an annual fee.

SMAs differ from mutual funds in the following ways:

- Unlike investors in mutual funds, investors in SMAs directly own the shares and therefore have control over which assets are bought and sold and over the timing of transactions.
- Unlike mutual funds, in which no consideration is given to the tax position of the investor, transactions in SMAs take into account the specific tax needs of the investor.
- The required minimum investment for an SMA is usually much higher than for a mutual fund.

Hedge Funds

Hedge funds and venture capital funds are discussed in greater detail in Reading 60.

Hedge funds were originally meant to offer plays against the market and hedge against a downside, usually through short selling and using derivatives. Today, the term hedge funds has evolved to encompass a host of funds that simply look to generate absolute returns for investors (as compared to other funds that define a specific benchmark whose return they try to match or exceed).

- Hedge funds differ from mutual funds in that most hedge funds are exempt from many of the reporting requirements for a typical public investment company.
- They require a minimum investment that is typically U.S. $250,000 for new funds and U.S. $1 million or more for well-established funds.
- They usually place restrictions on investors' ability to make withdrawals from the fund.
- Total management fee also has a performance-based component.

Hedge fund strategies may involve significant risk due to the use of leverage and derivatives. Some of these strategies are discussed below:

- **Convertible arbitrage funds** purchase securities such as convertible bonds and simultaneously take short positions in related equity securities.
- **Dedicated short bias funds** take more short positions than long positions.
- **Emerging market funds** invest in companies in emerging markets by purchasing corporate or sovereign securities.
- **Equity market neutral funds** eliminate exposure to overall market movements by taking short positions in overvalued securities and long positions (of nearly equal value) in undervalued securities.
- **Event driven funds** attempt to take advantage of specific company events, such as mergers and acquisitions.
- **Fixed-income arbitrage funds** take opposing positions in debt securities to profit from arbitrage opportunities and to limit interest rate risk.
- **Global macro funds** attempt to profit from changes in the overall macroeconomic environment using derivatives on currencies and interest rates.
- **Long/short funds** go long on securities that are expected to increase in value and short securities that are expected to decrease in value. These differ from equity market neutral funds in that they attempt to profit from movements in the broader market, as well as from identifying overvalued or undervalued securities.

Buyout and Venture Capital Funds

Leveraged buyout (LBO) funds raise money specifically for the purpose of buying public companies, taking them private, and restructuring them to make them more efficient and profitable concerns. The purchase of company shares is usually financed with a significant amount of debt. The idea is to service the debt by increasing the company's cash flow and then to exit the investment through an IPO or sale to another company.

A venture capital (VC) fund does not buy out a company, but provides financing to startups.

Buyout and venture capital funds have the following characteristics:

- They take equity positions in companies and play a very active role in managing those companies.
- The eventual exit strategy is an important consideration when funds evaluate potential investments.

LBO and VC funds are similar to hedge funds in that they have relatively high minimum investment requirements, investors are unable to withdraw money from these funds for a specified period, and management fees have a performance-based component.

Reading 42: Portfolio Risk and Return: Part I

Lesson 1: Investment Characteristics of Assets

LOS 42a: Calculate and interpret major return measures and describe their appropriate uses. **Vol 4, pp 272–295**

LOS 42b: Describe characteristics of the major asset classes that investors consider in forming portfolios. **Vol 4, pp 272–295**

LOS 42c: Calculate and interpret the mean, variance, and covariance (or correlation) of asset returns based on historical data. **Vol 4, pp 272–295**

Financial assets are generally defined by their risk and return characteristics. This makes it easier to value them and simplifies the process of determining which assets should be included in a portfolio.

Return

Financial assets may provide one or both of the following types of returns:
- Periodic income (e.g., dividends and interest income)
- Capital gains or losses resulting from changes in market price.

Holding Period Return

Holding period return is simply the return earned on an investment over a single specified period of time. It is calculated as:

$$R = \frac{P_t - P_{t-1} + D_t}{P_{t-1}} = \frac{P_t - P_{t-1}}{P_{t-1}} + \frac{D_t}{P_{t-1}} = \text{Capital gain} + \text{Dividend yield}$$

$$= \frac{P_T + D_T}{P_0} - 1$$

where:
P_t = Price at the end of the period
P_{t-1} = Price at the beginning of the period
D_t = Dividend for the period

Note: We have assumed that the dividend is paid at the end of the period. If the dividend is paid any time before t, we would also have to account for the return earned by investing the dividend for the remainder of the period. This would lead to a higher holding period return.

Holding period returns may also be calculated for more than one period by compounding single period returns:

$$R = [(1 + R_1) \times (1 + R_2) \times \dots \times (1 + R_n)] - 1$$

where:
$R_1, R_2, \dots, R_n$ are sub-period returns

Arithmetic or Mean Return

The arithmetic or mean return is a simple average of all holding period returns. It is calculated as:

$$R = \frac{R_{i1} + R_{i2} + \ldots + R_{iT}}{T} = \frac{1}{T}\sum_{t=1}^{T} R_{iT}$$

Arithmetic return is easy to calculate and has known statistical properties such as standard deviation, which is used to evaluate the dispersion of observed returns. However, the arithmetic mean return is biased upward as it assumes that the amount invested at the beginning of each period is the same. This bias is particularly severe if holding period returns are a mix of both positive and negative returns.

Geometric Mean Return

The geometric mean return accounts for compounding of returns, and does not assume that the amount invested in each period is the same. The geometric mean is lower than the arithmetic mean (due to the effects of compounding) unless there is no variation in returns, in which case they are equal.

The geometric mean return is calculated as:

$$R = \{[(1+R_1)\times(1+R_2)\times\ldots\times(1+R_n)]^{1/n}\} - 1$$

Basically, the geometric mean reflects a "buy-and-hold" strategy, whereas the arithmetic mean reflects a constant dollar investment at the beginning of each time period.

Money-Weighted Return or Internal Rate of Return

Unlike the return measures discussed above, the money-weighted return accounts for the amount of money invested in each period and provides information on the return earned on the actual amount invested. The money-weighted return equals the internal rate of return of an investment.

A drawback of the money-weighted return is that it does not allow for return comparisons between different individuals or different investment opportunities. For example, two investors in the same mutual fund could have different money-weighted returns if they invested varying amounts in different periods.

Example 1-1: Computation of Returns

An analyst gathered the following information regarding a mutual fund's returns over 5 years:

Year	Assets Under Management at the Beginning of the Year	Net Return
1	$40 million	25%
2	$35 million	10%
3	$55 million	−10%
4	$70 million	5%
5	$30 million	20%

---

1. Calculate the holding period return for the 5-year period.
2. Calculate the arithmetic mean annual return.
3. Calculate the geometric mean annual return. How does it compare with the arithmetic mean annual return?
4. Calculate the money-weighted annual return.

Solution

1. Holding period return = $[(1.25)(1.1)(0.9)(1.05)(1.2)] - 1 = 55.93\%$

2. Arithmetic mean annual return = $(0.25 + 0.1 - 0.1 + 0.05 + 0.2) / 5 = 10\%$

3. Geometric mean annual return = $\{[(1.25)(1.1)(0.9)(1.05)(1.2)]^{1/5}\} - 1 = 9.29\%$

4. In order to calculate the money-weighted annual return, we need to determine cash inflows and outflows. From the investor's perspective, amounts invested in the fund are negative cash flows and amounts withdrawn from the fund are positive cash flows. The dollar value of the holdings at the end of the investment horizon is also treated as a cash inflow to the investor.

Year	1	2	3	4	5
Balance from previous year	0	50	38.5	49.5	73.5
Net investment*	40	−15	16.5	20.5	−43.5
Net balance at the beginning of year	40	35	55	70	30
Investment return for the year	25%	10%	−10%	5%	20%
Investment gain/loss	10	3.5	−5.5	3.5	6
Balance at the end of year	50	38.5	49.5	73.5	36

* Net investment = Net balance at the beginning of year − Ending balance from previous year.

The following cash flows are used to compute the money-weighted rate of return.

$CF_0 = -\$40$; $CF_1 = \$15$; $CF_2 = -\$16.5$; $CF_3 = -\$20.5$; $CF_4 = \$43.5$; $CF_5 = \$36$

Use the following TI calculator key strokes to calculate the money-weighted annual return:

[CF] [2ND] CE|C]
40 [+/−] [ENTER] [↓]
15 [ENTER] [↓] [↓]
16.5 [+/−] [ENTER] [↓][↓]
20.5 [+/−] [ENTER] [↓][↓]
43.5 [ENTER] [↓] [↓]
36 [ENTER] [IRR] [CPT]
IRR = 7.97%

An investment may have a term less than one year long. In such cases, the return on the investment is annualized to enable comparisons across investment instruments with different maturities. Annualized returns are calculated as:

$$r_{annual} = (1 + r_{period})^n - 1$$

where:
r = Return on investment
n = Number of periods in a year

The assumption here is that the returns earned over these short investment horizons can be replicated over the year. However, this is not always possible.

Example 1-2: Annualized Returns

An analyst obtained the following rates of return for three investments:

Investment 1 offers a 5.5% return in 120 days
Investment 2 offers a 6.2% return in 16 weeks
Investment 3 offers a 7.3% return in 4 months

Calculate the annualized rates of return for these investments.

Solution

Investment 1:
$R = (1 + 0.055)^{365/120} - 1 = 17.69\%$

Investment 2:
$R = (1 + 0.062)^{52/16} - 1 = 21.59\%$

Investment 3:
$R = (1 + 0.073)^{12/4} - 1 = 23.54\%$

The return on a portfolio is simply the weighted average of the returns on individual assets. For example, the return of a two-asset portfolio can be calculated as:

$$R_p = w_1 R_1 + w_2 R_2$$

where:
R_p = Portfolio return
w_1 = Weight of Asset 1
w_2 = Weight of Asset 2
R_1 = Return of Asset 1
R_2 = Return of Asset 2

Other Return Measures and Their Applications

Gross and Net Returns

Gross returns are calculated before deductions for management expenses, custodial fees, taxes, and other expenses that are not directly linked to the generation of returns. Note that trading expenses (e.g., commissions) are accounted for in the computation of gross returns. Gross returns are an appropriate measure to evaluate portfolio performance.

Net returns deduct all managerial and administrative expenses that reduce an investor's return. Investors are primarily concerned with net returns.

Pre-Tax and After-Tax Nominal Returns

Pre-tax nominal returns do not adjust for taxes or inflation. Unless otherwise stated, always assume that stated returns are pre-tax nominal returns.

After-tax nominal returns account for taxes. Most investors are concerned with returns on an after-tax basis.

Real Returns

Nominal returns consist of the real risk-free rate of return, a premium for risk, and a premium for inflation. Investors calculate the real return because:

- It is useful in comparing returns across time periods as inflation rates may vary over time.
- It is useful in comparing returns among countries when returns are expressed in local currencies in which inflation rates vary between countries.
- The after-tax real return is what an investor receives as compensation for postponing consumption and assuming risk after paying taxes on investment returns.

Real after-tax returns are not usually computed by investment managers because it is difficult to estimate a general tax rate that is applicable to all investors.

Leveraged Return

The leveraged return is computed when an investor uses leverage (by either borrowing money or using derivative contracts) to invest in a security.

Leverage enhances returns, but also magnifies losses. See Example 1-3.

Example 1-3: Computation of Special Returns

Continuing from Example 1-1, suppose that the mutual fund spends a fixed amount of $600,000 every year on expenses that are unrelated to the manager's performance. Given that an investor faces a tax rate of 25% and that the inflation rate is 3%, answer the following questions:

1. What is the annual gross return for the fund in Year 1?
2. What is the after-tax net return for the investor in Year 2? Assume that all gains are realized at the end of the year and that taxes are paid immediately at that time.
3. What is the expected after-tax real return for the investor in Year 5?
4. What is the net return earned by investors in the fund over the 5-year period?

Solution

1. The fixed expenses of $600,000 would cause the gross return to be higher than net return by 1.5% (600,000 / 40,000,000). Therefore, gross return would equal 26.5%(1.5% + 25%).

2. After-tax return (Year 2) = 10% × (1 − 0.25) = 7.5%

3. After-tax return (Year 5) = 20% × (1 − 0.25) = 15%

   $$\text{After-tax real return (Year 5)} = \frac{(1+0.15)}{(1+0.03)} - 1 = 1.1165 - 1 = 0.1165 = 11.65\%$$

4. The HPY for the fund over the 5-year period is computed after considering all direct and indirect expenses. The net return is 55.93%.

Variance and Covariance of Returns

The risk of an asset or a portfolio of assets can be measured by its standard deviation, which is the positive square root of variance.

Variance of a Single Asset

Variance equals the average squared deviation of observed values from their mean. A higher variance indicates higher volatility or dispersion of returns. The population variance is calculated as follows:

$$\sigma^2 = \frac{\sum_{t=1}^{T}(R_t - \mu)^2}{T}$$

where:
R_t = Return for the period t
T = Total number of periods
μ = Mean of T returns

If only a representative sample of the population is available, we may calculate the sample variance as:

$$s^2 = \frac{\sum_{t=1}^{T} (R_t - \bar{R})^2}{T - 1}$$

where:

$\bar{R}$ = mean return of the sample observations

s^2 = sample variance

Standard Deviation of an Asset

The population and sample standard deviations are calculated as:

$$\sigma = \sqrt{\frac{\sum_{t=1}^{T} (R_t - \mu)^2}{T}} \qquad s = \sqrt{\frac{\sum_{t=1}^{T} (R_t - \bar{R})^2}{T - 1}}$$

Variance of a Portfolio of Assets

Earlier in this reading, we learned that the expected return on a portfolio of securities equals the weighted average of the individual securities' returns. However, calculation of portfolio variance and standard deviation is not as straightforward. In addition to being a function of individual asset variances and their weights in the portfolio, portfolio variance also depends on the covariance (and correlation) between the assets in the portfolio. The variance of a two-asset portfolio can be calculated as:

$$\sigma_p^2 = w_1^2 \sigma_1^2 + w_2^2 \sigma_2^2 + 2w_1 w_2 \sigma_1 \sigma_2 \rho_{1,2} \text{ or } w_1^2 \sigma_1^2 + w_2^2 \sigma_2^2 + 2w_1 w_2 \text{Cov}_{1,2}$$

The standard deviation of a portfolio of two risky assets is calculated as:

$$\sigma_p = \sqrt{w_1^2 \sigma_1^2 + w_2^2 \sigma_2^2 + 2w_1 w_2 \sigma_1 \sigma_2 \rho_{1,2}} \text{ or } \sqrt{w_1^2 \sigma_1^2 + w_2^2 \sigma_2^2 + 2w_1 w_2 \text{Cov}_{1,2}}$$

The first part of the formula for the two-asset portfolio standard deviation ($w_1^2 \sigma_1^2 + w_2^2 \sigma_2^2$) tells us that portfolio standard deviation is a *positive* function of the standard deviation and weights of the individual assets held in the portfolio. The second part ($2w_1 w_2 \text{Cov}_{1,2}$) shows us that portfolio standard deviation is also dependent on how the two assets move in relation to each other (covariance or correlation). See Example 1-4.

Example 1-4: Mean Return, Variance of Returns, Covariance of Returns, and Correlation.

An analyst gathered the following information regarding the returns on two stocks:

Year	Stock 1 Return	Stock 2 Return
2006	0.200	0.100
2007	0.100	0.150
2008	–0.150	–0.050
2009	–0.200	0.100
2010	0.050	0.050
2011	0.100	0.200

Calculate the mean return, sample variance, sample covariance, and correlation of returns for these two stocks.

Solution

Year	Stock 1 Return	Stock 2 Return	$R_t - R_1$	$R_t - R_2$	$(R_t - R_1)(R_t - R_2)$
2006	0.200	0.100	0.183	0.008	0.002
2007	0.100	0.150	0.083	0.058	0.005
2008	–0.150	–0.050	–0.167	–0.142	0.024
2009	–0.200	0.100	–0.217	0.008	–0.002
2010	0.050	0.050	0.033	–0.042	–0.001
2011	0.100	0.200	0.083	0.108	0.009
Sum	**0.100**	**0.550**			**0.036**

Stock 1:

The mean return is calculated by dividing the sum of the individual annual returns by the number of years in the sample.

$$\text{Mean Return} = \bar{R}_1 = \frac{\Sigma R_1}{n} = \frac{0.1}{6} = 1.67\%$$

Sample variance is calculated by dividing the sum of the squared deviations from the mean (sum of the contents of Column 4) by the number of years in the sample minus 1.

$$\text{Sample variance} = s^2 = \sum_{n=1}^{N} (R_t - \bar{R}_1)^2 / (N-1)$$

$$s_1^2 = \frac{[(0.183)^2 + (0.083)^2 + (-0.167)^2 + (-0.217)^2 + (0.033)^2 + (0.083)^2]}{(6-1)}$$

$$s_1^2 = 0.0247$$

Sample standard deviation is calculated as the square root of sample variance.

$$\text{Sample standard deviation} = s_1 = (0.0247)^{1/2} = 0.1572$$

Stock 2:

$$\text{Mean Return} = \bar{R}_2 = \frac{0.55}{6} = 9.17\%$$

$$\text{Sample variance} = s_2^2 = \frac{[(0.008)^2 + (0.058)^2 + (-0.142)^2 + (0.008)^2 + (-0.042)^2 + (0.108)^2]}{(6-1)}$$

$$s_2^2 = 0.0074$$

$$\text{Sample standard deviation} = s_2 = (0.0074)^{1/2} = 0.0860$$

Sample covariance is calculated by dividing the sum of the products of the deviations from the mean for the stocks (sum of the contents of Column 6) by the number of years in the sample minus 1.

$$\text{Sample covariance} = \text{Cov}_{1,2} = \frac{[\Sigma(R_t - R_1)(R_t - R_2)]}{(n-1)}$$

$$= \frac{0.036}{(6-1)}$$

$$= 0.0072$$

Finally, sample correlation is calculated by dividing the covariance of returns by the product of the standard deviations of returns of the two stocks.

$$\text{Sample correlation} = \frac{\text{Cov}_{1,2}}{s_1 s_2} \quad \frac{0.0072}{(0.1572 \times 0.0860)} = 05326$$

Historical Return and Risk

Historical Mean Return and Expected Return

Historical return refers to the return that was actually earned in the past, while expected return refers to the return that an investor expects to earn in the future. Historical returns are calculated from historical data, while expected returns are determined by the real risk-free interest rate, expected inflation, and expected risk.

Even though investors sometimes use historical returns to forecast expected returns, one must bear in mind that there is no guarantee that returns earned in the past will be earned in the future.

Risk-Return Trade-off

Every investment decision involves a trade-off between risk and return. Empirical evidence has shown that over the long run, market prices reward higher risk with higher returns.

Other Investment Characteristics

In order to evaluate investments using mean (expected return) and variance (risk), we need to make the following assumptions:

- Returns follow a normal distribution (which is fully described by its mean and variance).
- Markets are informationally and operationally efficient.

When these assumptions are violated we need to consider additional investment characteristics.

Distributional Characteristics

We have discussed the characteristics of a normal distribution in Reading 9. The mean-variance framework is only appropriate for evaluating investments whose returns are normally distributed. In reality however, returns are not always normally distributed. Deviations from normality may occur either because of skewness or kurtosis.

- *Skewness* refers to the asymmetry of a returns distribution.
  - When most of the distribution is concentrated on the left, it is referred to as right skewed or positively skewed.
  - When most of the distribution is concentrated to the right, it is referred to as left skewed or negatively skewed.

- *Kurtosis* refers to fat tails or higher than normal probabilities for extreme returns. This leads to an increase in an asset's risk that is not captured by the mean-variance framework.

Market Characteristics

Markets are not always operationally efficient. One limitation on operational efficiency in markets is liquidity. Liquidity has an impact on the bid-ask spread (illiquid stocks have a wider spread) and on the price impact of a trade (illiquid stocks suffer a greater price impact).

Informational efficiency is discussed in later readings on market efficiency.

LESSON 2: RISK AVERSION, PORTFOLIO SELECTION AND PORTFOLIO RISK

LOS 42d: Explain risk aversion and its implications for portfolio selection. Vol 4, pp 295–304

The Concept of Risk Aversion

Suppose an investor is offered two alternatives:

Option 1: He is guaranteed $25 in one year.
Option 2: There is a 50% chance that he will get $50 in one year, and a 50% chance that he will get nothing.

The expected value in both these cases is $25, but there are three possibilities regarding the investor's preferences.

1. The investor may play it safe and go with Option 1. This behavior is indicative of risk aversion. Risk-averse investors aim to maximize returns for a given level of risk and minimize risk for a given level or return. Historically, there has been a positive relationship between risk and return, which suggests that market prices are primarily determined by investors who are predominantly risk averse.

2. The investor may choose to gamble and go with Option 2. Such risk-seeking investors get extra utility or satisfaction from the uncertainty associated with their investments. Even though most individuals do exhibit risk-seeking behavior in isolated situations (e.g., gambling at casinos when the expected value of the payoff can even be negative), risk aversion is the standard assumption in the investment arena.

3. The investor may be indifferent between the two options. Such risk-neutral investors seek higher returns irrespective of the level of risk inherent in an investment.

Risk tolerance refers to the level of risk that an investor is willing to accept to achieve her investment goals.
- The lower the risk tolerance, the lower the level of risk acceptable to the investor.
- The lower the risk tolerance, the higher the risk aversion.

Utility Theory and Indifference Curves

In the investment management arena, utility is a measure of the relative satisfaction that an investor derives from a particular portfolio. For example, a risk-averse investor obtains a higher utility from a definite outcome relative to an uncertain outcome with the same expected value. In order to quantify the preferences for investment choices using risk and return, utility functions are used. An example of a utility function is:

$$U = E(R) - \frac{1}{2}A\sigma^2$$

where:
U = Utility of an investment
E(R) = Expected return
σ^2 = Variance of returns
A = Additional return required by the investor to accept an additional unit of risk

"A" is a measure of risk aversion. It is higher for investors who are more risk averse as they require larger compensation for accepting more risk.

The utility function listed on the previous page assumes the following:

- Investors are generally risk averse, but prefer more return to less return.
- Investors are able to rank different portfolios based on their preferences and these preferences are internally consistent. This means that if Investment A is preferred to Investment B, and Investment B is preferred to Investment C, Investment A must be preferred to Investment C.

We can draw the following conclusions from the utility function:

- Utility is unbounded on both sides—it can be highly negative or highly positive.
- Higher return results in higher utility.
- Higher risk results in lower utility.
- The higher the value of "A," the higher the negative effect of risk on utility.

Note that utility is not an absolute level of satisfaction. A portfolio with a utility, "U," of 2.5 is not necessarily two times as satisfying as a portfolio with a "U" of 1.25. However, the former would definitely be preferred to the latter.

Important Notes Regarding the Risk Aversion Coefficient, "A"

- "A" is positive for a risk-averse investor. Additional risk reduces total utility.
- It is negative for a risk-seeking investor. Additional risk enhances total utility.
- It equals zero for a risk-neutral investor. Additional risk has no impact on total utility.

Indifference Curves

The risk-return tradeoff that an investor is willing to bear can be illustrated by an indifference curve. An investor realizes the same total utility or satisfaction from every point on a given indifference curve. Since each investor can have an infinite number of risk-return combinations that generate the same utility, indifference curves are continuous at all points. Two points relating to indifference curves for risk-averse investors are worth noting:

1. They are *upward sloping*. This means that an investor will be indifferent between two investments with different expected returns only if the investment with the lower expected return entails a lower level of risk as well.
2. They are *curved*, and their slope becomes steeper as more risk is taken. The increase in return required for every unit of additional risk increases at an increasing rate because of the diminishing marginal utility of wealth.

> Utility cannot be compared across individuals because it is a personal concept. Consequently, it cannot be summed among individuals to determine utility from the societal standpoint.

> The risk-free asset, which has a variance (risk) of zero, generates the same utility for all types of investors.

Figure 2-1: Indifference Curves and Risk Aversion

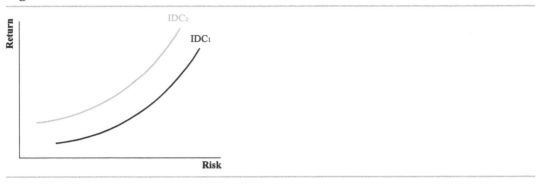

Figure 2-1 illustrates two indifference curves. While an investor would be equally happy at any point on IDC_1, she would prefer any point on IDC_2 to any point on IDC_1. This is because IDC_2 offers a higher level of return for every given level of risk compared to IDC_1. The utility of risk-averse investors increases as we move north-west.

The slope of an indifference curve represents the extra return required by the investor to accept an additional unit of risk. See Figure 2-2.

- A risk-averse investor would have a relatively steep indifference curve (significant extra return required to take on more risk).
- A less risk-averse investor would have a flatter indifference curve (lower extra return required to take on more risk).
- A risk-seeking investor would have an indifference curve with a negative slope. Her utility increases with higher return and higher risk.
- A risk-neutral investor would have a perfectly horizontal indifference curve. Her utility does not vary with risk.

> The risk aversion coefficient (in the utility function) and the slope of the indifference curve are positively related.

Figure 2-2: Indifference Curves of Various Types of Investors

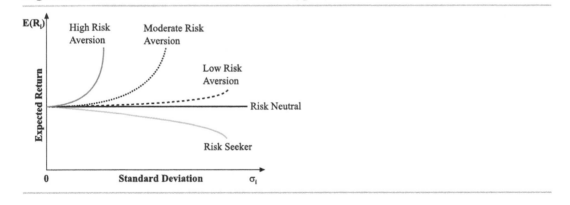

For the remainder of the section on portfolio management, we shall assume that all investors are risk-averse. See Example 2-1.

Example 2-1: Computation of Utility

Answer the questions below based on the following information:

Investment	Expected Return; E(r)	Standard Deviation (s)
A	8%	19%
B	10%	24%
C	17%	28%
D	24%	32%

Utility formula:

$$U = E(R) - \frac{1}{2} A\sigma^2$$

1. Which investment will a risk-averse investor with a risk aversion coefficient of 5 choose?
2. Which investment will a risk-averse investor with a risk aversion coefficient of 3 choose?
3. Which investment will a risk-neutral investor choose?
4. Which investment will a risk-loving investor choose?

Solution

The following table shows the utility for risk-averse investors with A = 5 and A = 3.

Investment	Expected Return; E(r)	Standard Deviation (σ)	Utility at A = 5	Utility at A = 3
A	8%	19%	−0.010	0.0259
B	10%	24%	−0.044	0.0136
C	17%	28%	−0.026	0.0524
D	24%	32%	−0.016	0.0864

1. A risk-averse investor with a risk aversion coefficient of 5 would choose Investment A.

2. A risk-averse investor with a risk aversion coefficient of 3 would choose Investment D.

3. A risk-neutral investor's risk aversion coefficient is 0. She wants the highest return possible and therefore, would choose Investment D.

4. A risk-loving investor likes both higher risk and higher return. Therefore, she would choose Investment D as well.

Application of Utility Theory to Portfolio Selection

The Risk-Free Asset

The expected return on a risk-free asset is entirely certain and therefore the standard deviation of its expected returns is zero ($\sigma_{RFR} = 0$). The return earned on the risk-free asset is the risk-free rate (RFR).

Expected Return for a Portfolio Containing a Risky Asset and the Risk-Free Asset

Let's assume that we invest a proportion of our investable funds (w_i) in a risky asset (i) that has an expected return, $E(R_i)$, and variance, σ_i^2, and the remainder ($1 - w_i$) in the risk-free asset that has an expected return of RFR and a variance of zero.

> The relevant portion of the CFA Program curriculum invests a weight of w_i in the risk-free asset. We assume that w_i equals the weight of the risky asset in the portfolio. The conclusion of the analysis is the same.

The expected return for the portfolio that includes the risk-free asset and a risky asset is simply the weighted average of their expected returns.

$$E(R_p) = w_i E(R_i) + (1 - w_i)RFR \quad \text{or} \quad E(R_p) = RFR + w_i[E(R_i) - RFR]$$

where:
w_i = Proportion of funds invested in the risky asset.
$E(R_i)$ = The expected rate of return on the risky asset.

Equation 1

Standard Deviation of a Portfolio Containing a Risky Asset and the Risk-Free Asset

Recall that the variance for a two-asset portfolio is given as:

$$\sigma_{portfolio}^2 = w_1^2\sigma_1^2 + w_2^2\sigma_2^2 + 2w_1 w_2\sigma_1\sigma_2\rho_{1,2}$$

Substituting the risk-free asset for Asset 1, and the risky asset (i) for Asset 2, this formula becomes:

$$S_{portfolio}^2 = (1 - w_i)^2 S_{RFR}^2 + w_i^2\sigma_i^2 + 2(1 - w_i)w_i S_{RFR}\sigma_i R_{RFR,i}$$

The variance of the risk-free asset is zero because it has a guaranteed return. Further, the return on the risk-free asset does not vary with the return on any risky asset. Therefore, the correlation between the risk-free asset and the risky asset is also zero ($R_{RFR,i} = 0$). Hence, the expression for the variance of a portfolio becomes:

$$\sigma_{port}^2 = w_i^2\sigma_i^2$$

The standard deviation of a portfolio that combines a risk-free asset with a risky asset is a linear proportion of the standard deviation of the risky asset.

$$\sigma_{port} = w_i\sigma_i$$

The expression for the standard deviation of the portfolio can be reorganized to get an expression for w_i:

$$w_i = \frac{\sigma_{port}}{\sigma_i}$$

Equation 2

Replacing w_i with $\dfrac{\sigma_{port}}{\sigma_i}$ in Equation 1, we can state the expected return on the portfolio as a function of portfolio risk:

$$E(R_p) = RFR + w_i[E(R_i) - RFR] \quad (Equation\ 1)$$

$$E(R_p) = RFR + \frac{\sigma_{port}}{\sigma_i}[E(R_i) - RFR]$$

$$E(R_p) = RFR + \sigma_{port}\frac{[E(R_i) - RFR]}{\sigma_i}$$

This equation that relates the return on a portfolio composed of the risk-free asset and a risky asset to the standard deviation of the portfolio is known as the capital allocation line (CAL). The CAL has an intercept of RFR and a constant slope that equals:

$$\boxed{\frac{[E(R_i) - RFR]}{\sigma_i}}$$

The expression for the slope of the CAL is the extra return required for each additional unit of risk and is also known as the market price of risk. See Figure 2-3.

Figure 2-3: Capital Allocation Line with Two Assets

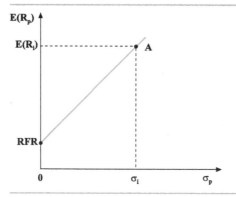

- At Point RFR, the portfolio only consists of the risk-free asset. Therefore, its expected return equals RFR and variance equals zero.
- At Point A, the portfolio only consists of the risky asset. Therefore its expected return equals $E(R_i)$ and variance equals σ_i^2
- Risk-return combinations beyond Point A can be obtained by borrowing at the risk-free rate $(1 - w_i < 0)$ and investing in the risky asset $(w_i > 1)$.

The next question is which of these numerous portfolios that lie along the CAL will actually be chosen by the investor? The answer lies in combining indifference curves with the CAL. Indifference curves represent the investor's utility function, while the CAL represents the risk-return combinations of the set of portfolios that the investor can invest in. Portfolios that lie below the CAL may be invested in, but then the investor would not be maximizing the potential return given the level of risk she is willing to take. Portfolios that lie above the CAL are desirable, but cannot be attained with the given assets.

Figure 2-4: Portfolio Selection

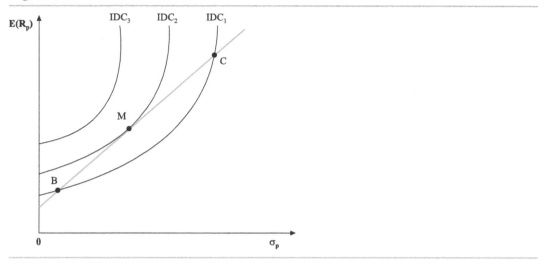

From Figure 2-4 notice that:

- IDC$_3$, which lies above the CAL, is most desirable but cannot be attained with the available assets.
- IDC$_1$ intersects the CAL at two different points, Point B and Point C. Both these points offer the same level of satisfaction to the investor, as they lie on the same indifference curve.
- IDC$_2$ is tangential to the CAL at Point M.

Given a choice between investing in a portfolio on IDC$_1$ (Points B or C) or in a portfolio on IDC$_2$ (Point M) an investor would choose the portfolio on IDC$_2$ as it offers a higher level of satisfaction (it lies to the northwest of IDC$_1$). Therefore, Point M (the point of tangency between the investor's indifference curve and the CAL) represents the optimal portfolio for this investor.

Portfolio Selection for Two Investors with Different Levels of Risk Aversion

The indifference curve of a relatively more risk-averse investor (Harry) would lie to the left of the indifference curve of a less risk-averse investor (Bob) because he has a lower tolerance for risk. Notice that Harry's optimal portfolio has a lower expected return and a lower level of risk than Bob's optimal portfolio. Further, for the same level of return, Harry's indifference curve has a higher slope, which suggests that he needs a greater incremental return than Bob for taking additional risk. See Figure 2-5.

Figure 2-5: Optimal Portfolios

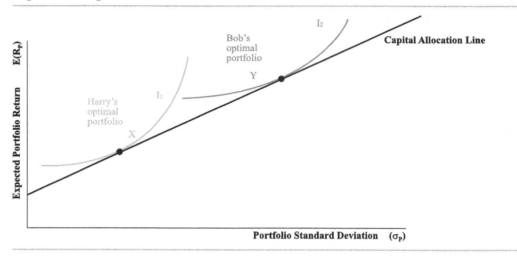

LOS 42e: Calculate and interpret portfolio standard deviation.
Vol 4, pp 304–315

LOS 42f: Describe the effect on a portfolio's risk of investing in assets that
are less than perfectly correlated. **Vol 4, pp 304–315**

Portfolio Risk

Earlier in this reading, we learned that in addition to being a function of individual asset
variances and their weights in the portfolio, *portfolio variance also depends on the
covariance (and correlation) between the assets in the portfolio.* The formula for the
standard deviation of a portfolio of risky assets is:

$$\sigma_p = \sqrt{\sigma_p^2} = \sqrt{\sum_{i=1}^{n} w_i^2 \sigma_i^2 + \sum_{i=1}^{n}\sum_{j=1}^{n} w_i w_j Cov_{i,j}} \qquad i \neq j$$

The formula for the standard deviation of a portfolio consisting of two risky assets is:

$$\sigma_p = \sqrt{w_1^2\sigma_1^2 + w_2^2\sigma_2^2 + 2w_1 w_2 \sigma_1 \sigma_2 \rho_{1,2}} \text{ or } \sqrt{w_1^2\sigma_1^2 + w_2^2\sigma_2^2 + 2w_1 w_2 Cov_{1,2}}$$

The formula for the standard deviation of a portfolio consisting of three risky assets is:

$$\sigma_p = \sqrt{w_1^2\sigma_1^2 + w_2^2\sigma_2^2 + w_3^2\sigma_3^2 + 2w_1 w_2 Cov_{1,2} + 2w_2 w_3 Cov_{2,3} + 2w_3 w_1 Cov_{3,1}}$$

The first part of the formula for the two-asset portfolio standard deviation ($w_1^2\sigma_1^2 + w_2^2\sigma_2^2$)
tells us that portfolio standard deviation is a *positive* function of the standard deviation
and weights of the individual assets held in the portfolio. The second part ($2w_1 w_2 Cov_{1,2}$)
shows us that portfolio standard deviation is also dependent on how the two assets move in
relation to each other (covariance or correlation).

From the two-asset portfolio standard deviation formula it is also important to understand that:

- The maximum value for portfolio standard deviation will be obtained when the correlation coefficient equals +1.
- Portfolio standard deviation will be minimized when the correlation coefficient equals −1.
- If the correlation coefficient equals zero, the second part of the formula will equal zero and portfolio standard deviation will lie somewhere in between.

Implications

- When asset returns are *negatively* correlated, the final term in the standard deviation formula is negative and serves to *reduce* portfolio standard deviation.
- If the correlation between assets equals zero, portfolio standard deviation is *greater* than when correlation is negative.
- When asset returns are positively correlated, the second part of the formula for portfolio standard deviation is also positive and portfolio standard deviation is higher than when the correlation coefficient equals zero. With a correlation coefficient of +1 (perfect positive correlation) there are no diversification benefits.

Let's go through a brief example to highlight some important points. Assets A and B have the following expected returns, portfolio weights, variances, and standard deviations:

Asset	E(R)	Weight	σ^2	σ
A	0.10	0.5	0.0081	0.09
B	0.05	0.5	0.0049	0.07

Portfolio standard deviations in various correlation scenarios are given below.

Scenario	Correlation Between Assets	Portfolio Standard Deviation
a	−1	0.01
b	−0.5	0.0409
c	0	0.057
d	0.5	0.0695
e	1	0.08

First of all, remember that the portfolio's expected return does *not* vary with the correlation coefficient of the two assets. The expected return for this portfolio equals 0.075 or 7.5%.

a. With perfectly negative correlation, the standard deviation of the portfolio is at its lowest (1%). The negative covariance term significantly offsets the individual asset variance terms.

b. With a correlation of −0.5 the standard deviation of the portfolio is not at its lowest, but is still relatively low (4.09%) due to the negative covariance term.

c. With zero correlation, portfolio standard deviation (5.7%) is higher than it is with negative correlation, but lower than it is with positive correlation.

d. With a correlation of 0.5 the standard deviation of the portfolio is still higher (6.95%).

e. With perfect positive correlation, the standard deviation of the portfolio (8%) is at its highest possible level. There are no diversification benefits from investing in the portfolio when correlation is +1. In this scenario, portfolio standard deviation is simply the weighted average of the standard deviations of the individual assets. This is because the expression for portfolio standard deviation is in the form of:

$$\sigma_{port} = \sqrt{(w_A \sigma_A)^2 + (w_B \sigma_B)^2 + 2(w_A \sigma_A)(w_B \sigma_B)(1)}$$

which can be simplified to:

$$\sigma_{port} = \sqrt{[(w_A \sigma_A) + (w_B \sigma_B)]^2} \Rightarrow \sigma_{port} = (w_A \sigma_A) + (w_B \sigma_B)$$

> Recall from high school algebra that an expression in the form of $(a + b)^2$ can be expanded to $(a^2 + b^2 + 2ab)$

Conclusion: The risk (standard deviation) of a portfolio of risky assets depends on the asset weights and standard deviations, *and most importantly on the correlation of asset returns.* The *higher* the correlation between the individual assets, the *higher* the portfolio's standard deviation.

Constant Correlation with Changing Weights

Using the same two assets, now let's change the weights of the individual assets in the portfolio, and use a constant correlation coefficient of zero to gauge the impact on portfolio standard deviation.

Portfolio	w_A	w_B	$E(R_{port})$	σ_{port}
f	0	1	0.05	0.07
g	0.25	0.75	0.0625	0.0571
h	0.5	0.5	0.075	0.57
i	0.75	0.25	0.0875	0.0697
j	1	0	0.1	0.09

Figure 2-6: Risk Return Tradeoff

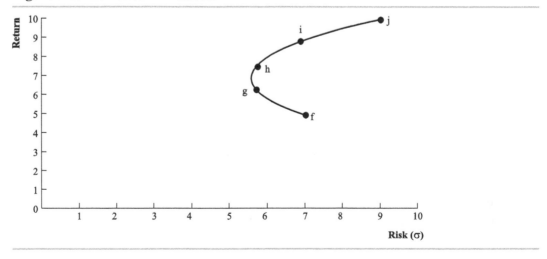

From Figure 2-6, notice the following:

- The set of risk-return combinations for the 5 portfolios traces an ellipse that starts at Portfolio f (Asset B's risk-return profile), and goes through the 50–50 point onto Portfolio j (Asset A's risk-return profile).
- With assets that have a correlation of less than +1, it is possible to form portfolios that have a *lower* risk than either of the individual assets. This holds true for Portfolios g, h, and i in our example.
- A conservative investor can experience both a higher return and a lower risk by diversifying into a higher-risk, higher-return asset if the correlation between the assets is fairly low. Suppose a conservative investor is fully invested in Asset B (Portfolio f), where she expects a return of 5% with a portfolio standard deviation of 7%. By shifting 25% of her assets into the higher-risk asset (Asset A) and investing in Portfolio g, she can increase her expected return to 6.25% and lower the standard deviation of her portfolio to 5.71%.

Figure 2-7 shows the change in curvature of the risk-return relationship between assets depending on their weights, as a function of the correlation between the two assets

Figure 2-7: Effect of Correlation on Portfolio Risk and Return

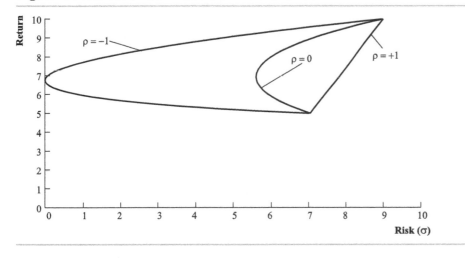

Notice that for any mix of asset weights, the maximum value that the portfolio standard deviation can take is equal to the higher of the individual assets' standard deviations.

Notice the following from Figure 2-7:

- When correlation equals +1, the risk-return combinations that result from altering the weights lie along a straight line between the two assets' risk-return profiles.
- As correlation falls, the curvature of this line increases.
- When correlation equals −1, the curve is represented by two straight lines that meet at the vertical axis. This point represents a zero-risk portfolio where portfolio return must equal the risk-free rate to prevent arbitrage.

Portfolios of Many Risky Assets

As more and more assets are added to a portfolio, the contribution of each individual asset's risk to portfolio risk diminishes. The covariance among the assets in the portfolio accounts for the bulk of portfolio risk.

Further, given that there are a large number of assets in the portfolio, if we assume that all assets in the portfolio have the same variance and the same correlation among assets, the portfolio can have a variance of zero (zero risk) if the individual assets are unrelated to one another.

Avenues for Diversification

Investors can diversify by:

- Investing in a variety of asset classes (e.g., large cap stocks, small cap stocks, bonds, commodities, real estate, etc.) that are not highly correlated.
- Using index funds that minimize the costs of diversification and grant exposure to specific asset classes.
- Investing among countries that focus on different industries, are undergoing different stages of the business cycle, and have different currencies.
- Choosing not to invest a significant portion of their wealth in employee stock plans, as their human capital is already entirely invested in their employing companies.
- Only adding a security to the portfolio if its Sharpe ratio is greater than the Sharpe ratio of the portfolio times the correlation coefficient.
- Only adding a security to the portfolio if the benefit (additional expected return, reduced portfolio risk) is greater than the associated costs (trading costs and costs of tracking a larger portfolio).
- Adding insurance to the portfolio by purchasing put options or adding an asset class that has a negative correlation with the assets in the portfolio (e.g., commodities).

LESSON 3: EFFICIENT FRONTIER AND INVESTOR'S OPTIMAL PORTFOLIO

LOS 42g: Describe and interpret the minimum-variance and efficient frontiers of risky assets and the global minimum-variance portfolio. Vol 4, pp 315–322

We have learned that combining risky assets may result in a portfolio that has lower risk than any of the individual assets in the portfolio (the third bullet on the previous page). As the number of assets available increases, they can be combined into a large number of different portfolios (each with different assets and weights), and we can create an opportunity set of investments.

Combinations of these assets can be formed into portfolios that entail the lowest level of risk for each level of expected return. An envelope curve that plots the risk-return characteristics of the lowest risk "domestic assets only" portfolios is labeled MVF_{DA} (minimum-variance frontier—domestic assets) on Figure 3-1. As international assets are added to the portfolio, portfolio risk for each level of return can be reduced further given that international assets are not perfectly positively correlated with domestic assets. Therefore, the minimum-variance frontier that includes international assets (MVF_{IA}) lies to the left of MVF_{DA}. Similarly, once all possible investments and asset classes are considered, the minimum-variance frontier (MVF) that plots the risk-return characteristics of portfolios that minimize portfolio risk at each given level of return lies further to the left. We will work with this minimum-variance frontier as we move forward and assume that all assets and asset classes have been considered in deriving this minimum-variance frontier. Note that no risk-averse investor would invest in any portfolio that lies to the right of the MVF, as it would entail a higher level of risk than a portfolio that lies on the MVF for a given level of return.

Figure 3-1: Investment Opportunity Set

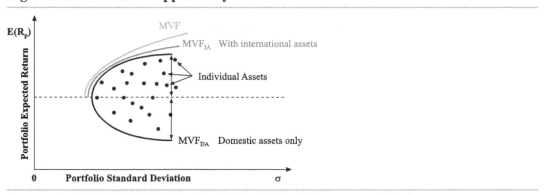

In Figure 3-2, notice that Portfolios A, B, and C all have the same expected return, $E(R_1)$. Portfolio A entails the lowest level of risk, but lies to the left of the minimum variance frontier so it cannot be attained given the investment opportunity set. The minimum risk that the investor can take to earn $E(R_1)$ is by investing in Portfolio B. A risk-averse investor would invest in Portfolio B over Portfolio C as it entails lower risk for the same expected return. Portfolio D defines the global minimum-variance portfolio. It is the portfolio of risky securities that entails the lowest level of risk among all the risky asset portfolios on the minimum-variance frontier.

Note the emphasis on "risky" assets. Later, the introduction of the risk-free asset will allow us to relax this constraint.

Figure 3-2: Minimum-Variance Frontier

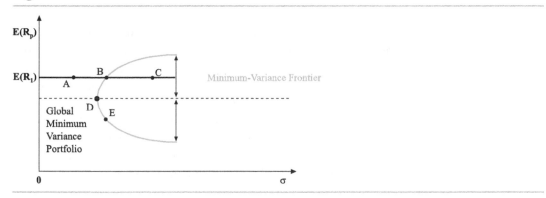

The minimum-variance frontier represents portfolios with the lowest level of risk for each level of expected return. Investors aim to maximize expected return for each level of risk. Given a choice between Portfolios B and E (that entail the same level of risk and lie on the minimum-variance frontier), an investor would prefer Portfolio B as it offers a higher return. Therefore, all portfolios on the MVF that lie above and to the right of the global minimum-variance portfolio dominate all portfolios on the MVF that lie below and to the right of the global minimum-variance portfolio.

This dominant portion of the MVF (the one above and to the right of the global minimum-variance portfolio) is known as the Markowitz efficient frontier. It contains all the possible portfolios that rational, risk-averse investors will consider investing in.

An important thing to note about the efficient frontier is that the slope of the curve decreases as we move to the right. The additional return attained as investors take on more risk (by successively moving to the right along the Markowitz efficient frontier to portfolios with more and more risk) declines.

A Risk-Free Asset and Many Risky Assets

Now let's bring the risk-free asset into our analysis. The risk-free asset has zero risk (so it plots on the y-axis), an expected return of RFR, and zero correlation with risky assets. Further, the risk-return characteristics of portfolios that combine the risk-free asset with a risky asset or a portfolio of risky assets lie along a straight line.

An investor can attain any point along CAL_A by investing a certain portion of her funds in the risk-free asset and the remainder in a portfolio of risky assets (Portfolio A). The set of portfolios that lies on CAL_A (combinations of the risk-free asset and Portfolio A with varying weights) dominates all the risky-asset portfolios on the efficient frontier below Point A because portfolios along CAL_A have a higher return than the portfolios on the efficient frontier with the same risk (standard deviation).

> The difference between the CALs that we are using here and the CAL described earlier in the reading is that back then we were combining the risk-free asset with a risky asset. Now that we are working with the Markowitz efficient frontier, we are combining the risk-free asset with different portfolios of risky assets.

Likewise, any position can be attained along CAL_B by investing in some combination of the risk-free asset and Portfolio B of risky assets. Again, these potential combinations of the risk-free asset and Portfolio B dominate all portfolio possibilities on the efficient frontier below Point B. Further, any portfolio that lies on CAL_B dominates any portfolio on CAL_A because portfolios that lie on CAL_B offer a higher expected return for any given level of risk compared to those on CAL_A.

Therefore, as the investor combines the risk-free asset with portfolios further up the efficient frontier, she keeps attaining better portfolio combinations. Each successive portfolio on the efficient frontier has a steeper line (higher slope) joining it to the risk-free asset. The slope of this line represents the additional return per unit of extra risk. The steeper the slope of the line, the better risk-return tradeoff the portfolio offers. The line with the steepest slope is the one that is drawn from the risk-free asset to Portfolio M (which occurs at the point of tangency between the efficient frontier and a straight line drawn from the risk-free rate). This particular line offers the best risk-return tradeoff to the investor. Any combination of the risk-free asset and Portfolio M dominates all portfolios below CAL_M.

It is essential to understand what we have accomplished here. By adding the risk-free asset, we have narrowed down the risky asset portfolio that an investor would invest in to a single optimal portfolio, Portfolio M, which is at the point of tangency between CAL_M and the efficient frontier.

- At Point RFR, an investor has all her funds invested in the risk-free asset.
- At Point M she has all of her funds invested in Portfolio M (which is entirely composed of risky securities).
- At any point between RFR and M, she holds both Portfolio M and the risk-free asset (i.e., she is lending some of her funds at the risk-free rate).

However, an investor may want to attain a higher expected return than available at Point M, where all her funds are invested in the risky-asset portfolio. Adding leverage to the portfolio by borrowing money at the RFR and investing it in the risky asset portfolio will allow her to attain risk-return profiles beyond (to the right of, or above) Point M on the CAL_M (e.g., Point L). See Figure 3-3.

Figure 3-3: Optimal Risky Portfolio

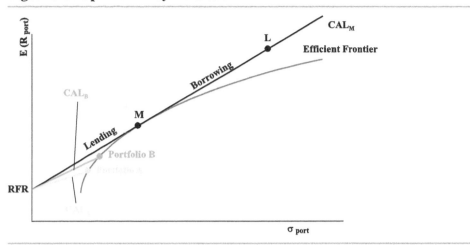

The Two-Fund Separation Theorem

The two-fund separation theorem states that regardless of risk and return preferences, all investors hold some combination of the risk-free asset and an optimal portfolio of risky assets. Therefore, the investment problem can be broken down into two steps:

1. The investing decision, where an investor identifies her optimal risky portfolio.
2. The financing decision, where she determines where exactly on the optimal CAL, she wants her portfolio to lie. Her risk preferences (as delineated by her indifference curves) determine whether her desired portfolio requires borrowing or lending at the risk-free rate.

Example 3-1: Choosing the Right Portfolio

Based on the information in Figure 3-4 and the table that follows, answer the following questions:

Figure 3-4: Choosing the Right Portfolio

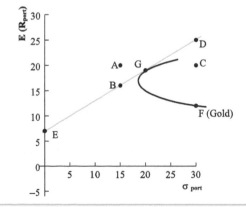

Point	Return (%)	Risk (%)
A	20	15
B	16	15
C	20	30
D	25	30
E	7	0
F (Gold)	12	30
G	19	20

1. Which of the above points is not achievable?
2. Which of the portfolios will not be chosen by a rational, risk-averse investor?
3. Which of these portfolios is most suitable for a risk-neutral investor?
4. Why is gold held by many rational investors as part of a larger portfolio, when it is shown in the graph to lie on the inefficient part of the feasible set?

Solution

1. Portfolio A lies outside the feasible set and therefore is not achievable.

2. Portfolios C and F will not be chosen by a rational, risk-averse investor. This is because Portfolio D provides higher return (25%) than both of them for the same level of risk (30%). Portfolios C and F are the only investable points that do not lie on the capital allocation line.

3. Portfolio D is most suitable for a risk-neutral investor who does not care about risk and wants the highest possible return.

4. Although gold lies on the inefficient part of the feasible set, it is still held by many rational investors as part of a larger portfolio. This is because gold has low or negative correlation with many risky assets, which helps to reduce the overall risk of the portfolio.

LOS 42h: Discuss the selection of an optimal portfolio, given an investor's utility (or risk aversion) and the capital allocation line. Vol 4, pp 322–327

Optimal Investor Portfolio

The line CAL_M in Figures 3-3 and 3-5 represents the best portfolios available to an investor. The portfolios along this line contain the risk-free asset and the optimal portfolio, Portfolio M, with varying weights. An individual's optimal portfolio depends on her risk-return preferences, which are incorporated into her indifference curves.

Figure 3-5 shows an investor's indifference curve, which is tangent to the CAL_M at Point C. Therefore, the optimal investor portfolio for this particular investor is Portfolio C on the CAL_M.

For a more risk-averse investor, the optimal investor portfolio would lie closer to the y-axis (a higher proportion invested in the risk-free asset), while a less risk-averse investor's optimal portfolio would lie closer to Portfolio M, and further away from the y-axis. An investor with an even higher tolerance for risk might borrow money at the risk-free rate to invest in Portfolio M. Her optimal portfolio would lie to the right of Portfolio M on CAL_M.

The thing to notice is that we have been able to account for all types of investors' risk preferences by using just two items—the risk-free asset and Portfolio M that consists of risky assets. Portfolio M is the optimal risky asset portfolio and will be selected by a rational, risk-averse investor regardless of her preferences. The only decision that the investor makes is how to divide her funds between the risk-free asset and the Portfolio M.

Figure 3-5: Optimal Investor Portfolio

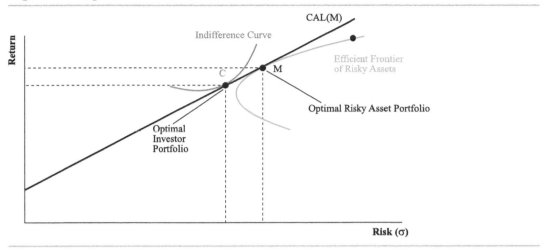

READING 43: PORTFOLIO RISK AND RETURN: PART II

LESSON 1: CAPITAL MARKET THEORY

Before getting into the LOS for this reading, we summarize some of the important takeaways from the previous sections on portfolio management:

- Risky assets can be combined into portfolios that may have a lower risk than each of the individual assets in the portfolio if assets are not perfectly positively correlated.
- An investor's investment opportunity set includes all the individual risky assets and risky asset portfolios that she can invest in.
- The minimum-variance frontier reduces the investment opportunity set to a curve that contains only those portfolios that entail the lowest level of risk for each level of expected return.
- The global minimum-variance portfolio is the portfolio of risky assets that entails the lowest level of risk among all portfolios on the minimum-variance frontier.
- Investors aim to maximize return for every level of risk. Therefore, all portfolios above and to the right of the global minimum-variance portfolio dominate those that lie below and to the right of the global minimum-variance portfolio.
- The section of the minimum-variance frontier that lies above and to the right of the global minimum-variance portfolio is referred to as the Markowitz efficient frontier.

A risk-free asset has an expected return of the risk-free rate (RFR), a standard deviation (risk) of zero, and a correlation with any risky asset of zero. Once the risk-free asset is introduced into the mix:

LOS 43a: Describe the implications of combining a risk-free asset with a portfolio of risky assets. **Vol 4, pp 342–346**

- Any portfolio that combines a risky asset portfolio that lies on the Markowitz efficient frontier and the risk-free asset has a risk-return tradeoff that is linear (CAL is represented by a straight line).
- The point at which a line drawn from the risk-free rate is tangent to the Markowitz efficient frontier defines the optimal risky asset portfolio. This line is known as the optimal CAL.
- Each investor will choose a portfolio (optimal investor portfolio) that contains some combination of the risk-free asset and the optimal risky portfolio. The weights of the risk free asset and the optimal risky portfolio in the optimal investor portfolio depend on the investor's risk tolerance (indifference curve).
- The optimal investor portfolio is defined by the point where the investor's indifference curve is tangent to the optimal CAL.

LOS 43b: Explain the capital allocation line (CAL) and the capital market line (CML). Vol 4, pp 342–350

Going forward, we shall assume that all investors have homogenous expectations. Given that all investors in the market have identical expectations regarding the risk-return distribution for each asset, only one optimal risky portfolio exists. If investors have different expectations regarding various assets, there would be different optimal risky portfolios.

If markets are informationally efficient (i.e., market price is an unbiased estimate of the sum of the discounted values of a security's expected cash flows), investors would not be able to earn a rate of return that exceeds the required rate of return from the investment. In this case, investors should adopt passive investment strategies as they entail lower costs and are easy to administer.

If however, an investor has more confidence in her abilities to forecast cash flows and estimate growth rates and discount rates, she might consider an active investment strategy. She would use her forecasts to determine whether an asset is fairly priced by the market and trade on any perceived mispricing.

When we refer to the "market" we are referring to all assets (e.g., stocks, bonds, real estate, commodities, etc.) that are tradable and investable. For our purposes, going forward, we will define the term "market" quite narrowly as the S&P500 Index. The terms "market return" and "market risk premium" therefore refer to the return on the S&P500 and the U.S. equity risk premium (difference between the S&P500 return and the U.S. long-term interest rate) respectively.

The Capital Market Line

A capital allocation line (CAL), which was described in the previous reading, includes all combinations of the risk-free asset and **any risky asset portfolio**. The capital market line (CML) is a special case of the capital allocation line where the risky asset portfolio that is combined with the risk-free asset is the **market portfolio**.

Graphically, the market portfolio occurs at the point where a line from the risk-free asset is tangent to the Markowitz efficient frontier. The market portfolio is the optimal risky asset portfolio given homogenous expectations. All portfolios that lie below the CML offer a lower return than portfolios that plot on the CML for each level of risk.

An interesting point is that the slopes of the CML and CAL are constant even though they represent combinations of two assets. The important thing to note is that they are not combinations of two risky assets, but of a risk-free asset and a risky portfolio.

The risk and return characteristics of portfolios that lie on the CML can be computed using the risk and return formulas for two-asset portfolios.

Expected return on portfolios that lie on CML

$$E(R_p) = w_f R_f + (1 - w_f)E(R_m)$$

Variance of portfolios that lie on CML

$$\sigma^2 = w_f^2 \sigma_f^2 + (1 - w_f)^2 \sigma_m^2 + 2w_f(1 - w_f)Cov(R_f, R_m)$$

The derivation of this expression relating the expected return of portfolios that lie on the CML to their variance (risk) is very similar to the derivation of the CAL equation in Reading 42. The only difference is that the risky asset, i, in the CAL is replaced by the market portfolio, m, in the CML.

Equation of CML

$$E(R_p) = R_f + \frac{E(R_m) - R_f}{\sigma_m} \times \sigma_p$$

where:
y-intercept = R_f = risk-free rate

$$\text{slope} = \frac{E(R_m) - R_f}{\sigma_m} = \text{market price of risk}$$

Figure 1-1 illustrates the CML.

Figure 1-1: Capital Market Line

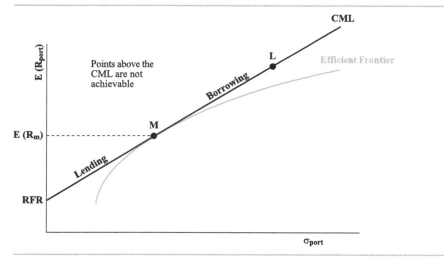

- At Point RFR, an investor has all her funds invested in the risk-free asset.
- At Point M she has all of her funds invested in the market portfolio (which only contains risky securities).
- At any point between RFR and M, she holds both the market portfolio and the risk-free asset (i.e., she is lending some of her funds at the risk-free rate).

However, an investor may want to attain a higher expected return than available at Point M, where all her funds are invested in the market portfolio. Adding leverage to the portfolio by borrowing money at the RFR and investing it in the market portfolio will allow her to attain a risk-return profile beyond (to the right of, or above) Point M on the CML (e.g., Point L).

The particular point that an investor chooses on the CML depends on her utility function, which in turn is determined by her risk and return preferences. See Example 1-1.

Example 1-1: Risk and Return of a Leveraged Portfolio

Sasha Miles is evaluating how to allocate funds between the risk-free asset and the market portfolio. She gathers the following information:
- Risk-free rate of return = 6%
- Expected return on the market portfolio = 14%
- Standard deviation of returns of the market portfolio = 23%

Calculate the expected risk and return of a portfolio that is:
a. 75% invested in the market portfolio.
b. 140% invested in the market portfolio.

Solution

Portfolio return and standard deviation can be calculated using the following equations:

$$E(R_p) = w_1 R_f + (1 - w_1)E(R_m)$$

$$\sigma_p = (1 - w_1)\sigma_m$$

Recall that the standard deviation of the risk-free asset, and the covariance of returns between the risk-free asset and the market portfolio, both equal 0.

---

a. $E(R_p) = w_1R_f + (1-w_1)E(R_m)$

$E(R_p) = (0.25 \times 0.06) + (0.75 \times 0.14) = 12\%$

$\sigma_p = (1-w_1)\sigma_m$

$\sigma_p = (0.75 \times 0.23) = 17.25\%$

b. $E(R_p) = (-0.4 \times 0.06) + (1.4 \times 0.14) = 17.2\%$

$\sigma_p = (1.4 \times 0.23) = 32.2\%$

A weight of 140% in the market portfolio implies that the investor borrows 40% of the funds at the risk-free rate (6%).

Leveraged Positions with Different Lending and Borrowing Rates

In the previous section, we assumed that an investor could borrow or lend unlimited amounts of funds at the risk-free rate. Practically speaking, an investor's ability to repay is not as certain as that of the U.S. government, so the rate at which she would be able to borrow would be higher than the rate at which she would be able to lend. Given the disparity in borrowing and lending rates, the CML would no longer be a straight line (see Figure 1-2).

The slope of the CML to the left of Point M (when she invests a portion of her portfolio in the risk-free asset at R_f) would be:

$$\frac{E(R_m) - R_f}{\sigma_m}$$

While the slope CML to the right of Point M (where she is borrowing at R_b) would be:

$$\frac{E(R_m) - R_b}{\sigma_m}$$

All passively managed portfolios would lie on the kinked CML even though an investor's investment in the risk free asset may be:

- Positive (the investor's optimal portfolio would lie between RFR and Point M)
- Zero (the investor's optimal portfolio would lie at Point M)
- Negative (the investor's optimal portfolio would lie to the right of Point M)

The risk and return for a leveraged portfolio is higher than that of an unleveraged portfolio. Further, given that the investor's borrowing rate is higher than the risk-free rate, for each additional unit of risk taken beyond Point M (when the portfolio is leveraged), the investor gets a lower increase in expected return compared with portfolios to the left of Point M (where the portfolio is not leveraged).

Figure 1-2: CML with Different Lending and Borrowing Rates

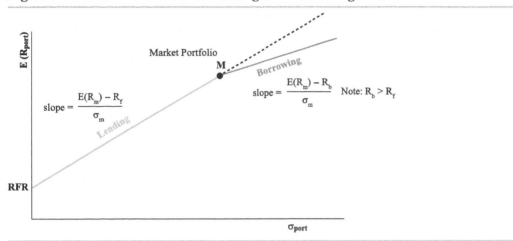

LOS 43c: Explain systematic and nonsystematic risk, including why an investor should not expect to receive additional return for bearing nonsystematic risk. **Vol 4, pp 354–356**

Systematic and Nonsystematic Risk

When investors diversify across assets that are not perfectly positively correlated, the portfolio's risk is lower than the weighted average of the individual assets' risks. In the market portfolio, all the risk unique to individual assets comprising the portfolio has been diversified away. The risk that disappears due to diversification in the portfolio construction process is known as unsystematic risk (also known as unique, diversifiable, or firm-specific risk). The risk inherent in all risky assets (caused by macro-economic variables) that cannot be eliminated by diversification is known as systematic risk (also known as nondiversifiable or market risk).

> Total Risk = Systematic risk + Unsystematic risk

Complete diversification of a portfolio requires the elimination of all unsystematic or diversifiable risk. Once unsystematic risk has been eliminated and only systematic risk remains, a completely diversified portfolio would correlate perfectly with the market.

By adding assets to a portfolio that are not perfectly correlated with the assets already in the portfolio, we can reduce the overall standard deviation of the portfolio. However, we cannot eliminate the variability and uncertainty of macroeconomic factors that affect returns on all risky assets. We do not have to include all the assets in the market portfolio to diversify away unsystematic risk. Studies have shown that a portfolio consisting of 12 to 30 different stocks can diversify away 90% of unsystematic risk. Whatever the exact number of different stocks required to eliminate unsystematic risk, it is significantly lower than *all* the risky assets comprising the market portfolio. Further, we can attain a lower level of systematic risk by diversifying globally versus only diversifying within one country, because some of the domestic systematic risk factors (such as monetary policy) are not perfectly correlated with systematic risk variables in other countries.

In capital market theory, taking on a higher degree of unsystematic risk will not be compensated with a higher return because unsystematic risk can be eliminated, without additional cost, through diversification. Only if an investor takes on a higher level of risk that cannot be easily diversified away (systematic risk) should she expect to be rewarded in the form of a higher return. Systematic risk is measured as the contribution of a security to the risk of a well diversified portfolio.

This conclusion has very important implications for asset pricing and expected returns. If risk is measured in terms of the standard deviation of returns of a stock, the riskiest stock will not necessarily have the highest expected return. For example, consider a tech firm whose entire business is reliant on the success of one particular technology. If the innovation is a success, the returns on the company's stock would be phenomenal, but if its product does not penetrate the market, the company would go out of business. The two scenarios facing this company are extreme. It is a stock with a high standard deviation of expected returns and high total risk.

Compare an investment in this tech company to an investment in a large manufacturing company that has a relatively well-known brand. This company may not seem to be a very risky investment in terms of total risk (standard deviation of expected returns), but it is relatively more sensitive to changes in the macroeconomic environment than the tech company.

Most of the risk inherent in the tech company's stock is firm specific in nature. Market factors like the rate of economic growth make up a relatively small proportion of the total risk of this company. The major chunk of its total risk (measured by standard deviation) can be diversified away by adding other stocks to the portfolio. For the manufacturing company, most of its standard deviation in expected returns (total risk) arises from macroeconomic risk factors that cannot be diversified away.

Even though the tech stock has a higher level of total risk, capital market theory dictates that the market will expect a higher return on the investment that has a higher level of systematic risk, regardless of total risk. Unsystematic risk is not rewarded by an efficient market because it can be diversified away at no cost. *Therefore, the expected return on an individual security only depends on its systematic risk.*

As we have seen earlier, portfolios on the CML offer a better risk-return tradeoff than portfolios that plot below it, so it effectively becomes the new efficient frontier for investors. The CML leads all investors to invest in the same risky asset portfolio, Portfolio M. Investors only differ regarding their exact position on the CML, which depends on their risk preferences.

LOS 43d: Explain return generating models (including the market model) and their uses. Vol 4, pp 356–359

Return-Generating Models

A return-generating model is a model that is used to forecast the return on a security given certain parameters. A multi-factor model uses more than one variable to estimate returns.

- Macroeconomic factor models use economic factors (e.g., economic growth rates, interest rates, and inflation rates) that correlate with security returns to estimate returns.
- Fundamental factor models use relationships between security returns and underlying fundamentals (e.g., earnings, earnings growth, and cash flow growth) to estimate returns.

- Statistical factor models use historical and cross-sectional returns data to identify factors that explain returns and use an asset's sensitivity to those factors to project future returns.

A general return generating model may be expressed as:

$$E(R_i) - R_f = \sum_{j=1}^{k} \beta_{ij} E(F_j) = \beta_{i1}[E(R_m) - R_f] + \sum_{j=2}^{k} \beta_{ij} E(F_j)$$

where:
$E(F_1), E(F_2),\ldots E(F_k)$ = Various factors in the model. There are k number of factors in the model
B_{ij} = Factor weights, or loads associated with each factor.
$E(R_i) - R_f$ = Excess return
$E(R_m)$ = Market return

The Market Model

The market model is an example of a single-index return generation model. It is used to estimate beta risk and to compute abnormal returns. The market model is given as:

$$R_i = \alpha_i + \beta_i R_m + e_i$$

First, the intercept α_i and slope coefficient β_i are estimated using historical asset and market returns. These estimates are then used to predict returns in the future. See Example 2-1.

Example 2-1: Using the Market Model to Calculate Abnormal Returns

A regression of ABC Stock's historical monthly returns against the return on the S&P500 gives an α_i of 0.002 and a β_i of 1.05. Given that ABC Stock rises by 3% during a month in which the market rose 1.25%, calculate the abnormal return on ABC Stock.

Solution

ABC Stock's expected return for the month = $0.002 + 1.05 \times 0.0125 = 0.015125$ or 1.51%

ABC's company-specific return (abnormal return) = $0.03 - (0.015125) = 0.014875$ or 1.49%

LOS 43e: Calculate and interpret beta. **Vol 4, pp 359–363**

Calculation and Interpretation of Beta

Beta is a measure of the sensitivity of an asset's return to the market's return. It is computed as the covariance of the return on the asset and the return on the market divided by the variance of the market. See Example 2-2.

$$\beta_i = \frac{Cov(R_i, R_m)}{\sigma_m^2} = \frac{\rho_{i,m}\sigma_i\sigma_m}{\sigma_m^2} = \frac{\rho_{i,m}\sigma_i}{\sigma_m}$$

Example 2-2: Calculating Asset Beta

Given that the standard deviation of the returns on the market is 18%, calculate beta for the following assets:
- Asset A, which has a standard deviation twice that of the market and zero correlation with the market.
- Asset B, which has a standard deviation of 24% and its correlation of returns with the market equals −0.2.
- Asset C, which has a standard deviation of 20% and its covariance of returns with the market is 0.035.

Solution

We use the following formula for calculating beta:

$$\beta_i = \frac{\rho_{i,m}\sigma_i}{\sigma_m}$$

Since the correlation of Asset A with the market equals zero, its beta also equals zero.

Asset B's beta = (−0.2 × 0.24) / 0.18 = −0.267

Asset C's beta = 0.035 / 0.18² = 1.08

Important Points Regarding Beta

- Beta captures an asset's systematic or nondiversifiable risk.
- A positive beta suggests that the return on the asset follows the overall trend in the market.
- A negative beta indicates that the return on the asset generally follows a trend that is opposite to that of the current market trend.
- A beta of zero means that the return on the asset is uncorrelated with market movements.
- The market has a beta of 1. Therefore, the average beta of stocks in the market also equals 1.

Estimating Beta Using Regression Analysis

The market model described previously can also be used to compute beta. Historical market and asset returns are used to determine α_i and β_i (see Figure 2-1.). The length of the period from which the inputs to the regression model are drawn from is extremely important. If data over a short time period are used, beta estimates may be affected by special events during that period. If data over a longer time period are used, they can be a poor gauge of future performance if major changes have occurred in the asset.

Figure 2-1: Beta Estimation with a Plot of Security and Market Returns

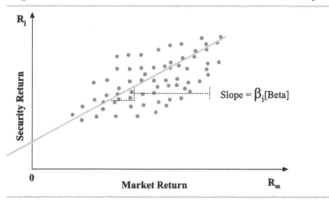

LESSON 3: THE CAPITAL ASSET PRICING MODEL

LOS 43f: Explain the capital asset pricing model (CAPM), including its assumptions, and the security market line (SML). Vol 4, pp 363–368

LOS 43g: Calculate and interpret the expected return of an asset using the CAPM. Vol 4, pp 368–369

The Capital Asset Pricing Model

The capital asset pricing model (CAPM) is a single-index model that is widely used to estimate returns given security betas. The CAPM is expressed as:

$$E(R_i) = R_f + \beta_i[E(R_m) - R_f]$$

Assumptions of the CAPM

- Investors are utility-maximizing, risk-averse, rational individuals.
- Markets are frictionless and there are no transaction costs and taxes.
- All investors have the same single-period investment horizon.
- Investors have homogenous expectations and therefore arrive at the same valuation for any given asset.
- All investments are infinitely divisible.
- Investors are price-takers. No investor is large enough to influence security prices.

The SML illustrates the CAPM equation. Its y-intercept equals the risk-free rate and its slope equals the market risk premium, $(R_m - R_f)$.

Recall that the CAL and the CML are only applied to efficient portfolios, not to individual assets or inefficient portfolios. They used total risk on the x-axis, and since only systematic risk is priced, they could only be used for efficient portfolios (those with no unsystematic risk and whose total risk therefore was the same as their systematic risk).

> Efficient portfolios are those that offer the highest return for each level of risk.

The SML and the CAPM on the other hand, apply to any security or portfolio, regardless of whether it is efficient. This is because they are based only on a security's systematic risk, not total risk.

The CAPM equation tells us that the expected (required) rate of return for a risky asset is determined by the risk-free rate plus a risk premium. The risk premium for an asset is determined by the systematic risk of the asset, (β_i), and the prevailing market risk premium, $(R_m - R_f)$. See Example 3-1.

Example 3-1: Using the SML to Compute Expected Returns

Assume that the risk-free rate in an economy is 5% and the return on the market portfolio is expected to be 10%. Compute the expected rates of return for the following 5 securities:

Stock	Beta
A	0.75
B	1.00
C	1.15
D	1.5
E	−0.25

Solution

$$E(R_i) = R_f + \beta_i[E(R_m) - R_f]$$

$$E(R_A) = R_f + \beta_A[E(R_m) - R_f] = 0.05 + 0.75(0.10 - 0.05) = 8.75\%$$

$$E(R_B) = R_f + \beta_B[E(R_m) - R_f] = 0.05 + 1.00(0.10 - 0.05) = 10\%$$

$$E(R_C) = R_f + \beta_C[E(R_m) - R_f] = 0.05 + 1.15(0.10 - 0.05) = 10.75\%$$

$$E(R_D) = R_f + \beta_D[E(R_m) - R_f] = 0.05 + 1.5(0.10 - 0.05) = 12.5\%$$

$$E(R_E) = R_f + \beta_E[E(R_m) - R_f] = 0.05 + (-0.25)(0.10 - 0.05) = 3.75\%$$

- Security C and D's betas are greater than market beta (1). These securities have a higher level of systematic risk than the market, meaning that they are more risky than the market portfolio. The expected return on these assets is therefore greater than the return on the market.

- Security A and E's betas are lower than market beta. These securities have a lower level of systematic risk than the market, meaning that they are less volatile than the market portfolio. Therefore the expected return on these assets is lower than the return on the market.

- A security with a negative beta (Stock E) is quite rare in practice. Notice that its required or expected return is even lower than the risk-free rate. This is because its negative beta *reduces* systematic portfolio risk.

- Stock B's beta equals market beta, so its expected return equals the rate of return expected from the market (10%).

Portfolio Beta

The CAPM can also be applied to portfolios of assets.

- The beta of a portfolio equals the weighted average of the betas of the securities in the portfolio.
- The portfolio's expected return can be computed using the CAPM (see Example 3-2):

$$E(R_p) = R_f + \beta_p[E(R_m) - R_f]$$

Example 3-2: Portfolio Beta and Return

Allison invests 25% of her money in the risk-free asset, 35% in the market portfolio, and 40% in Alpha Corp, a U.S. stock that has a beta of 1.5. Given that the risk-free rate and the expected return on the market are 5% and 14% respectively, calculate the portfolio's beta and expected return.

Solution

The beta of the risk-free asset and that of the market equal 0 and 1 respectively. The beta of the portfolio is calculated as:

$$\beta_{Portfolio} = w_1\beta_1 + w_2\beta_2 + w_3\beta_3$$

$$\beta_{Portfolio} = (0.25 \times 0) + (0.35 \times 1) + (0.4 \times 1.5) = 0.95$$

Expected return of the portfolio = $R_f + \beta(R_m - R_f)$

Expected return of the portfolio = 5% + 0.95 (14% − 5%) = 13.55%

LOS 43h: Describe and demonstrate applications of the CAPM and the SML. Vol 4, pp 368–374

Applications of the CAPM

Estimate of expected return: The expected rate of return computed from the CAPM is used by investors to value stocks, bonds, real estate, and other assets. In capital budgeting, where the NPV is used to make investing decisions, the CAPM is used to compute the required rate of return, which is then used to discount expected future cash flows. See Example 3-3.

Example 3-3: Application of the CAPM to Capital Budgeting

The directors of Mercury Inc. are considering investing in a new project. The project requires an initial investment of $550 million in one year. The probability of success is 60%. If it is successful, the project will provide an income of $350 million at the end of Year 2, but will also require a further investment of $200 million. Further, it will generate net income of $250 million in each of Years 3 and 4. At the end of Year 4, the company will sell the project for $300 million. If the project is unsuccessful, the company will not earn anything. Given that the market return is 14%, risk-free rate is 4%, and beta of the project is 1.5, answer the following questions:

1. Calculate the annual cash flows using the probability of success.
2. Calculate the expected return.
3. Calculate the net present value.

Solution

1. Year 1 = −$550m
   Year 2 = 0.6 × ($350m − $200m) = $90m
   Year 3 = 0.6 × $250m = $150m
   Year 4 = 0.6 × ($250m + $300m) = $330m

2. Using the CAPM, the expected or required rate of return is calculated as:

   Required return = 4% + [1.5 × (14% − 4%)] = 19%

3. Use the following TI calculator keystrokes to calculate NPV.

   [CF] [2ND] [CE|C]
   [↓] 550 [+/−] [ENTER] [↓][↓]
   90 [ENTER] [↓][↓]
   150 [ENTER] [↓][↓]
   330 [ENTER] [NPV]
   19 [ENTER] [↓] [CPT]

   NPV = −$145.06 million

Portfolio Performance Evaluation:

The *Sharpe ratio* is used to compute excess returns per unit of total risk. It is calculated as:

$$\text{Sharpe ratio} = \frac{R_p - R_f}{\sigma_p}$$

Notice that the Sharpe ratio basically equals the slope of the CAL. A portfolio with a higher Sharpe ratio is preferred to one with a lower Sharpe ratio given that the numerator of the portfolios being compared is positive. If the numerator is negative, the ratio will be closer to zero (less negative) for riskier portfolios, resulting in distorted rankings. Two drawbacks of the Sharpe ratio are that it uses total risk as a measure of risk even though only systematic risk is priced, and that the ratio itself is not informative.

The *Treynor ratio* basically replaces total risk in the Sharpe ratio with systematic risk (beta). It is calculated as:

$$\text{Treynor ratio} = \frac{R_p - R_f}{\beta_p}$$

For the Treynor ratio to offer meaningful results, both the numerator and the denominator must be positive. Neither the Sharpe nor the Treynor ratio offer any information about the significance of the differences between the ratios for portfolios.

M-squared (M^2) is also based on total risk, not beta risk. It is calculated as:

$$M^2 = (R_p - R_f)\frac{\sigma_m}{\sigma_p} - (R_m - R_f)$$

M^2 offers rankings that are identical to those provided by the Sharpe ratio. However, these rankings are easier to interpret as they are in percentage terms. A portfolio that matches the market's performance will have an M^2 of zero, while one that outperforms the market will have a positive M^2. The M^2 also enables us to tell which portfolios beat the market on a risk-adjusted basis.

Jensen's alpha is based on systematic risk (like the Treynor ratio). It first estimates a portfolio's beta risk using the market model, and then uses the CAPM to determine the required return from the investment (given its beta risk). The difference between the portfolio's actual return and the required return (as predicted by the CAPM) is called Jensen's alpha. Jensen's alpha is calculated as:

> Jensen's alpha is the maximum that an investor should be willing to pay the portfolio manager.

$$\alpha_p = R_p - [R_f + \beta_p(R_m - R_f)]$$

Jensen's alpha for the market equals zero. The higher the Jensen's alpha for a portfolio, the better its risk-adjusted performance (see Example 3-4).

Example 3-4: Portfolio Performance Evaluation

The following table provides information about the portfolio performance of three investment managers:

Manager	Return	σ	β
A	13%	20%	0.6
B	11%	15%	1.1
C	12%	10%	0.8
Market (M)	10%	16%	
Risk-free rate (R_f)	4%		

1. Calculate the following for each of the investment managers:

   a. Expected return
   b. Sharpe ratio
   c. Treynor ratio
   d. M^2
   e. Jensen's alpha

2. Comment on your answers and rank the managers' performance.

Solution

1. We illustrate the calculations for Manager A. The table that follows summarizes the results for all managers.

   Manager A

   Expected return $= R_f + \beta(R_m - R_f) = 4\% + [0.6 \times (10\% - 4\%)] = 7.6\%$

   $$\text{Sharpe ratio} = \frac{R_A - R_f}{\sigma_A} = \frac{13\% - 4\%}{20\%} = 0.45$$

   $$\text{Treynor ratio} = \frac{R_A - R_f}{\beta_A} = \frac{13\% - 4\%}{0.6} = 0.15$$

   $$M^2 = (R_A - R_f)\frac{\sigma_m}{\sigma_A} - (R_A - R_f) = (13\% - 4\%)\frac{16\%}{20\%} - (10\% - 4\%) = 1.2\%$$

   Jensen's alpha $= R_A - [R_f + \beta(R_m - R_f)] = 13\% - [4\% + 0.6(10\% - 4\%)] = 5.4\%$

Manager	Expected Return	Sharpe Ratio	Treynor Ratio	M^2	Jensen's Alpha
A	7.6%	0.45	0.150	1.20%	5.4%
B	10.6%	0.47	0.064	1.47%	0.4%
C	8.8%	0.8	0.1	6.80%	3.2%
Market	10%	0.375	0.060	0	0
R_f	4%	–	–	–	0

Ranking of portfolios by performance

Rank	Sharpe Ratio	Treynor Ratio	M^2	Jensen's Alpha
1	C	A	C	A
2	B	C	B	C
3	A	B	A	B
4	M	M	M	M
5	–	–	–	R_f

2. When considering total risk (relevant when the portfolio is not fully diversified), we look at the Sharpe ratio and M^2. C performs the best as she has both the highest Sharpe ratio (0.8) and the highest M^2 (6.8).

When we consider systematic risk (relevant when the portfolio is well diversified), we look at the Treynor ratio and Jensen's alpha. Manager A performs the best as she has both the highest Treynor ratio (0.15) and the highest Jensen's alpha (5.4%).

Notice that all three managers outperform the benchmark as the risk-return profiles of their performance lie above the SML, as shown in Figure 3-1:

Figure 3-1: Portfolio Performance Versus SML

We can see from the graph that A performs the best on a risk-adjusted basis as it lies northwest relative of the other portfolios.

All these measures assume that an appropriate portfolio is used as the benchmark portfolio.

A question arises as to when analysts should use measures like the Sharpe ratio and M^2 (that are based on total risk) and when they should use the Treynor ratio or Jensen's alpha (that are based on beta risk). Total risk is relevant when an investor holds an inefficient portfolio (one that is not fully diversified)

Security Characteristic Line

The security characteristic line (SCL) plots the excess returns of a security against the excess returns on the market. The equation of the SCL is given as:

$$R_i - R_f = \alpha_i + \beta_i(R_m - R_f)$$

Note that Jensen's alpha is the y-intercept, and beta is the slope of the SCL.

Security Selection: Identifying Mispriced Securities

Table 3-1 uses the same five stocks that we used in Example 2-1. We now calculate the expected return on these five securities based on their expected dividends, expected prices in one year, and current market prices.

Table 3-1: Calculation of Expected Return

Stock	Beta	Required Return from SML	Current Price (P_0)	Expected Dividend (D_1)	Expected Price (P_1)	Expected Return $[(P_1 + D_1)/P_0] - 1$
A	0.75	8.75%	25	1	26.31	[(26.31+1)/25] −1 = **9.24%**
B	1.00	10%	32	0.75	34.45	[(34.45+0.75)/32] −1 = **10%**
C	1.15	10.75%	15	0.80	15.7	[(15.70+0.80)/15] −1 = **10%**
D	1.5	12.5%	7	Nil	7.95	[(7.95+0)/7] −1 = **13.57%**
E	−0.25	3.75%	48	1.5	48.3	[(48.30+1.50)/48] −1 = **3.75%**

To determine whether a security is undervalued or overvalued, we compare the return that the security offers (based on its expected future price and dividend payments over the holding period) to the return it should offer to compensate investors for its systematic risk (beta). For example, based on our forecasts, Stock A offers a return of 9.24%. Based on the CAPM, the return required form Stock A to compensate for its beta risk is 8.75%. Stock A's current price is too low, which is why its expected return is higher than the required return (according to the CAPM). Therefore, Stock A is *undervalued* and investors should buy it.

Our forecasted return for Stock C (10%) is lower than the return required by investors for investing in a stock with a beta of 1.15 (10.75%). Stock C's current price is too high. Therefore, investors should *sell* the stock based on the given forecasts.

- If the expected return using price and dividend forecasts is *higher* than the investor's required return given the systematic risk in the security, the security is *undervalued* and the investor should *buy* it.
- If the expected return using price and dividend forecasts is *lower* than the investor's required return given the systematic risk in the security, the security is *overvalued* and the investor should *sell* it.

Let's plot the forecasted returns on these securities on the same graph as the SML (which illustrates the required return from securities with various levels of systematic risk). See Figure 3-2.

Figure 3-2: Mispriced Securities

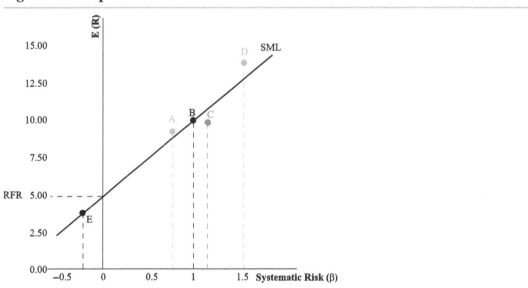

- Notice from Figure 3-2 that Stock A and D plot *above* the SML. This is because the expected return on these stocks is *greater* than their required return. Securities that plot *above* the SML are *undervalued* and should be *purchased*.

- Stock B and E plot on the SML. This means that the expected return on these securities equals the return required from these securities. These stocks are *fairly valued*.

- Stock C plots *below* the SML. The expected return for this stock falls short of the return required to compensate investors for the systematic risk inherent in the security. This stock is *overvalued* and should be *sold*.

Constructing a Portfolio

The CAPM tells us that investors should hold a portfolio that combines the risk-free asset with the market portfolio. Let's assume that we begin with the S&P 500 as our risky asset portfolio. The S&P 500 index only contains large-cap U.S. stocks, but does not encompass the entire global market. Therefore, we might want to consider a security not included in the S&P 500 for inclusion in the portfolio. The decision regarding whether the particular security should be included in our portfolio depends on the α_i of the security (based on the CAPM and the S&P 500 as the market portfolio). Positive α_i securities (even if they are correctly priced) should be added to the portfolio.

Further, within the set of securities included in the S&P 500, some may be undervalued (expected to generate positive alpha) and others may be overvalued (expected to generate negative alpha) based on investor expectations. The weight of undervalued securities should be increased and that of overvalued securities should be reduced. See Example 3-5.

> The information ratio $\left(\dfrac{\alpha_i}{\sigma_{ei}}\right)$ measures the abnormal return per unit of risk added by the security to a well-diversified portfolio. The larger the information ratio is, the more valuable the security.

The weight of each nonmarket security in the portfolio should be proportional to:

$$\frac{\alpha_i}{\sigma_{ei}^2}$$

where:

α_i = Jensen's alpha

σ_{ei}^2 = Nonsystematic variance of the security

Example 3-5: Optimal Investor Portfolio with Heterogeneous Beliefs

An investor gathers the following information regarding three stocks, which are not in the market portfolio:

Stocks	Expected Return	Standard Deviation	Beta
A	16%	29%	1.7
B	20%	24%	1.4
C	18%	21%	1.2

Given that the return on the market portfolio is 13% with a standard deviation of 15%, and the risk-free rate of return is 5%, answer the following questions:

1. Calculate Jensen's alpha for Stocks A, B, and C.
2. Calculate nonsystematic variance for A, B, and C.
3. If an investor holds the market portfolio, should she add any of these three stocks to her portfolio? If so, which stock should have the highest weight in the portfolio?

Solution

1. $\alpha_A = R_A - [R_f + \beta(R_m - R_f)] = 13\% - [4\% + 0.6(10\% - 4\%)] = 5.4\%$

    $\alpha_A = 16\% - [5\% + 1.7(13\% - 5\%)] = -0.026$

    $\alpha_B = 20\% - [5\% + 1.4(13\% - 5\%)] = 0.038$

    $\alpha_C = 18\% - [5\% + 1.2(13\% - 5\%)] = 0.034$

2. Nonsystematic variance = Total variance − Systematic variance

    $\sigma_{ei}^2 = \sigma_i^2 - \beta_i^2 \sigma_m^2$

    A's nonsystematic variance $= (0.29)^2 - (1.7^2 \times 0.15^2) = 0.0191$

    B's nonsystematic variance $= (0.24)^2 - (1.4^2 \times 0.15^2) = 0.0135$

    C's nonsystematic variance $= (0.21)^2 - (1.2^2 \times 0.15^2) = 0.0117$

3. Stock A should not be included in the portfolio as it has a negative alpha. It should only be included if the investor can short the stock.

    On the other hand, Stocks B and C have positive alphas and should be included in the portfolio. Their weights are determined as follows:

    Weight of Stock B = 0.038 / 0.0135 = 2.815

    Weight of Stock C = 0.034 / 0.0117 = 2.906

    In relative terms, the weight of Stock C will be greater than that of Stock B by 3.23% (2.906 / 2.815 − 1).

Beyond the CAPM

Limitations of the CAPM

Theoretical limitations
- The CAPM is a single-factor model; only systematic risk is priced in the CAPM
- It is only a single period model.

Practical limitations
- A true market portfolio is unobservable as it would also include assets that are not investable (e.g., human capital)
- In the absence of a true market portfolio, the proxy for the market portfolio used varies across analysts, which leads to different return estimates for the same asset (not permissible in the CAPM world).

Extensions of the CAPM

Theoretical models like the arbitrage pricing theory (APT) expand the number of risk factors. *Practical models* use extensive research to uncover risk factors that explain returns.

LESSON 1: PORTFOLIO PLANNING

LOS 44a: Describe the reasons for a written investment policy statement (IPS). **Vol 4, pp 394–395**

In order to construct a portfolio that satisfies the client's investment objectives, investment managers first need to devise a plan. This plan is documented in an investment policy statement (IPS).

The Investment Policy Statement

An investment policy statement is an invaluable planning tool that adds discipline to the investment process. Before developing an IPS, an investment manager must conduct a fact finding discussion with the client to learn about the client's risk tolerance and other specific circumstances.

The IPS can be thought of as a roadmap that serves the following purposes:

- It helps the investor decide on realistic investment goals after learning about financial markets and associated risks.
- It creates a standard according to which the portfolio manager's performance can be judged.
- It guides the actions of portfolio managers, who should refer to it from time to time to assess the suitability of particular investments for their clients.

A typical investment policy statement specifies investment objectives and constraints, and the types of risks that the investor is willing to take in order to meet those goals.

Investment goals are expressed in terms of both risk and return. This is because every investment decision involves a trade-off between risk and return. An investor's willingness and ability to take more risk in pursuit of higher returns depends on her individual situation and preferences. However, a manager must ensure that a client's return objectives and risk tolerance are consistent with each other. A client should not expect to earn a relatively high return without taking a relatively high level of risk.

Investment constraints are factors that the investment manager needs to consider when making investments for the client's portfolio. These typically include the following:

- Liquidity requirements.
- Time horizon.
- Tax concerns.
- Regulatory requirements.
- Unique needs and circumstances.

The investment policy statement should be reviewed on a regular basis and updated when there are major economic changes or changes in the client's needs and circumstances.

LOS 44b: Describe the major components of an IPS. Vol 4, p 395

An investment policy statement does not have a single standard format. It generally includes the following sections:

The sections that are most closely linked to a client's distinctive needs, and probably the most important from a planning perspective, are those dealing with investment objectives and constraints.

- An introduction that describes the client.
- A statement of purpose.
- A statement of duties and responsibilities, which describes the duties and responsibilities of the client, the custodian of the client's assets, and the investment manager.
- Procedures that outline the steps required to keep the IPS updated and steps required to respond to various contingencies.
- The client's investment objectives.
- The client's investment constraints.
- Investment guidelines regarding how the policy should be executed (e.g., whether use of leverage and derivatives is permitted) and specific types of assets that must be excluded.
- Evaluation and review guidelines on obtaining feedback on investment results.
- Appendices that describe the strategic asset allocation and the rebalancing policy.

LOS 44c: Describe risk and return objectives and how they may be developed for a client. Vol 4, pp 396–402

Risk Objectives

It is very important for the portfolio manager to ensure that the risk of the portfolio is suitable for the client. Quantitative risk objectives may be absolute, relative, or a combination of both.

Note that this objective is not related to investment market performance, good or bad, and is absolute in the sense of being self-standing.

- An example of an absolute risk objective would be that the client does not want to lose more than 5% of her capital over a particular period. A more practical way of stating the same objective would be as a probability statement (e.g., the portfolio should not lose more than 5% of its value over a 12-month period with 95% probability). Measures of absolute risk include the variance, standard deviation, and value at risk.
- Relative risk objectives relate risk to a certain benchmark that represents an appropriate level of risk. For example, investments in large-cap U.K. equities could be benchmarked to the FTSE 100. Tracking risk or tracking error is the appropriate measure of risk relative to a benchmark.

Risk objectives for institutional clients may be stated in terms of minimizing the probability of failing to meet their liabilities when they are due.

Risk tolerance is a function of both a client's ability to take risk and her willingness to take risk. The ability to take risk is a function of several factors including time horizon, expected income, and net worth. Generally speaking, a client with a longer time horizon, high expected income, and greater net worth has a greater ability to bear risk. A client's willingness to bear risk, on the other hand, is based on more subjective factors including her psychological makeup and level of understanding of financial markets.

LOS 44d: Distinguish between the willingness and the ability (capacity) to take risk in analyzing an investor's financial risk tolerance.
Vol 4, pp 407–410

- When the client's ability to take risk is below average and her willingness to take risk is also below average, the investor's overall risk tolerance is below average.
- When the client's ability to take risk is above average and her willingness to take risk is also above average, the investor's overall risk tolerance is above average.
- When the client's ability to take risk is below average and her willingness to take risk is above average, the investor's overall risk tolerance is below average.
- When the client's ability to take risk is above average and her willingness to take risk is below average, the investment manager should explain the conflict and implications to the client.

When there is a mismatch between a client's ability and willingness to take risk, the prudent approach is to conclude that the client's tolerance for risk is the lower of the two factors. Further, any decisions made must be documented.

Return Objectives

Return objectives may also be stated in absolute or relative terms.

- Absolute return objectives state the percentage return desired by the client. The return may be expressed on a real or nominal basis.
- Relative return objectives express the required return relative to a stated benchmark. A good benchmark should be investable (i.e., an investor should be able to replicate it).

The return objective may be stated before or after fees and on a pre- or post-tax basis. Further, it could also be expressed in terms of a required return (i.e., the amount an investor needs to earn over the investment horizon to meet a specified future goal).

The portfolio manager must ensure that the client's return objective is realistic in light of her tolerance for risk.

LOS 44e: Describe the investment constraints of liquidity, time horizon, tax concerns, legal and regulatory factors, and unique circumstances and their implications for the choice of portfolio assets. Vol 4, pp 402–407

Liquidity

This refers to the ability to readily convert investments into cash at a price close to fair market value. Investors may require ready cash to meet unexpected needs and could be forced to sell their assets at unfavorable terms if the investment plan does not consider their liquidity needs. Therefore, an IPS should state any likely requirements to withdraw funds from the portfolio.

Time Horizon

This refers to the time period between putting funds into an investment and requiring them for use. A close relationship exists between an investor's time horizon, liquidity needs, and ability to take risk. The shorter the time horizon, the harder it would be for an investor to overcome losses. Therefore, low-risk investments are more appropriate for investors with short time horizons.

Tax Concerns

Taxes play a very important role in investment planning because, unlike tax-exempt investors, taxable investors are really only concerned with after-tax returns on their portfolios. The tax code in most countries is very complex. For example, dividend income, interest income, and rental income may be taxed at the investor's marginal tax rate, while capital gains might be taxed at a different rate. Further, capital gains are only taxable after the asset has been sold (the capital gain realized), but unrealized capital gains are not taxable (the tax liability can be deferred indefinitely).

Legal and Regulatory Factors

Investors also need to be aware of legal and regulatory factors. For example, some countries impose a limit on the proportion of equity securities in a pension fund's portfolio. Further, an individual working for a company may be constrained from selling her shares for a period of time if she has access to material nonpublic information about the company (e.g., members of a company's board of directors are prohibited from trading the company's stock before financial results are released).

Unique Circumstances

There may be a number of individual and unusual considerations that affect investors. For example, many investors may want to exclude certain investments from their portfolios based on personal or socially conscious reasons. Because each investor is unique, the implications of this constraint differ for each investor. For example, an investor may not want to invest additional funds in the company she works for if she already has stock options in the company.

LESSON 2: PORTFOLIO CONSTRUCTION

LOS 44f: Explain the specification of asset classes in relation to asset allocation. Vol 4, pp 411–418

LOS 44g: Discuss the principles of portfolio construction and the role of asset allocation in relation to the IPS. Vol 4, pp 410–424

> An asset class is a category of assets that have similar characteristics, attributes, and risk-return relationships.

Portfolio Construction

Once the IPS has been compiled, the investment manager begins constructing the portfolio. How the portfolio funds are allocated across different asset classes is referred to as the portfolio's strategic asset allocation (SAA). A portfolio's SAA is important because it is a portfolio's allocation across various asset classes (not its allocation across securities within those asset classes) that is the primary determinant of portfolio returns.

Capital Market Expectations

Capital market expectations refer to a portfolio manager's expectations regarding the risk and return prospects of various asset classes. Capital market expectations are quantified in terms of expected returns, standard deviation of returns, and correlations among asset classes. Return expectations can be developed from historical data, economic analysis, or valuation models, while standard deviation and correlation estimates are primarily obtained from historical data.

The Strategic Asset Allocation

The strategic asset allocation defines how the investor's funds are divided across different asset classes. Traditionally, cash, equities, bonds, and real estate were defined as the major asset classes. Recently, hedge funds, private equity, and commodities have been added to the list. Further each asset class can be subdivided into several sub-classes. For example, bonds can be divided into government and corporate debt. Further, government bonds can be subdivided into domestic and foreign government bonds, while corporate bonds can be divided into investment-grade and high-yield bonds.

When defining asset classes, the following must be considered:

- Each asset class should contain assets that carry a similar expected return and risk and correlations among the assets within a class should be relatively high.
- Each asset class should provide diversification benefits. The correlation of an asset class with other asset classes should be relatively low.
- Asset classes should be mutually exclusive and should cover all investment alternatives.

Sometimes asset classes will be subdivided into smaller classes which are relatively highly correlated with each other. For example, the European and U.S. equity markets have a relatively high correlation, but they may still be treated as separate asset classes for the purposes of portfolio construction because different managers/products may be used to manage investments in U.S. equities and European equities.

The risk-return characteristics of the strategic asset allocation depend on the expected returns and risk of the individual asset classes, and on the correlations between the asset classes. Typically, risk-averse investors will place a higher weight on government bonds and cash in their SAA's, while those with a higher risk tolerance will have a higher weight invested in equities.

A theoretical framework for developing the SAA for a client is by developing the client's utility function and using capital market expectations to determine the risk-return profiles of all investable portfolios available to the client. As illustrated in a previous reading, the utility function can be used to draw up indifference curves, while capital market expectations can be used to determine the efficient frontier. The point of tangency between the two represents the optimal asset allocation for the investor. A change in capital market expectations would cause a movement in the efficient frontier, while a change in the investor's objectives or constraints would result in a shift in her indifference curves. A change in either of both the efficient frontier and the investor's indifference curves would require the strategic asset allocation to be adjusted.

Note that the framework described above may not be followed exactly in practice due to the following reasons:

- An IPS does not explicitly express the client's investment objectives and constraints in terms of a utility function. It usually only provides threshold levels of risk and return along with a description of constraints.
- The constraints listed in the IPS make it more appropriate to use multi-period models. This framework is a single period model.

Steps Toward an Actual Portfolio

1. Risk budgeting: This is the process of subdividing the desired level of portfolio risk (which has been determined in the IPS) across the different sources of investment returns (i.e., the strategic asset allocation, tactical asset allocation, and security selection).

2. Tactical asset allocation: This refers to an allocation where the manager deliberately deviates from the strategic asset allocation for the short term. For example, if a manager believes that equities are in for a difficult few months, she might invest more (than stated in the SAA) of the portfolio in bonds on a temporary basis to enhance portfolio return.

> Deviating from the prescribed weights and aiming to select securities that will outperform the benchmark leads to additional risk over and above the risk in the policy portfolio.

3. Security selection: A manager may be able to outperform the asset class benchmark by investing in particular securities within the asset class that she expects to do well (better than the benchmark).

4. Portfolio rebalancing: Changes in security prices will lead to changes in the weights of different asset classes in the portfolio and cause them to deviate or "drift" from policy weights. Therefore, the portfolio should be rebalanced periodically and brought in line with policy weights. The set of rules that lay out guidelines for rebalancing the portfolio is known as the rebalancing policy and is an important element of risk management.

Additional Portfolio Organizing Principles

The top-down investment framework described in this reading has two drawbacks:

- If several managers are hired to manage different subclasses within the same asset class, it may result in underutilization of the risk budget.
- Each manager would trade within the portfolio under her management so the portfolio overall may not be efficient from a capital gains tax point of view.

In order to avoid this, managers invest most of their funds in passive investments and trade a minority of assets actively. This approach is known as the "core-satellite" approach.

READING 45: MARKET ORGANIZATION AND STRUCTURE

LESSON 1: THE FUNCTIONS OF THE FINANCIAL SYSTEM, ASSETS, CONTRACTS, FINANCIAL INTERMEDIARIES AND POSITIONS

LOS 45a: Explain the main functions of the financial system. **Vol 5, pp 6–14**

A financial system consists of markets and financial intermediaries that facilitate the transfer of financial assets, real assets, and financial risks in various forms from one entity to another. There are three main functions of a financial system.

1. To help people achieve their purposes in using the financial system.
2. To facilitate the discovery of the rate of return where aggregate savings equal aggregate borrowings.
3. Allocating capital to its most efficient uses.

1. Helping people achieve their purposes in using the financial system

- The financial system helps in the saving process by creating investment vehicles (e.g., bank deposits, notes, stocks, etc.) that investors can buy or sell in the market without incurring heavy transaction costs.
- The financial system facilitates borrowing by aggregating funds from savers. A well-functioning financial system reduces transaction costs (e.g., the costs of arranging, monitoring, and recovering loans) and makes the borrowing process more efficient.
- Institutions in the financial system help companies in raising equity capital. Further, they value the securities that companies sell and ensure that financial information is accurate and properly disclosed. Transparency and liquidity in markets encourage investor participation.
- The financial system helps to manage various risks (e.g., default risk, exchange rate risk, interest rate risk, and other risks) by offering contracts to hedge those risks. Further, investment banks and exchanges ensure that these instruments trade in liquid markets.
- The financial system facilitates the exchange of assets by creating liquidity in spot markets (markets where assets are traded for immediate delivery). Liquidity reduces transaction costs for traders.
- The financial system facilitates information-based trading by creating liquid markets with low transaction costs. Further, accounting standards and regulatory requirements reduce the cost of information for investors.

2. Determining rates of return

Savers try to move money from the present to the future, while borrowers try to move money from the future to the present. The higher the expected return on saving, the more savers will forgo current consumption and move money to the future. On the other hand, the higher the cost of borrowing, the lower the amount of money borrowers would want to move from the future to the present. The rate at which the aggregate demand for funds (borrowing) equals the aggregate supply of funds (saving) is called the equilibrium interest rate, and determining this rate is one of the most important functions of the financial system.

> The required rates of return for securities vary by their risk characteristics, terms, and liquidity.

3. Allocating capital efficiently

Allocative efficiency is reached when the scarce capital in an economy is allocated to the most productive uses. A financial system seeks to ensure that only the best projects obtain the funds available from savers. Investors are wary of making losses so they try to carefully study the prospects of various investments available to them in order to make well-informed decisions regarding where to invest.

LOS 45b: Describe classifications of assets and markets. Vol 5, pp 14–16

Assets may be classified as financial or physical assets:

> Different classifications of assets are described in the next LOS.

- Financial assets include securities, currencies, and contracts.
- Physical assets include commodities and real assets.

Markets may be classified on the basis of:

- The timing of delivery.
  - Markets for immediate delivery are referred to as spot markets.
  - Markets where delivery occurs at some point in the future include forward, futures, and options markets.

- Who the seller is.
  - Markets in which securities are sold by issuers (where funds flow from the purchaser to the issuer) are known as primary markets.
  - Markets in which securities are sold by investors (where funds flow between traders) are called secondary markets.

- The maturity of instruments that are traded.
  - Markets that trade debt instruments maturing in one year or less are referred to as money markets.
  - Markets that trade instruments of longer maturities are referred to as capital markets.

- The types of securities:
  - Publicly traded debt, equities, and shares in pooled investment vehicles that hold these securities are referred to as traditional investment markets.
  - Hedge funds, private equity, commodities, real estate securities and properties, and securitized debt are part of alternative investment markets.

LOS 45c: Describe the major types of securities, currencies, contracts, commodities, and real assets that trade in organized markets, including their distinguishing characteristics and major subtypes. **Vol 5, pp 16–28**

Securities

Securities include bonds, notes, commercial paper, mortgages, common stock, preferred stock, warrants, mutual fund shares, unit trusts, and depository receipts. They may be classified as:

- **Public securities** that trade in public markets (e.g., exchanges). Issuers of public securities are usually required to comply with strict rules and regulatory standards.
- **Private securities** that can typically only be purchased by qualified investors. Private securities are relatively illiquid.

Fixed Income Securities

Fixed income instruments are promises to repay borrowed money. Payments (which include interest and principal amounts) may be pre-specified or may vary according to a fixed formula based on a reference rate. Fixed income instruments may be classified as:

- *Notes:* Fixed income securities with maturities of 10 years or less.
- *Bonds:* Fixed income securities with maturities greater than 10 years.
- *Bills:* These are issued by governments and have maturities of one year or less.
- *Certificates of deposit:* These are issued by banks and usually mature within a year.
- *Commercial paper:* These are issued by corporations and usually mature within a year.
- *Repurchase agreements:* These are short-term lending instruments.
- *Money market instruments:* These are traded in the money market and have maturities of one year or less.

Equities

Equity owners have ownership rights in a company. Equity securities include:

- *Common shares:* Holders of common shares can participate in the company's decision-making process. They are entitled to receive dividends declared by the company, and if the company goes bankrupt they have a claim on the company's assets after all other claims have been satisfied.

- *Preferred shares:* Preferred shareholders have a higher priority in claims on dividends and on the company's assets in case of liquidation. They are entitled to receive fixed dividends on a regular basis.

- *Warrants:* Holders of warrants have the right to purchase an entity's common stock at a pre-specified price at or before the warrants' expiration date.

Pooled Investments

Pooled investment vehicles (e.g., mutual funds, depositories, and hedge funds) issue securities that represent shared ownership in the assets held by them. People invest in these vehicles to benefit from their investment management expertise and to diversify their portfolios.

- *Asset-backed securities:* Companies often use pools of loans or receivables (e.g., auto loans and leases, consumer loans, credit cards, etc.) as underlying assets to issue securities known as asset-backed securities. These securities then transfer any interest and principal payments from the underlying assets to their holders on a monthly basis.

Currencies

These are monies issued by national monetary authorities and primarily trade in the foreign currency market. Retail currency trades occur through ATM machines, credit cards, and debit cards when transactions are executed in currencies different from the currency held in customers' accounts.

Contracts

Contracts are agreements between two or more parties to do something in the future. A contract's value depends on the value of its underlying, which may be a commodity, a security, an index, an interest rate, or even another contract.

Contracts may be settled in cash or may require physical delivery, and may be classified on the basis of:

- The nature of the underlying asset:
    - If the underlying asset is a physical asset, the contract is referred to as a physical contract.
    - If the underlying asset is a financial asset, the contract is referred to as a financial contract.

- The timing of delivery:
    - If the contract requires immediate delivery (i.e., in three days or less), it is referred to as a spot contract and trades in the spot market.
    - If the contract requires delivery to be made in the future (i.e., after three days or more), it may be a forward, futures, swap, or an options contract.

Forward Contracts

A forward is a contract between two parties, where one (the long position) has the obligation to buy, and the other (the short position) has an obligation to sell an underlying asset at a fixed price (established at the inception of the contract) at a future date. Market participants usually enter a forward contract to hedge a pre-existing risk.

Futures Contracts

Futures contracts are similar to forward contracts in that they may also be deliverable or cash-settled, but there are also significant differences between the two. Unlike forward contracts:

- Futures contracts are standardized and trade on organized exchanges.
- A clearinghouse is the counterparty to all futures contracts.

Swap Contracts

A swap is an agreement between two parties to exchange a series of cash flows at periodic settlement dates over a certain period of time. A swap may also be looked upon as a series of forward contracts.

Option Contracts

Option contracts give their holders the right to buy or sell a security at a predetermined price (exercise price) some time in the future.

- **Call options** give their holders the right to purchase the underlying asset at some future date at the option's exercise price. Holders are likely to exercise their call options when the price of the underlying asset is greater than the exercise price.

- **Put options** give their holders the right to sell the underlying asset at some future date at the option's exercise price. Holders are likely to exercise their put options when the price of the underlying asset is lower than the exercise price.

Options that can only be exercised at their expiration dates are known as European options, while options that can be exercised anytime until or at their expiration dates are known as American options.

Other Contracts

People often enter into insurance contracts to protect themselves from unexpected losses. Insurance contracts include credit default swaps (CDSs) that promise to pay their holders the amount of principal in case a company defaults on its bonds.

Commodities

Commodities include precious metals, energy products, industrial metals, agricultural products, and carbon credits.

Commodities may trade in the spot market (for immediate delivery) or in the forward or futures market (for delivery in the future). The primary traders in commodities spot markets are producers and processors of industrial metals and agricultural products as they have the ability to store the physical products and take or make delivery. Further, as part of their normal business operations, they obtain information that gives them an advantage as information-motivated traders.

Investment managers and other information-motivated traders participate in commodity futures markets to hedge risks and/or to speculate on future prices. These traders usually deal in futures markets, as they do not have the capacity to handle the physical products. Further, the fact that futures markets are relatively more liquid enables them to close or exit their positions easily.

Real Assets

Real assets include tangible properties such as real estate, airplanes, machinery, and lumber stands. These assets are normally held by operating companies (e.g., real estate developers and airplane leasing companies). However, institutional investors are increasingly adding them to their portfolios either directly (through direct ownership of the asset), or indirectly (through investments in securities of companies that invest in these assets). Real assets are attractive because:

- They may have low correlations with other assets in the investor's portfolio, thus providing diversification benefits.
- They offer income and tax benefits to investors.

However, real asset valuation is very difficult due to the heterogeneous nature of each investment. Further, real assets tend to be relatively illiquid and entail high management costs.

Indirect investments in real estate can be made by purchasing shares in real estate investment trusts (REITs) and master limited partnerships (MLPs). These entities pool funds from investors and invest in different types of real estate. Because these securities are relatively more homogeneous and divisible than the underlying real assets, they trade in relatively liquid markets.

LOS 45d: Describe types of financial intermediaries and services that they provide. Vol 5, pp 28–38

Financial intermediaries allow buyers and sellers of assets and contracts to transfer risk and capital between them, often without any knowledge of each other. Financial intermediaries include the following:

Brokers, Exchanges, and Alternative Trading Systems

Brokers are agents who fulfill orders for their clients. They reduce costs of trading for their clients by finding counterparties for their trades.

- *Block brokers* provide brokerage services to large traders. It is difficult to fulfill large orders, as there are not many potential counterparties for large trades. In order to induce counterparties to trade, large buy orders generally execute at a premium, while large sell orders generally trade at a discount to market prices. Large trades, if known to the public before being executed, may have a significant impact on market price and therefore must be managed carefully.

- *Investment banks* provide a variety of services to companies, including:
  - Arranging initial and seasoned security offerings.
  - Issuing securities to finance their business.
  - Identifying and acquiring other companies.

Exchanges provide a platform where traders can carry out their trades. Over time, the distinction between exchanges and brokers has become rather vague, as electronic order matching systems are increasingly being used by both to arrange trades for clients.

Alternative Trading Systems (ATSs) (also known as electronic communications networks [ECNs] and multilateral trading facilities [MTFs]) are trading venues just like exchanges. However, they differ from exchanges in that they do not exercise regulatory authority over their members except with respect to the conduct of their trading in their trading networks. Many ATSs are known as "dark pools" because they do not display orders sent to them.

Dealers

Unlike brokers, dealers fulfill orders for their clients by actually taking positions as counterparties for their trades. After executing a trade, they hope to close their positions by taking the opposite side of the original transaction with another client. Essentially, they indirectly connect two traders who arrive in the market at different points in time. By acting as counterparties to trades, dealers create liquidity in the market. They profit when their average purchase price is less than their average selling price.

Dealers may also often act as brokers and vice-versa, so practitioners often use the term **broker-dealer** to refer to brokers and dealers. Sometimes however, there may be a conflict of interest with respect to how broker-dealers fill orders. As brokers they must strive to find the best possible price for their clients, but as dealers they aim to maximize their own profits. Therefore, customers often specify how they want their orders to be filled (whether they want it filled by the broker or traded with another trader) when dealing with a broker-dealer.

Dealers with whom the central bank trades when conducting monetary policy are referred to as **primary dealers**. The central bank buys from and sells securities to these dealers who then trade with other market participants.

Securitizers

Securitization is the process of buying assets, placing them in a pool, and issuing securities that represent ownership of the assets in the pool. Entities that undertake this process are known as securitizers. They create and sell securitized instruments and act as financial intermediaries by connecting borrowers and lenders.

Depository Institutions and Other Financial Corporations

Depository institutions include commercial banks, savings and loan banks, credit unions, and other institutions that gather funds from depositors and lend them to borrowers. These institutions pay interest to depositors and provide transaction services (check writing and check cashing, etc.) to them. Borrowers go to these institutions in the hope of borrowing funds from them.

Brokers also act as financial intermediaries when they lend funds deposited by their clients to other clients who wish to buy securities on margin. Such brokers are known as **prime brokers**.

Insurance Companies

Insurance companies create and sell contracts that protect buyers of these contracts from risks that they seek protection from. Basically, insurance companies provide a payment to the owner of the insurance policy if the risk that she is concerned with materializes and results in a loss. Examples of insurance contracts include auto, fire, theft, and life insurance contracts.

Insurance companies are financial intermediaries as they connect the buyers of insurance contracts with investors, creditors, and reinsurers who are willing to bear the insured risks. Insurance buyers benefit as they are able to transfer risks to entities that are willing to assume them, while owners, creditors, and reinsurers of the insurance company (who assume these risks) benefit from being able to sell their tolerance to risk without having to manage the contracts. Managing insurance contracts requires the insurance company to manage fraud, moral hazard, and adverse selection.

- Fraud occurs when people deliberately report fake losses.
- Moral hazard occurs when people are less careful about avoiding losses, as they are covered by insurance.
- Adverse selection occurs as only those who are most at risk usually buy insurance.

Arbitrageurs

The law of one price states that two securities that generate identical cash flows in the future, regardless of future events, should have the same price today. Arbitrageurs are constantly on the lookout for violations of this law. They trade on mispricings until they are eliminated and asset prices converge to their "correct levels."

Arbitrageurs, who buy and sell the same security in two different markets (at different prices), act as financial intermediaries as they effectively connect sellers in one market with buyers in another market. They also bring liquidity to markets.

Settlement and Custodial Services

Clearinghouses arrange for the final settlement of trades. They also serve as guarantors of performance in futures markets and as escrow agents in other markets. Further, they ensure that their members have adequate capital to settle trades, and also place limits on the aggregate net order quantities (buy minus sell) of their members. All of these functions performed by the clearinghouse help limit counterparty risk.

Banks and broker-dealers may offer custodial services for holding securities on behalf of their clients. This helps prevent the loss of securities through fraud or oversight.

LOS 45e: Compare positions an investor can take in an asset.
Vol 5, pp 38–41

A position in an asset refers to the quantity of the asset that an entity owns or owes.

- A person with a long position owns an assets or a contract. She benefits when there is an increase in the price of the asset or contract.
- A person with a short position has sold an asset that she does not own, or has written or sold a contract. She benefits when there is a decrease in the price of the asset or contract.

Short positions are usually taken by information-motivated traders who believe that an asset or a contract will decrease in value. However, they may also be taken by hedgers who seek to eliminate/reduce a pre-existing risk. For example, a person holding gold inventories faces the risk of a fall in the price of gold. In order to protect herself from the risk of a fall in gold prices, she will take a short position on gold futures contracts. If the price of gold falls, she would incur a loss on her inventory of gold, which would be offset by a profit on her short futures position.

Positions on Forwards and Futures

The long position in a forward or a futures contract is the side that is obligated to take physical delivery of the asset or its cash equivalent at contract expiration. She will benefit from an increase in the price of the underlying asset.

The short position in a forward or a futures contract is the side that is obligated to make physical delivery of the asset or its cash equivalent at contract expiration. She will benefit from a decrease in the price of the underlying asset.

Positions on Options

The long position on an options contract is the party that holds the right to exercise the option. The short side refers to the writer of the option, who must satisfy any obligations arising from the contract.

- The long position on a call option will benefit when the underlying rises in value.
- The short position on a call option will benefit when the underlying falls in value.
- The long position on a put option will benefit when the underlying falls in value.
- The short position on a put option will benefit when the underlying rises in value.

Swap Contracts

The two parties in a swap contract simply agree to exchange contractually determined cash flows. There is no real buyer or seller, which makes it difficult to determine the long and short side of the contract. Usually, the party that benefits from an increase in the quoted price is referred to as the long.

Currency Contracts

A party that purchases one currency simultaneously sells another currency (the other currency in the price quote or exchange rate). Therefore, whenever we mention a long or a short position in a currency contract, we must mention the other currency as well. For example, we may state that a party is long on the dollar against the yen.

Short Positions

Short positions in contracts are created by selling contracts that the short seller does not own. The short seller is basically the issuer of the contract. For example, a company creates a short position on bonds (a contract between the company and bondholders or lenders) when it issues bonds in exchange for cash.

Short positions in securities are created by selling securities that the short seller does not own. In order to sell the securities, the short seller borrows the securities from long holders to deliver them to buyers. To unwind the position, the short seller then repurchases the security (hopefully at a lower price) from the market and returns it to the long holder.

The maximum profit for the holder of a long position on an asset is unlimited, while her losses are limited to the price she purchased the asset for. In contrast, the maximum profit for a short seller of an asset is limited to her selling price, while her losses are unlimited.

LOS 45f: Calculate and interpret the leverage ratio, the rate of return on a margin transaction, and the security price at which the investor would receive a margin call. Vol 5, pp 41–44

Levered Positions

Many markets allow investors to borrow funds from brokers to purchase securities. The investor borrows a portion of the price of the stock, contributes the rest of the funds herself, and puts up the stock as collateral. The borrowed money is known as the margin loan and the interest rate paid on it is the call money rate.

Traders who purchase securities on margin face minimum margin requirements. The initial margin requirement refers to the proportion of the total cost of the asset that an investor must invest with her own equity. This requirement may be determined by the government, the exchange, or the clearinghouse.

When traders borrow money to purchase securities, they are said to be leveraging their positions. The leverage ratio is the ratio of the value of the position to the value of the equity investment in it. The maximum leverage ratio for a position financed by a margin loan equals one divided by the minimum margin requirement.

Leverage enhances a trader's returns, but also magnifies losses, as illustrated in Example 1-1.

Example 1-1: Computing Total Return to a Leveraged Stock Purchase

Susan purchases 100 shares of Alpha Corp on margin for $30 per share. She sells her shares after one year at $24 per share. The following information is also available:

Dividend received on the stock = $0.30 per share
Commission paid = $0.10 per share
Leverage ratio = 2.0
Call money rate = 6%

1. What is the total return on this investment?
2. Why is the loss greater than the 20% decrease in the market price?

Solution

1. Total purchase price = 100 × 30 = $3,000

    Using her leverage ratio, we can calculate her equity investment as follows:

    Equity investment = 1 / 2.0 = 50%

    Therefore, she borrowed $1,500 ($3,000 × 50%).

    Commission paid on purchase transaction = 100 × 0.1 = $10

    Therefore, her total initial investment = $1,500 + 10 = $1,510

    Equity remaining after the sale is computed as follows:

Initial investment	$1,510
Purchase commission	−10
Trading gains/losses	−600
[(24 × 100) − 3,000]	
Margin interest paid	−90
(1,500 × 0.06)	
Dividends received	30
(0.3 × 100)	
Sales commission paid	−10
Remaining equity	$830

Or

Proceeds on sale (24 × 100)	2,400
Payoff loan	−1,500
Margin interest paid	−90
Dividends received	30
Sales commission paid	−10
Remaining equity	$830

Therefore, total return = (830 − 1,510) / 1,510] = −45.03%

2. The realized loss is greater than the 20% decrease in the market price primarily because of leverage and also because of interest paid on borrowed funds. Based on leverage alone (i.e., ignoring the other cash flows), the expected return on equity would be −40% (= 2.0 × −20%).

In addition to the initial margin requirement, traders who invest on margin must also adhere to maintenance margin requirements. After the purchase of a stock, an increase or decrease in the price translates into a change in the value of the collateral backing the margin loan. If the proportion of the value of the security financed by the investor's own equity (after adjusting for the price change) falls below the maintenance margin, the investor will receive a margin call, and she would have to deposit enough funds into her account to at least meet the maintenance margin level. If she fails to do so, her broker can sell the stock to pay off the margin loan. See Example 1-2.

The price at which an investor who goes long on a stock receives a margin call is calculated as:

$$P_0 \times \frac{(1 - \text{Initial margin})}{(1 - \text{Maintenance margin})}$$

Example 1-2: Margin Calls

Determine the share price at which an investor will receive a margin call given that the share price at the time of purchase was $60, the initial margin requirement is 50%, maintenance margin is 25%, and the investor has purchased 200 shares.

Solution

$$\text{Trigger price} = \frac{\$60(1 - 0.5)}{1 - 0.25} = \$40$$

The investor will receive a margin call when the stock price falls to $40.

Traders who sell securities short are also subject to margin requirements, as they have borrowed securities to take their positions.

LOS 45g: Compare execution, validity, and clearing instructions.
Vol 5, pp 44–50

LOS 45h: Compare market orders with limit orders. Vol 5, pp 44–45

The prices at which dealers and other proprietary traders are willing to buy securities are called bid prices and those at which they are willing to sell are called ask (or offer) prices. The quantities that market participants are willing to trade at the bid and ask prices are called bid sizes and ask sizes respectively.

The highest bid in the market is the highest price that a dealer is willing to pay for the security and is known as the best bid. On the other hand, the lowest ask price is the best offer. The difference between the best bid and the best offer is the market bid-ask spread. Liquid markets with low transaction costs generally have small bid-ask spreads.

Execution Instructions

Execution instructions indicate how an order should be filled. They include:

- Market orders, which instruct brokers or the exchange to fill an order immediately at the best available price. Market orders generally execute immediately as long as there are traders willing to take the other side of the trade. However, they may be expensive to execute, especially when the order size is large relative to the normal trading activity in the market.

- Limit orders, which instruct the broker or the exchange to fill an order at a specified price or better. These specified prices (maximum price for a limit buy order and minimum price for a limit sell order) are referred to as limit prices. Limit orders prevent trades from executing at unacceptable prices. However, this also means that they may not execute at all if the limit price on a buy order is too low or the limit price on a sell order is too high.

  - A limit buy order is aggressively priced when the limit price is high relative to the market "bid" and "ask" prices.
  - A limit buy order placed above the best offer is likely to be at least partially executed immediately and is called a marketable limit order.
  - A limit buy order placed above the best bid but below the best offer is said to have created a new market by establishing the new best bid.
  - A limit buy order placed at the best bid is said to make market. This order will have to wait for all buy orders (that were placed earlier) at that price to execute first.
  - A limit buy order placed below the best bid is referred to as behind the market and will not execute unless market prices drop. These orders are known as standing limit orders.

Although aggressively priced orders execute sooner, the prices at which they trade are inferior.

Some execution instructions include limitations on order size. For example, all-or-nothing orders (AON) can only trade if their entire sizes can be traded. Traders can also specify minimum fill sizes.

Exposure Instructions

Exposure instructions specify whether, how, and to whom orders may be exposed.

Hidden orders are exposed only to the brokers or exchanges that receive them. Other traders can discover hidden size only after submitting orders that will trade with that size. However, hidden orders may not execute at all as other traders do not know about them. Therefore, traders may sometimes indicate a specific display size (which is lower than the actual order size) with their orders to signal to other traders that someone is willing to trade at the displayed price. As most of the order size is hidden, these orders are also referred to as iceberg orders.

Validity Instructions

Validity instructions indicate when an order may be filled. They include:

- Day orders, which are only valid for the day on which they are submitted. These orders expire if not filled at the close of business.
- Good-till-cancelled orders, which are valid until cancelled by the broker.
- Immediate or cancel orders, which may only be filled, completely or in part, immediately and are otherwise cancelled. These are also known as fill or kill orders.
- Good-on-close orders, which only execute at the close of trading and are also called market-on-close orders.
- Stop orders (often referred to as stop-loss orders), which are placed by investors to protect themselves from adverse price movements. A stop-loss buy order is placed by short sellers above the market price. If the price of the asset moves against the short seller's expectations, the stop buy order will ensure that her losses do not exceed a particular limit. For example, if Veronica goes short on a stock that is currently priced at $50, she might place a stop buy order at $55. If the stock were to move up to $55, her stop loss buy order would execute and limit her loss to $5. On the other hand, a trader who is bullish on the market would place a stop-sell order below the current market price. If prices were to move down contrary to her expectations, the stop-sell order would limit her losses.

Clearing Instructions

Clearing instructions indicate how the final settlement of trades should be arranged. They include details of the entities responsible for clearing and settling the trade. Further, security sale orders must also indicate whether the sale is a long sale or a short sale.

Primary Markets

Primary markets are markets where issuers first sell their securities to investors. When a security is issued to the public for the first time, it is referred to as an initial public offering (IPO). On the other hand, when additional units of a previously issued security are sold, it is referred to as a seasoned offering (or a secondary offering) and the issue is called a seasoned issue.

Public Offerings

Companies generally issue securities to the public through an investment bank. The investment bank performs the following functions:
- Through a process called book building, it lines up subscribers who wish to purchase the security.
- It provides investment information about the issuer to its clients and to the public.

The issuer's arrangement with the investment bank may take one of the following forms:
- In an underwriting offer, the investment bank guarantees the sale of the issue at an offering price negotiated with the issuer. If the issue is not fully subscribed, the investment bank commits to purchasing the leftover securities at the offer price.
- In a best efforts offering, the investment bank merely acts as a broker. It tries its best to sell the securities at the negotiated price, but does not promise to purchase unsold securities.

Underwritten offerings lead to a conflict of interest for investment banks regarding pricing. As an agent the investment bank must strive to obtain the best (highest) possible price for issuers. However, since the investment bank is obligated to purchase leftover securities in case the issue is not fully subscribed, it would prefer the issue to be priced lower.

First-time issuers usually accept relatively low offer prices because they do not want to leave their issue undersubscribed as it sends out a negative signal about the company. For seasoned issues, it is easier to determine the price as the securities are already being traded in the secondary market.

Private Placements

In a private placement securities are not offered to the public. Companies sell securities directly to a group of qualified investors, usually through an investment bank. Qualified investors are generally those who understand associated risks and have sufficient wealth to withstand significant losses. Private placements are typically cheaper than public offerings as they do not require as much public disclosure. However, since privately placed securities do not trade on organized secondary markets, investors require a higher rate of return from them.

- Companies that issue securities via a *shelf registration* make all the public disclosures that are required in a regular offering, but they do not need to issue all the shares at once. They can sell them directly in the secondary market over time, which offers them flexibility as they can raise capital when they need it.
- Companies that issue securities through *dividend reinvestment plans (DRPs)* allow shareholders to reinvest their dividends by purchasing shares of the company. These shares may be newly issued or purchased from the open market.
- Companies sometimes offer *rights* to existing shareholders to purchase additional shares of the company in proportion to their current holdings at a fixed price.

Secondary Markets

The secondary market is that part of the financial market where previously issued securities and financial instruments are traded. Secondary markets play a very important role in that they provide liquidity to investors who purchased their securities in the primary market. Investors will hesitate to participate in the primary market if they cannot subsequently sell their holdings in the secondary market.

Secondary markets are also important for seasoned security issuers, as the prices of their new offerings are derived from the secondary market prices of currently outstanding securities that trade on the secondary market.

LOS 45j: Describe how securities, contracts, and currencies are traded in quote-driven, order-driven, and brokered markets. Vol 5, pp 54–58

Trading Sessions

In a call market, all bid and ask prices for an asset are gathered to determine one price where the quantity offered for sale is close to the quantity demanded. All transactions take place at this single price. Call markets are popular in smaller markets. However, they are also used on larger exchanges to determine the opening price of a trading session.

In a continuous market, transactions can take place whenever the market is open. Prices are set either through an auction process or by dealer bid-ask quotes. Most global stock exchanges are continuous markets.

The advantage of a call market is that it makes it easier for buyers and sellers to find each other by gathering all traders at the same place at the same time. In a continuous market, if a buyer and seller (or their orders) are not present at the same time, they cannot trade. The advantage of a continuous market is that a willing buyer and seller can trade anytime the market is open. In a call market they would only be able to trade when the market is called.

Execution Mechanisms

A pure auction market (order-driven market) is one where participants submit their bid and ask prices to a central location. Matching bids and offers are paired together and orders are executed. Order-driven matching mechanisms are characterized by two sets of rules:

- Order matching rules match buy orders to sell orders. They rank buy and sell orders based on:
    - Price precedence: Highest priced buy orders and lowest priced sell orders are ranked first.
    - Display precedence: Displayed quantities have precedence over undisplayed quantities at the same price.
    - Time precedence: Orders that arrived first have precedence over orders that arrived later with the same price and with the same display status.

- Trade pricing rules determine the prices at which matched trades take place. Prices may be determined based on the any of the following:
    - Under a uniform pricing rule, the same price is used for all trades. This rule is used by call markets where the market chooses the price that maximizes total quantity traded.
    - Under a discriminatory pricing rule, the limit price of the order or quote that arrived first (the standing order) determines the trade price. Continuous trading markets use this rule.
    - A derivative pricing rule uses the mid-point of the best bid and ask quotes from another market. Crossing networks (which may themselves be organized as call or continuous trading markets) use this pricing rule.

> **Crossing networks** are trading systems that match buyers and sellers who are willing to trade at prices obtained from other markets.

A dealer market (quote-driven market or price-driven market) consists of individual dealers who are assigned specific securities. These dealers create liquidity by purchasing and selling against their own inventory of securities. Competition between dealers ensures that competitive prices are available.

In a brokered market, brokers arrange trades among their clients. Brokers organize markets for unique items (e.g., real estate properties and fine art masterpieces) that only interest a limited number of people.

Market Information Systems

Markets may be structured based on the type and quantity of information they disseminate to the public.
- Pre-trade transparent markets publish real-time data about quotes and orders.
- Post-trade transparent markets publish data about trade prices soon after trades occur.

LESSON 3: WELL-FUNCTIONING FINANCIAL SYSTEMS AND MARKET REGULATION

LOS 45k: Describe the characteristics of a well-functioning financial system. Vol 5, pp 58–60

As mentioned previously, a well-functioning financial system helps:

- Investors to save for the future.
- Entities to borrow funds.
- Hedgers to manage various risks.
- The exchange of assets by creating liquidity in spot markets.

A financial system helps to achieve these goals by establishing financial markets and financial intermediaries. A financial market is a platform that brings together buyers and sellers to facilitate transfers of assets. A well-functioning securities market has the following features:

- Timely and accurate disclosures so that market participants can make well-informed decisions.
- Liquidity so that costs of trading are minimized.
- Complete markets that allow people solve their financial problems.
- External or informational efficiency, where prices respond to changes in fundamental values.

Financial intermediaries are also an integral part of the financial system. They:

- Match buyers and sellers by organizing trading venues, such as exchanges, brokerages, alternative trading systems, and so on.
- Provide liquidity.
- Lower borrowing costs by securitizing assets.
- Manage banks that match investors and borrowers by taking deposits and making loans.
- Manage insurance companies that pool uncorrelated risks.
- Provide investment advisory services to investors at a low cost.
- Organize clearinghouses that ensure the settlement of trades.
- Organize depositories that ensure safety of assets.

A well-functioning financial system leads to informationally efficient prices. Market participants analyze securities and push up (push down) prices of undervalued (overvalued) securities. However, this depends on the cost of obtaining fundamental information and market liquidity.

- Accounting standards help to lower the cost of obtaining relevant information by requiring companies to make timely financial disclosures.
- Liquid markets enable traders to act on that information and make investment decisions.

As a result of efficient markets, capital is allocated to its most productive use in society (i.e., allocative efficiency is reached).

Sidebar:

If all the assets or contracts needed to achieve these four objectives are available to trade, the financial system is said to have complete markets.

If the costs of trading are low, the financial market is said to be operationally efficient.

If assets and contracts are properly priced (given all available relevant information) the financial market is said to be informationally efficient.

LOS 45l: Describe the objectives of market regulation. Vol 5, pp 61–63

The following problems could arise in financial markets if they were left unregulated:

- Fraud and theft.
- Insider trading.
- Increase in the cost of information.
- Increase in the number of defaults.

In light of these problems, it is imperative that financial markets are regulated. Regulation of the financial system has the following objectives:

- To control fraud or deception of market participants.
- To control agency problems by setting minimum standards of competence for agents and by defining and enforcing minimum standards of practice.
- To promote fairness by creating a level playing field for market participants.
- To set mutually beneficial standards for financial reporting.
- To prevent undercapitalized financial firms from exploiting their investors by making excessively risky investments.
- To ensure that long-term liabilities are funded. For example, regulation seeks to ensure that insurance companies and pension funds have sufficient capital to honor their long term commitments.

Regulation may be provided by governments or industry groups (self-regulating organizations or SROs).

READING 46: SECURITY MARKET INDICES

LESSON 1: INDEX DEFINITION, CALCULATIONS, CONSTRUCTION AND MANAGEMENT

LOS 46a: Describe a security market index. Vol 5, pp 78–79

A security market index consists of individual securities (also called constituent securities) that represent a given security market, market segment, or asset class. Each security market index may have two versions depending on how returns are calculated:
- A price return index only reflects the prices of constituent securities.
- A total return index not only reflects prices, but also assumes reinvestment of all income received since inception.

The values of both versions of an index are the same at inception. However, as time passes, the total return index will be greater in value than the price return index by an increasing amount.

LOS 46b: Calculate and interpret the value, price return, and total return of an index. Vol 5, pp 79–82

The value of a price return index is calculated as follows:

$$V_{PRI} = \frac{\sum_{i=1}^{N} n_i P_i}{D}$$

where:
V_{PRI} = Value of the price return index
n_i = Number of units of constituent security i held in the index portfolio
N = Number of constituent securities in the index
P_i = Unit price of constituent security i
D = Value of the divisor

The divisor is initially chosen as a value that gives the index a convenient initial value (e.g., 1,000). However, over time the divisor must be adjusted to ensure that changes in the index only reflect changes in prices of constituent securities. For example, if some constituent securities are replaced by others in the index, the divisor must be adjusted so that the value of the index remains unchanged.

Index return calculations may measure price return or total return:

- Price return measures only the percentage change in price.
- Total return measures the percentage change in price plus interest, dividends, and other distributions.

The price return of an index can be calculated as:

$$PR_I = \frac{V_{PRI1} - V_{PRI0}}{V_{PRI0}}$$

where:
PR_I = Price return of the index portfolio (as a decimal number)
V_{PRI1} = Value of the price return index at the end of the period
V_{PRI0} = Value of the price return index at the beginning of the period

The price return of each constituent security is calculated as:

$$PR_i = \frac{P_{i1} - P_{i0}}{P_{i0}}$$

where:
PR_i = Price return of constituent security i (as a decimal number)
P_{i1} = Price of the constituent security i at the end of the period
P_{i0} = Price of the constituent security i at the beginning of the period

The price return of the index equals the weighted average price return of the constituent securities. It is calculated as:

$$PR_I = w_1 PR_1 + w_2 PR_2 + ... + w_N PR_N$$

where:
PR_I = Price return of the index portfolio (as a decimal number)
PR_i = Price return of constituent security i (as a decimal number)
w_i = Weight of security i in the index portfolio
N = Number of securities in the index

Total Return

The total return of an index can be calculated as:

$$TR_I = \frac{V_{PRI1} - V_{PRI0} + Inc_I}{V_{PRI0}}$$

where:
TR_I = Total return of the index portfolio (as a decimal number)
V_{PRI1} = Value of the total return index at the end of the period
V_{PRI0} = Value of the total return index at the beginning of the period
Inc_I = Total income from all securities in the index held over the period

The total return of each constituent security is calculated as:

$$TR_i = \frac{P_{1i} - P_{0i} + Inc_i}{P_{0i}}$$

where:
TR_i = Total return of constituent security i (as a decimal number)
P_{1i} = Price of constituent security i at the end of the period
P_{0i} = Price of constituent security i at the beginning of the period
Inc_i = Total income from security i over the period

The total return of the index equals the weighted average total return of the constituent securities. It is calculated as:

$$TR_I = w_1 TR_1 + w_2 TR_2 + \ldots + w_N TR_N$$

where:
TR_I = Total return of the index portfolio (as a decimal number)
TR_i = Total return of constituent security i (as a decimal number)
w_i = Weight of security i in the index portfolio
N = Number of securities in the index

Given a series of price returns for an index, the value of a price return index can be calculated as (see Example 1-1):

$$V_{PRIT} = V_{PRI0}(1+PR_{I1})(1+PR_{I2})\ldots(1+PR_{IT})$$

where:
V_{PRI0} = Value of the price return index at inception
V_{PRIT} = Value of the price return index at time t
PR_{IT} = Price return (as a decimal number) on the index over the period

Similarly, the value of a total return index may be calculated as:

$$V_{TRIT} = V_{TRI0}(1+TR_{I1})(1+TR_{I2})\ldots(1+TR_{IT})$$

where:
V_{TRI0} = Value of the index at inception
V_{TRIT} = Value of the index at time t
TR_{IT} = Total return (as a decimal number) on the index over the period

---

Example 1-1: Price Return and Total Return Indices

An analyst obtained the following information regarding an equity market index created at the beginning of 2008:

	2008	2009
Price return	7.5%	8.3%
Total return	12.6%	13.4%

Given that the index value at inception is 1,000, calculate the values of price return and total return indices at the end of 2008 and 2009.

Solution

Price return index

Value at the end of 2008 = $1,000 \times 1.075 = 1,075$

Value at the end of 2009 = $1,000 \times 1.075 \times 1.083 = 1,164.225$

Total return index

Value at the end of 2008 = $1,000 \times 1.126 = 1,126$

Value at the end of 2009 = $1,000 \times 1.126 \times 1.134 = 1,276.884$

LOS 46c: Describe the choices and issues in index construction and management. **Vol 5, p 82**

Constructing and managing a security market index involves:

- Target market selection.
- Security selection.
- Index weighting.
- Rebalancing.
- Reconstitution.

Target Market and Security Selection

When constructing a security market index, the first decision that must be made relates to which market, market segment, or asset class the index should represent. The target market may be based on:
- Asset class (e.g., equities, fixed income, or real estate)
- Geographic region (e.g., Japan, South Africa, or Europe)
- The exchange on which the securities are traded (e.g., New York, London, or Tokyo)
- Other characteristics (e.g., economic sector, company size, and investment style)

An index may consist of all the securities in the target market or just a representative sample of the target market. Some indices (e.g., S&P 500) fix the number of securities to be included in the index, while others (e.g., TOPIX) allow the number of securities to vary to reflect changes in the target market or to maintain a certain percentage of the target market.

LOS 46d: Compare the different weighting methods used in index construction. **Vol 5, pp 82–91**

LOS 46e: Calculate and analyze the value and return of an index given its weighting method. **Vol 5, pp 82–91**

Price Weighting

In a price-weighted index the weight of each constituent security is determined by dividing its price by the sum of the prices of all constituent securities:

$$w_i^P = \frac{P_i}{\sum_{i=1}^{N} P_i}$$

The value of a price-weighted index is computed by dividing the sum of the security prices by the divisor. See Example 1-2. At inception, the divisor is typically set to the number of securities in the index.

Example 1-2: Price-Weighted Index

A price-weighted equity index consists of one share each of five securities. The prices of these securities at the end of 2008 and 2009 are given below:

Securities	Price at the End of 2008 ($)	Price at the End of 2009 ($)
A	30	34
B	22	28
C	35	31
D	50	54
E	48	44

1. Calculate the value of the index at the beginning of 2009.
2. Calculate the weights of each security at the beginning of 2009.
3. Calculate the price return of the index for 2009.

Solution

In the examples relating to various weighting methods, we have concentrated on determining only the price return on the index to keep it simple. Total return index calculations are similar, the only difference being that total returns for each constituent security are used instead of price returns.

1. Value of the index at the beginning of 2009:

$$= \frac{(30 \times 1) + (22 \times 1) + (35 \times 1) + (50 \times 1) + (48 \times 1)}{5} = 37$$

2. Weight of security A = 30/185 = 16.22%
   Weight of security B = 22/185 = 11.89%
   Weight of security C = 35/185 = 18.92%
   Weight of security D = 50/185 = 27.03%
   Weight of security E = 48/185 = 25.95%

3. Value of the index at the end of 2009:

$$= \frac{(34 \times 1) + (28 \times 1) + (31 \times 1) + (54 \times 1) + (44 \times 1)}{5} = 38.2$$

Price return of the index for 2009 = (38.2 − 37) / 37 = 3.24%

The advantage of a price-weighted index is its simplicity. One of the issues with a price-weighted index is that a stock split or stock dividend by one of the constituent securities changes the weights of all securities in the index. To prevent stock splits and stock dividends from changing the value of the index, the divisor of a price-weighted index must be adjusted. This is illustrated in Example 1-3.

Example 1-3: Calculation of Index Divisor After a Stock Split

A price-weighted market index includes four stocks: A, B, C, and D. Stock B issues a four-for-one stock split. The table below lists the prices of the stocks before and after the split.

Stock	Before Split	After Stock Split by Stock B
A	40	40
B	80	20
C	70	70
D	50	50
	240	**180**
		$180 \div x = 60$
	Index $= 240 \div 4 = 60$	$x = 3$

If the divisor is not adjusted for the stock split, the index will fall from 60 to 45 (180/4) even though there has been no change in prices other than to adjust for the split. To reflect the fact that stock values really have not changed, the index divisor must be adjusted. This new divisor, x, is calculated as $(40 + 20 + 70 + 50) / 60 = 3$.

Price-weighted indices suffer from a *downward* bias. Companies that split their stock are typically those that have witnessed substantial increases in their stock prices. As their stock prices fall to adjust for the split, their weight in the index also falls.

Equal Weighting

In an equal-weighted index, each constituent security is given an identical weight in the index at inception. The weights are calculated as:

$$w_i^E = \frac{1}{N}$$

where:
w_i = Fraction of the portfolio that is allocated to security i or weight of security i
N = Number of securities in the index

The number of shares of each security included in the index is calculated as the value allotted to each constituent security divided by the price of the security. Unlike a price-weighted index, where the weights are arbitrarily determined by market prices, the weights in an equal-weighted index are effectively determined by the index provider (in choosing the particular weighting mechanism). See Example 1-4.

Example 1-4: Equal-Weighted Index

An equal-weighted equity index with an initial value of 10,000 consists of five securities whose prices as at the end of 2008 and 2009 are given below:

Securities	Price at the End of 2008 ($)	Price at the End of 2009 ($)
A	30	34
B	22	28
C	35	31
D	50	54
E	48	44

1. Calculate the number of shares of each security included in the equal-weighted index.
2. Calculate the index value at the end of 2009.
3. Calculate the price return of the index for 2009.

Solution

Since the index consists of five securities, each security will be assigned a weight of 20% in the index. As the total value of the index is 10,000, the value assigned to each security will be 2,000.

1. Number of shares of Stock A = 2,000/30 = 66
   Number of shares of Stock B = 2,000/22 = 90
   Number of shares of Stock C = 2,000/35 = 57
   Number of shares of Stock D = 2,000/50 = 40
   Number of shares of Stock E = 2,000/48 = 41

> The number of shares of each security in this example has been rounded off for simplicity.

2. The value of the index position in each security at the end of 2009 is calculated as:

   Security A: 66 × 34 = 2,244
   Security B: 90 × 28 = 2,520
   Security C: 57 × 31 = 1,767
   Security D: 40 × 54 = 2,160
   Security E: 41 × 44 = 1,804

   Therefore, the total value of the index at the end of 2009 is calculated as:
   2,244 + 2,520 + 1,767 + 2,160 + 1,804 = 10,495

3. The price return of the index for 2009 = (10,495 / 10,000) − 1 = 4.95%

Equal-weighted indices are also preferred because of their simplicity. However, they have a few disadvantages:

- Assigning an equal weight to all securities under-represents (over-represents) those securities that constitute a relatively large (small) fraction of the target market.
- The index does not remain equally weighted once the prices of the constituent securities change. Frequent adjustments must be made to maintain equal weighting.

Market-Capitalization Weighting

A market-capitalization weighted (value weighted) index is based on the total market value (current stock price times the total number of shares outstanding) of all stocks in the index. The proportion of each constituent security is determined by dividing its market capitalization by the total market capitalization of all the securities in the index:

$$w_i^M = \frac{Q_i P_i}{\sum_{j=1}^{N} Q_j P_j}$$

where:
w_i = Fraction of the portfolio that is allocated to security i or weight of security i
Q_i = Number of shares outstanding of security i
P_i = Share price of security i
N = Number of securities in the index

The initial market value is assigned a base number (e.g., 100) and a new market value is computed periodically. The change in the index is measured by comparing the new market value to the base market value. See Example 1-5.

Example 1-5: Market Capitalization-Weighted Index

A market-capitalization-weighted equity index consists of five securities whose prices and number of shares outstanding are given below:

Securities	Price at the End of 2008 ($)	Price at the End of 2009 ($)	Shares Outstanding
A	30	34	4,000
B	22	28	6,000
C	35	31	2,000
D	50	54	2,500
E	48	44	3,000

---

1. Calculate the weight of each security in the index at the beginning of 2009.
2. Calculate the value of the divisor that gives an index value of 1,000 at the beginning of 2009.
3. Calculate the price return of the index for 2009.

Solution

1. Total market capitalization at the beginning of 2009:

$$= (30 \times 4,000) + (22 \times 6,000) + (35 \times 2,000) + (50 \times 2,500) + (48 \times 3,000) = 591,000$$

The weights of each of the 5 securities are calculated below:

Security A = (30 × 4,000) / 591,000 = 20.30%
Security B = (22 × 6,000) / 591,000 = 22.34%
Security C = (35 × 2,000) / 591,000 = 11.84%
Security D = (50 × 2,500) / 591,000 = 21.15%
Security E = (48 × 3,000) / 591,000 = 24.37%

2. Value of the divisor = 591,000 / 1,000 = 591

3. Total market capitalization at the end of 2009:

$$= (34 \times 4,000) + (28 \times 6,000) + (31 \times 2,000) + (54 \times 2,500) + (44 \times 3,000) = 633,000$$

Price return of the index for 2009 = (633,000/591) / 1,000 − 1 = 7.11%

Value-weighted indices automatically adjust for stock splits and stock dividends.

Float-Adjusted Market-Capitalization Weighting

In a float-adjusted market-capitalization weighted index, the proportion of each constituent security is determined by adjusting its market capitalization for its market float.

Market float generally refers to the number of shares of the constituent security that are available to the investing public. Shares held by controlling shareholders, other corporations, and governments are subtracted from the total number of outstanding shares to determine the market float. See Example 1-6.

The float-adjusted market-capitalization weight of each constituent security is calculated as:

$$w_i^M = \frac{f_i Q_i P_i}{\displaystyle\sum_{j=1}^{N} f_j Q_j P_j}$$

where:
f_i = Fraction of shares outstanding in the market float
w_i = Fraction of the portfolio that is allocated to security i or weight of security i
Q_i = Number of shares outstanding of security i
P_i = Share price of security i
N = Number of securities in the index

Example 1-6: Float-Adjusted Market-Capitalization Weighted Indices

A float-adjusted market-capitalization weighted equity index consists of five securities. Further information is provided in the table below:

Securities	Price at the End of 2008 ($)	Price at the End of 2009 ($)	Shares Outstanding	Percentage of Shares in Market Float
A	30	34	4,000	40
B	22	28	6,000	70
C	35	31	2,000	80
D	50	54	2,500	50
E	48	44	3,000	60

1. Calculate the number of shares of each security that will be included in the index.
2. Calculate the total float-adjusted market-capitalization at the beginning of 2009.
3. Calculate the price return of the index for 2009.

Solution

1. The number of shares of each security to be included in the index is calculated as:

   Security A = 4,000 × 40% = 1,600
   Security B = 6,000 × 70% = 4,200
   Security C = 2,000 × 80% = 1,600
   Security D = 2,500 × 50% = 1,250
   Security E = 3,000 × 60% = 1,800

2. The total float-adjusted market-capitalization at the beginning of 2009 is calculated as:

   $(30 \times 1,600) + (22 \times 4,200) + (35 \times 1,600) + (50 \times 1,250) + (48 \times 1,800) = 345,300$

> 3. The total float-adjusted market-capitalization at the end of 2009 is calculated as:
>
> $$(34 \times 1,600) + (28 \times 4,200) + (31 \times 1,600) + (54 \times 1,250) + (44 \times 1,800) = 368,300$$
>
> Price return of the index for 2009 = (368,300 / 345,300) − 1 = 6.66%

The primary advantage of market capitalization weighting (and float-adjusted market capitalization weighting) is that securities are held in proportion to their value in the target market. A disadvantage is that stocks with larger market values have a larger impact on the index. Stocks that have seen their prices rise (fall) will see their relative weight in the index increase (decline). The effect of market value weighting is therefore similar to that of a momentum trading strategy.

Fundamental Weighting

Instead of using prices of constituent securities, a fundamental weighted index uses other measures of a company's size (that are independent of the stock price) such as book value, cash flow, revenues, and earnings to determine weights of securities in the index. Some fundamental indices use a single measure to weight the constituent securities, while others combine weights from several measures to form a composite value that is used for weighting. See Example 1-7.

The fundamental weight on security i can be calculated as:

$$w_i^F = \frac{F_i}{\sum\limits_{j=1}^{N} F_j}$$

where:
F_i = A given fundamental size measure of company i

Earnings yield equals earnings per share for the most recent 12-month period divided by the current market price per share. The earnings yield (which is the inverse of the P/E ratio) shows the percentage of each dollar invested in the stock that was earned by the company.

The earnings yield is used by many investment managers to determine optimal asset allocations.

Example 1-7: Fundamental Weighting

Consider two stocks, A and B, which are the only securities in an index. Market capitalization and earnings information for the stocks is given below:

	Stock A	Stock B	Total
Market capitalization ($)	1.4 billion	600 million	2 billion
Earnings ($)	40 million	40 million	80 million

The earnings yield of Stock A is 2.86% (0.04b/1.4b) and that of Stock B is 6.67% (40m/600m).

The weights assigned to the two stocks in a market-capitalization weighted and fundamental weighted index (based on earnings) are given below:

	Stock A	Stock B
Market-capitalization weighted	1.4/(1.4 + 0.6) = 70%	0.6 /(1.4 + 0.6) = 30%
Fundamental weighted	40/(40 + 40) = 50%	40/(40 + 40) = 50%

Notice that compared to a value-weighted index, a fundamental weighted index assigns a higher weight to Stock B (50% versus 30%) and a lower weight to Stock A (50% versus 70%). Stocks with a higher earnings yield than that of the overall market weighted portfolio will be more heavily weighted under fundamental weighting compared to market value weighting. Fundamental weighting therefore, results in a "value tilt."

In contrast to market-capitalization weighted indices, in which the weight of a stock in the index moves in the same direction as its price, fundamental weighted indices have a "contrarian" effect in that the portfolio weights move away from securities whose prices have risen (as higher prices result in a lower earnings yield).

LOS 46f: Describe rebalancing and reconstitution of an index. Vol 5, pp 92–93

Rebalancing

We have seen that the weights assigned to constituent securities at inception of an index change as their prices change. In order to keep the weights of constituent securities consistent with the index's weighting method, security weights must be adjusted or rebalanced.

- In equal-weighted indices, the weights of securities that have witnessed price appreciation increase over time, and weights of securities that have underperformed decrease over time. Rebalancing an equal-weighted index would require reducing the weight of securities that have outperformed and increasing the weight of securities that have underperformed.
- Price-weighted indices do not need to be rebalanced, as the weight of each constituent security is determined by its price.
- Market-capitalization weighted indices rebalance themselves to reflect changes in the market-capitalization of constituent securities. They only need to be rebalanced to reflect mergers, acquisitions, liquidations, and so on.

Reconstitution

This refers to the process of changing the constituent securities in an index. Constituent securities need to be examined on a regular basis to evaluate whether they still meet the criteria for inclusion in the index. If they no longer meet the criteria, they must be replaced with securities that do meet the criteria. Index reconstitution is performed in order to:

- Reflect changes in the target market as a result of bankruptcies, de-listings, mergers, and so on.
- Reflect the judgment of the selection committee.

Reconstitution creates turnover within the index (especially for market value weighted indices), as once the revised list of constituent securities is determined, the weights of all constituent securities must be recalculated. Further, the frequency of reconstitution is a major issue for widely used indices and their constituent securities. Even before a scheduled reconstitution is undertaken by the index provider, investors speculate on which securities will be added to or removed from the index. If investors bet on a particular security being added to a popular index (by purchasing significant quantities of that particular security), the stock can see a dramatic increase in its price before it is actually added to the index.

LESSON 2: USES OF MARKET INDICES AND TYPES OF INDICES

LOS 46g: Describe uses of security market indices. Vol 5, pp 93–95

- Indices are good indicators of the collective opinion of market participants and are used to gauge market sentiment. However, indices typically only include a sample of stocks and therefore do not reflect the behavior of investors who trade in other stocks.

- They are used as proxies for measuring and modeling returns, systematic risk, and risk-adjusted performance. For example, when applying the CAPM, the S&P 500 is used as a proxy for the market portfolio in the United States.

- By exhibiting the risk and return profiles of select groups of securities, indices act as proxies for asset classes in asset allocation models. They provide the historical data used to model the risks and returns of different asset classes.

- In the field of performance evaluation, indices are used as benchmarks for actively managed portfolios. For example, the performance of a portfolio consisting of global small-capitalization stocks might be compared to the performance of the FTSE Global Small Cap Index, which includes 4,600 small-capitalization stocks across 48 countries.

- Security market indices serve as the basis for the creation of numerous investment products. For example, they led to the development of index portfolios, which subsequently led to the introduction of exchange-traded funds (ETFs). ETFs in turn led to the development of new indices to serve the other needs of investors.

LOS 46h: Describe types of equity indices. Vol 5, pp 95–98

Equity indices include the following:

Broad market indices: A broad equity market index contains securities representing more than 90% of the selected market. For example, the Russell 3000 consists of the largest 3,000 stocks (by market capitalization), and represents 99% of the U.S. equity market.

Multi-market indices: Multi-market indices consist of security market indices from different countries and may represent multiple national markets, geographic regions, economic development groups, or even the entire world. A number of index providers, including MSCI- Barra publish multi-market indices. Index providers weight constituent securities in each country by market capitalization and determine the weight of each country in the overall index based on relative GDPs, effectively creating fundamental weighting in these indices.

Sector indices: Sector indices only include securities representing a particular economic sector (e.g., finance, health care, technology, etc.) where the economic sector may be classified on a national, regional, or global basis. These play an important role in evaluating a portfolio manager's performance and determining whether she is better at stock selection or sector allocation. Further, they serve as model portfolios for sector-specific ETFs and other investment portfolios.

Style indices: Financial firms like Dow Jones and Standard & Poor's have developed different indices based on specific investment strategies used by portfolio managers. These indices include those based on size (e.g., small-cap versus large-cap equities) and others based on style (e.g., growth versus value stocks). Stocks may need to be reclassified over time based on changing valuation ratios or market capitalizations. Therefore, style indices generally have much higher turnover than broad market indices.

LOS 46i: Describe types of fixed-income indices. Vol 5, pp 98–101

Creating bond-market indices presents the following challenges:

- There is a broader universe of bonds than of stocks.
- The universe of bonds is constantly changing as a result of new issues, calls, and maturities.
- The price volatility of a bond (as measured by duration) is constantly changing. Duration changes with a bond's maturity and market yields.
- Current and continuous transaction prices are not available for bonds.

Types of Fixed-Income Indices

Fixed-income securities can be classified along the following dimensions:

- Type of issuer (government, government agency, corporation).
- Type of financing (general obligation, collateralized).
- Currency of payments.
- Maturity.
- Credit quality (investment grade, high yield, credit agency ratings).
- Absence or presence of inflation protection.

Fixed-income indices can be categorized as follows:

- Aggregate or broad market indices.
- Market sector indices.
- Style indices.
- Economic sector indices.
- Specialized indices such as high-yield, inflation-linked, and emerging market indices.

Due to the wide variety of instruments, fixed-income indices may be subdivided based on a variety of dimensions. For example, indices categorizing securities as investment-grade and high-yield may be subdivided by maturity and credit rating.

LOS 46j: Describe indices representing alternative investments.
Vol 5, pp 101–103

Investments in asset classes other than equities and fixed-income have gained popularity as investors have looked to diversify their portfolios. Several indices have been created to represent the performance of these asset classes.

Commodity indices: Commodity indices consist of futures contracts on one or more commodities and have the following characteristics:

- They do not have an obvious weighting method so index providers create their own weighting methods. Commodities may either be weighted equally, or on the basis of price, or may have fixed weights as determined by a committee. The returns of different commodity indices that contain the same commodities may differ due to differences in weighting methods.

- Different weighting methods lead to different exposures to specific commodities, which result in very different risk and return profiles of commodity indices. Equity and fixed-income indices that target the same markets share similar risk and return profiles.

- The performance of commodity indices may differ from that of the underlying commodities because indices consist of futures contracts on commodities rather than the actual commodities. Aside from being affected by changes in prices of the underlying commodities, index returns are also affected by the risk-free rate, changes in futures prices, and roll yield.

Real estate investment trust indices: Real estate indices represent the market for real estate and real estate securities. They can be categorized as:

- Appraisal indices
- Repeat sales indices
- Real estate investment trust (REIT) indices

REIT indices consist of shares of publicly traded REITs (public or private organizations that combine individual investors' funds and provide them access to real estate investments). Shares issued by REITs trade on various exchanges around the world and are priced continuously.

Hedge fund indices: Hedge fund indices are designed to represent the performance of hedge funds (private investment vehicles that typically use leverage and long and short investment strategies) on a very broad, global level or the strategy level. Hedge fund indices have the following characteristics:

- They rely on voluntary disclosures from funds, as it is not mandatory for hedge funds to disclose performance to any party other than investors.

- If they do decide to disclose performance, hedge funds have a choice regarding which index or indices they report their performance to. Therefore, rather than index providers determining the constituents, the constituents determine the index. Further, different hedge fund indices may reflect very different performance for the hedge fund industry over the same period of time based on the hedge funds represented in those indices.

- Poorly performing hedge funds may stop reporting their performance to hedge fund indices or may cease to exist altogether. This leads to survivorship bias and an upward bias in hedge fund performance as represented by these indices.

LOS 46k: Compare types of security market indices. Vol 5, pp 103–104

Table 2-1: Representative Indices Worldwide[1]

As indicated in this reading, the choice of indices to meet the needs of investors is extensive. Investors using security market indices must be careful in their selection of the index or indices most appropriate for their needs. The following table illustrates the variety of indices reflecting different asset classes, markets, and weighting methods.

Index	Representing	Number of Securities	Weighting Method	Comments
Dow Jones Industrial Average	U.S. blue-chip companies	30	Price	The oldest and most widely-known U.S. equity index. Wall Street Journal editors choose 30 stocks from among large, mature, blue-chip companies.
Nikkei Stock Average	Japanese blue-chip companies	225	Modified price	Known as the Nikkei 225 and originally formulated by Dow Jones & Co. Because of extreme variations in price levels of component securities, some high price shares are weighted as a fraction of share price. Index contains some illiquid stocks.
TOPIX	All companies listed on the Tokyo Stock Exchange First Section	Varies	Float-adjusted market cap	Represents about 93 percent of the market value of all Japanese companies. Contains a large number of very small, illiquid stocks, making exact replication difficult.
MSCI All Country World Index	Stocks of 23 developed and 22 emerging markets	Varies	Free-float-adjusted market cap	Composed of companies representative of the market structure of developed and emerging market countries in the Americas, Europe/Middle East, and Asia/Pacific regions. Price return and total return versions available in both USD and local currencies.

1 - Representative Indices Worldwide, Volume 5, CFA Program Curriculum 2014

Table 2-1: Representative Indices Worldwide *(continued)*

Index	Representing	Number of Securities	Weighting Method	Comments
S&P Developed Ex-U.S. BMI Energy Sector Index	Energy sector of developed global markets outside the United States	Varies	Float-adjusted market cap	Serves as a model portfolio for the SPDR® S&P Energy Sector Exchange-Traded Fund (ETF).
Barclays Capital Global Aggregate Bond Index	Investment-grade bonds in the North American, European, and Asian markets	Varies	Market cap	Formerly known as Lehman Brothers Global Aggregate Bond Index
Markit iBoxx Euro High-Yield Bond Indices	Sub-investment-grade euro-denominated corporate bonds	Varies	Market cap and variations	Rebalanced monthly. Represents tradable part of market. Price and total return versions available with such analytical values as yield, duration, modified duration, and convexity. Provides platform for research and structured products.
FTSE EPRA/NAREIT Global Real Estate Index	Real estate securities in the North American, European, and Asian markets	335	Float-adjusted market cap	The stock of REITs that constitute the index trade on public stock exchanges and may be constituents of equity market indices.
HFRX Global Hedge Fund Index	Overall composition of the HFR database	Varies	Asset weighting	Comprise all eligible hedge fund strategies. Examples include convertible arbitrage, distressed securities, market neutral, event driven, macro, and relative value arbitrage. Constituent strategies are asset weighted on the basis of asset distribution within the hedge fund industry.
HFRX Equal Weighted Strategies EUR Index	Overall composition of the HFR database	Varies	Equal weighting	Denominated in euros and is constructed from the same strategies as the HFRX Global Hedge Fund Index.
Morningstar Style Indices	U.S. stocks classified by market cap and value/growth orientation	Varies	Float-adjusted market cap	The nine indices defined by combinations of market cap (large, mid, and small) and value/growth orientation (value, core, growth) have mutually exclusive constituents and are exhaustive with respect to the Morningstar U.S. Market Index. Each is a model portfolio for one of the iShares Morningstar ETFs.

LESSON 1: THE CONCEPT OF MARKET EFFICIENCY AND FORMS OF MARKET EFFICIENCY

LOS 47a: Describe market efficiency and related concepts, including their importance to investment practitioners. Vol 5, pp 117–119

An informationally efficient market (an efficient market) is one where security prices adjust rapidly to reflect any new information. It is a market where asset prices reflect all past and present information.

Investment managers and analysts are interested in market efficiency because it dictates how many profitable trading opportunities may abound in the market.

- In an efficient market, it is difficult to find inaccurately priced securities. Therefore, superior risk-adjusted returns cannot be attained in an efficient market, and it would be wise to pursue a passive investment strategy, which entails lower costs.
- In an inefficient market, securities may be mispriced and trading in these securities can offer positive risk-adjusted returns. In such a market, an active investment strategy may outperform a passive strategy on a risk-adjusted basis.

In an efficient market, the time frame required for security prices to reflect any new information is very short. For example, in the foreign exchange market and developed equity markets, prices reflect new information in less than a minute. In a relatively inefficient market, the time frame of the price adjustment is long enough to allow many traders to earn profits with little risk.

Finally, in an efficient market, prices only adjust to new or unexpected information (surprises). Investors absorb the new information and revise their expectations regarding the security's risk and return accordingly. They then take positions on the asset in light of their new forecasts. If the expected return is adequate compensation for the security's perceived risk, investors will purchase the asset, and if the expected return does not offer sufficient compensation for the asset's perceived risk, they will liquidate positions in the asset or even short it.

LOS 47b: Distinguish between market value and intrinsic value. Vol 5, pp 119–120

The market value or market price of the asset is the price at which the asset can currently be bought or sold. It is determined by the interaction of demand and supply for the security in the market. Intrinsic value or fundamental value is the value of the asset that reflects all its investment characteristics accurately. Intrinsic values are estimated in light of all the available information regarding the asset; they are not known for certain.

In an efficient market, investors widely believe that the market price reflects a security's intrinsic value. On the other hand, in an inefficient market, investors may try to develop their own estimates of intrinsic value in order to profit from any mispricing (difference between the market price and intrinsic value).

The challenge for investors lies in estimating an asset's intrinsic value. Estimates of intrinsic value are derived by forecasting the amount and timing of the security's future cash flows, and then discounting them at an appropriate discount rate (which reflects the riskiness of these cash flows). As new, relevant information continues to flow to investors, estimates of intrinsic value and market prices keep changing.

LOS 47c: Explain factors that affect a market's efficiency. **Vol 5, pp 120–123**

Markets cannot strictly be classified as efficient or inefficient. Market efficiency should be viewed as falling on a continuum between these two extremes. A relatively efficient market reflects new information in market prices more quickly and more accurately than a relatively inefficient market.

Factors Contributing to and Impeding a Market's Efficiency

Market participants: Generally speaking, the greater the number of active market participants (investors and financial analysts) that analyze an asset or security, the greater the degree of efficiency in the market. Restrictions that prevent investors from trading in a market or in a particular security impede market efficiency.

Information availability and financial disclosure: The availability of accurate and timely information regarding trading activities and traded companies contributes to market efficiency. For a market to be considered efficient, investors should have access to the information necessary to value securities that trade in the market. Further, all investors should have fair and equal opportunity to act on this information.

Limits to trading: The activities of arbitrageurs, who seek opportunities to trade on mispricings in the market to earn arbitrage (riskless) profits, contribute to market efficiency. Arbitrageurs purchase securities that they believe are undervalued (bidding their prices up to their intrinsic values) and short securities that they believe are overvalued (bringing their prices down to their intrinsic values). Limitations on arbitrage trading (e.g., difficulty in executing trades immediately and high costs of trading) reduce market efficiency.

Transactions costs and information-acquisition costs: Investors should consider transaction costs and information-acquisition costs in evaluating the efficiency of a market.

Two securities that should trade for the exact same price in an efficient market may trade at different prices if the costs of trading on the mispricing (to make a profit) for the lowest-cost traders are greater than the potential profit. In such cases, these prices are still "efficient" within the bounds of arbitrage. The bounds of arbitrage are relatively narrow in highly liquid markets (e.g., U.S. T-bills), but wider in relatively illiquid markets.

Further, there are always costs associated with gathering and analyzing information. Net of information acquisition costs and the return offered on a security should be commensurate with the security's level of risk. If superior returns can be earned after deducting information-acquisition costs, the market is relatively inefficient.

LOS 47d: Contrast weak-form, semi-strong form, and strong-form market efficiency. **Vol 5, pp 124–129**

Weak-Form Efficient Market Hypothesis

Weak-form EMH assumes that current stock prices reflect *all security market information* including historical trends in prices, returns, volumes, and other market-generated information such as block trades and trading by specialists. Under this hypothesis, because current stock market prices have essentially factored in all historical data, future returns on a stock should be independent of past returns or patterns.

Proponents of weak-form EMH assert that abnormal risk-adjusted returns cannot be earned by using trading rules and technical analysis, which make investing decisions based on historical security market data.

On the whole, various tests for weak-form EMH have backed the theory that current market prices reflect all available security market information and lead to the conclusion that the markets tend to be weak-form efficient. However, there is evidence that in countries with developing markets (e.g., China, Bangladesh, and Turkey) opportunities to profit from technical analysis do exist.

> Abnormal returns are returns in excess of those implied by the SML for a stock with a given level of risk.

Semi-Strong Form Efficient Market Hypothesis

Semi-strong form EMH assumes that current security prices fully reflect *all security market information* and other public information. It encompasses weak-form EMH and also includes nonmarket public information such as dividend announcements, various financial ratios, and economic and political news in the set of information that is already factored into market values.

Proponents of the hypothesis assert that investors cannot earn abnormal risk-adjusted returns if their investment decisions are based on important material information after it has been made public. They stress that security prices rapidly adjust to reflect all public information.

Overall, semi-strong form EMH has received considerable support from studies in developed markets. In these markets, it has been found that abnormal risk-adjusted returns cannot be earned based on public information because security prices adjust for the information very quickly. However, there is some evidence that developing countries may not have semi-strong form efficient markets.

Strong-Form Efficient Market Hypothesis

Strong-form EMH contends that stock prices reflect *all public and private information*. It implies that no group of investors has sole access to any information that is relevant in price formation. Basically, there is no information out there that has not already been accounted for in current market prices.

Strong-form EMH encompasses weak-form and semi-strong form EMH and assumes perfect markets where information is cost free and available to all. Under strong-form EMH, no one can consistently achieve abnormal risk-adjusted returns, not even company insiders.

Studies have found that securities markets are not strong-form efficient. Abnormal risk-adjusted returns can be earned if material nonpublic information is used.

See Table 1-1 for a summary.

Table 1-1: Summary of Assertions of Various EMH

Form of EMH	Prices Fully Reflect	Types of Investors Who Cannot Earn Abnormal Returns Consistently
Weak form	All market (public) information.	Technical traders.
Semi-strong form	All market and nonmarket public information.	Technical traders and fundamental investors.
Strong form	All public and private information.	All investors.

Markets that are semi-strong form efficient must be weak-form efficient as well since public information includes market information. Similarly, markets that are strong-form efficient must also be semi-strong form efficient and weak-form efficient.

However, markets that are weak-form efficient may or may not be semi-strong form and strong-form efficient. Similarly, markets that are semi-strong form efficient may or may not be strong-form efficient.

LOS 47e: Explain the implications of each form of market efficiency for fundamental analysis, technical analysis, and the choice between active and passive portfolio management. Vol 5, pp 128–129

Implications of Efficient Market Hypothesis

- Securities markets are weak-form efficient. Therefore, past trends in prices cannot be used to earn superior risk-adjusted returns.
- Securities markets are also semi-strong from efficient. Therefore, investors who analyze information should consider what information is already factored into a security's price, and how any new information may affect its value.
- Securities markets are not strong-form efficient. This is because insider trading is illegal.

Efficient Markets and Technical Analysis

Technical analysts utilize charts to identify price patterns, which are used to make investment decisions. If the market is weak-form efficient, prices already reflect all available security market public information, and technical trading systems that depend only on past trading and price data cannot hold much value. Since tests have predominantly confirmed weak-form efficiency of markets, technical trading rules should not generate abnormal risk-adjusted profits after accounting for risks and transaction costs.

Efficient Markets and Fundamental Analysis

Fundamental analysts are concerned with the company that underlies the stock. They evaluate a company's past performance and examine its financial statements. They compute many performance ratios that aid them in assessing the validity of the stock's current price. They believe that a company's stock price can differ from its true intrinsic value, and investors who recognize the discrepancy can profit from it.

Fundamental analysis is necessary in a well-functioning securities market, as it helps market participants understand the implications of any new information. Further, fundamental analysis can help generate abnormal risk-adjusted returns if an analyst is superior to her peers in valuing securities.

Efficient Markets and Portfolio Management

If markets are weak and semi-strong form efficient, active management is not likely to earn superior risk-adjusted returns on a consistent basis. Therefore, passive portfolio management would outperform active management. Studies have shown that on a risk-adjusted basis, mutual funds perform as well as the market before considering fees and expenses, but underperform the market after considering these costs.

The implication here is that the role of the portfolio manager is not necessarily to beat the market, but to manage the portfolio in light on the investor's risk and return objectives.

LESSON 2: MARKET PRICING ANOMALIES AND BEHAVIORAL FINANCE

LOS 47f: Describe selected market anomalies. Vol 5, pp 129–136

There is considerable evidence to suggest that markets are generally efficient. However, research has also highlighted a number of potential inefficiencies or anomalies that result in securities being mispriced. An anomaly occurs when a change in the price of an asset cannot be explained by the release of new information into the market.

- If markets are efficient, trading strategies designed to exploit market anomalies will not generate superior risk-adjusted returns on a consistent basis.
- An exception to the notion of market efficiency (an anomaly) would occur if a mispricing can be used to earn superior risk adjusted returns consistently.

Observed anomalies can be placed into three categories.

1. Time-Series Anomalies

Calendar Anomalies

January effect: Studies have shown that since the 1980s, investors have earned significantly higher returns in the equity market during January compared to other months of the year. Tax reasons and "window-dressing" by portfolio managers have been held out as reasons to explain the January effect. However, recent evidence has suggested that the January effect is not persistent and does not produce superior returns on a risk-adjusted basis. Therefore, it is not a pricing anomaly. See Table 2-1 for other calendar anomalies.

Table 2-1: Other Calendar-Based Anomalies[1]

Anomaly	Observation
Turn-of-the-month effect	Returns tend to be higher on the last trading day of the month and the first three trading days of the next month.
Day-of-the-week effect	The average Monday return is negative and lower than the average returns for the other four days, which are all positive.
Weekend effect	Returns on weekends tend to be lower than returns on weekdays.
Holiday effect	Returns on stocks in the day prior to market holidays tend to be higher than other days.

Momentum and Overreaction Anomalies

Certain short-term share price patterns arise as a result of investors overreacting to the release of new information. Investors tend to inflate (depress) stock prices of companies that have released good (bad) news. Studies have shown that "losers" (stocks that have witnessed a recent price decline due to the release of bad news) have outperformed the market in subsequent periods, while winners have underperformed in subsequent periods.

However, other studies have also shown that securities that have outperformed in the short term continue to generate high returns in subsequent periods (carrying on price momentum).

The overreaction and momentum anomalies go against the assertions of weak-form efficiency in markets.

2. Cross-Sectional Anomalies

Size Effect

Studies conducted in the past showed that shares of smaller companies outperformed shares of larger companies on a risk-adjusted basis. However, recent studies have failed to reach the same conclusion.

Value Effect

Studies have found that low P/E stocks have experienced higher risk-adjusted returns than high P/E stocks. These results go against semi-strong form market efficiency. However, when the Fama and French three-factor model is used instead of the CAPM to predict stock returns, the value stock anomaly disappears.

---

1 - Exhibit 4, Volume 5, CFA Program Curriculum 2014

3. Other Anomalies

Closed-End Investment Fund Discounts

Several studies have shown that closed-end funds tend to trade at a discount (sometimes exceeding 50%) to their per-share NAVs. Theoretically, investors could purchase all the shares in the fund, liquidate the fund, and make a profit by selling the constituent securities at their market prices. However, after accounting for management fees, unrealized capital gains taxes, liquidity, and transaction costs, any profit potential is eliminated.

Earnings Surprises

Several studies have shown that although earnings surprises are quickly reflected in stock prices most of the time, this is not always the case. Investors may be able to earn abnormal returns using publicly available earnings information by purchasing stocks of companies that have announced positive earnings surprises. However, recent evidence has suggested that abnormal returns observed after earnings surprises do not control for transaction costs and risk.

Initial Public Offerings (IPOs)

Evidence suggests that investors who are able to acquire the shares of a company in an IPO at the offer price may be able to earn abnormal profits. However, this has not always proven to be the case. Further, over the long run, performance of IPOs has generally been below average.

Predictability of Returns Based on Prior Information

Considerable research has suggested that equity returns are based on factors such as interest rates, inflation rates, stock volatility, and so on. However, the fact that equity returns are related to economic fundamentals is not evidence of market inefficiency.

Implications for Investment Strategies

Although there is some evidence to support the existence of valid anomalies, it is difficult to consistently earn abnormal returns by trading on them. On average, markets are efficient. Further, it is possible that identified anomalies may not be violations of market efficiency, but the result of the statistical methodologies used to detect them.

LOS 47g: Contrast the behavioral finance view of investor behavior to that of traditional finance. Vol 5, pp 136–139

Behavioral Finance

Behavioral finance is a field of study that examines investor behavior and evaluates the impact of investor behavior on financial markets. The conclusions from behavioral finance studies regarding investor behavior are different from those assumed by valuation models in the following respects:

Most asset-pricing models assume that markets are rational and that the intrinsic value of a security reflects the rationality. But market efficiency and asset-pricing models do not require that each individual is rational –rather, only that the market is rational.

- In most financial models investors are assumed to be risk averse. Behavioralists assert that the dislike for risk is not symmetrical by pointing to loss aversion observed in investor behavior (i.e., investors dislike losses more than they like comparable gains).

- Another bias pointed out by behavioralists is overconfidence bias (i.e., investors have an inflated view of their ability to process new information appropriately). Since the bias asserts that most investors are incorrect in valuing securities given new information, stocks will be mispriced. Evidence has suggested that overconfidence has led to mispricing in most major markets around the world, but the bias has been observed predominantly in high-growth securities, whose prices are slow to factor in any new information.

- Other behavioral biases that have been put forward include:
  - Representativeness, where investors assess probabilities of future outcomes based on how similar they are to the current state.
  - Gambler's fallacy, where investors' estimates of future probabilities are affected by recent outcomes.
  - Mental accounting, where investors keep track of gains and losses from different investments in separate mental accounts.
  - Conservatism, where investors are slow to react to changes.
  - Disposition effect, where investors are quick to realize gains (by selling winners), but avoid realizing losses (by selling losers).
  - Narrow framing, where investors focus on issues in isolation.

The reason that behavioralists put forward these biases is because they assert that investor beliefs about a given asset's value may not be homogenous, which is why anomalies are observed in the market.

Concluding Remarks

Whether investor behavior can explain market anomalies is a subject open to debate.
- If investors must be rational for the market to be efficient, then markets cannot be efficient.
- If markets are defined as being efficient, investors cannot earn superior risk-adjusted profits consistently, available evidence suggests that markets are efficient even though investors do exhibit irrational behavior, such as herding.

READING 48: OVERVIEW OF EQUITY SECURITIES

LESSON 1: OVERVIEW OF EQUITY SECURITIES

Equities in Global Financial Markets. **Vol 5, pp 150–155**

In order to evaluate the importance of equity securities in global financial markets, we must look at the total market capitalization and trading volumes of global equity markets and the prevalence of equity ownership across various geographic regions.

- In 2008, on a global level, the equity market capitalization to GDP ratio was close to 100% (more than twice the long run average of 50%). This shows that investors attach a significant value to publicly traded equities relative to the aggregate market value of goods and services produced globally every year (global GDP).
- Studies have shown that during 1900 to 2011, government bonds and bills earned annualized real returns of less than 2%, which is in line with the inflation rate. On the other hand, equity markets earned real returns in excess of 4% per year in most markets. Equity securities entail higher risk than government bonds and bills, but they earn higher returns to compensate for the higher risk. Note that equity securities also tend to be more volatile over time.
- In most developed countries, equity ownership as a percentage of the population was between 20% and 50%. This illustrates how heavily weighted equity securities are in most investor portfolios.

LOS 48a: Describe characteristics of types of equity securities.
Vol 5, pp 155–161

LOS 48b: Describe differences in voting rights and other ownership characteristics among different equity classes. **Vol 5, pp 155–161**

A company may issue debt or equity securities to finance its operations. Issuing debt creates a liability for the company, as it is contractually obligated to make regular payments to its creditors. Investors who purchase debt securities are primarily interested in interest income.

On the other hand, issuing equity does not give rise to a liability. Shareholders have a residual claim on the company's assets after all liabilities have been paid. Investors who purchase equity securities are interested in capital appreciation as well as dividend income and therefore focus on the long-term performance of the company.

A company may issue the following types of equity securities:

Common Shares

Investors in common shares have an ownership interest in the company. They share the operating performance of the company, participate in the governance process through voting rights, and have a residual claim on the company's net assets in case of liquidation.

Voting rights enable common shareholders to have their say in major corporate decisions, including the election of the board of directors, and whether to merge with or acquire another company. In elections for the board of directors, companies may use statutory voting, where each share represents one vote, or cumulative voting, where total voting rights are based on the number of shares owned multiplied by the number of board directors being elected. Shareholders may apply all of their votes to a single candidate or spread them across the candidates in any proportion. Cumulative voting provides better representation of minority shareholders on the board.

Companies may issue different classes of common shares, each with different ownership and voting rights. Further, these different classes of shares might be entitled to different claims on the company's net assets in case of liquidation.

Common shares may also be callable or putable.
- **Callable** common shares give the issuing company the right, but not the obligation, to buy back shares from investors at a later date at the call price (which is specified when the shares are originally issued). Companies are likely to buy back shares when their market price is higher than the call price. This is beneficial for the company as it is able to:
  - ○ Buy shares at a lower price and resell them at the higher market price.
  - ○ Save on dividend payments and preserve its capital.

Callable common shares are also beneficial for the investors as they get a guaranteed return on their investments when the shares are called.

- **Putable** common shares give investors the right, but not the obligation, to sell their shares back to the issuing company at the put price (which is specified when the shares are originally issued). Investors are likely to exercise this right when the market price of shares is lower than the put price. Putable common shares limit investor losses. As far as the company is concerned, they make it easier to raise capital, as the put feature makes the shares more appealing to investors.

Preference Shares

Preference shares (also known as preferred stock) have the following characteristics:

- They do not give holders the right to participate in the operating performance of the company and they do not carry voting rights unless explicitly allowed for at issuance.
- They receive dividends before ordinary shareholders. Further, preferred dividends are fixed and are usually higher than dividends on common shares. However, the company is still not contractually obligated to make regular payments to holders of preferred stock.
- In case of liquidation, they have a higher priority in claims on the company's net assets than common shares. However, they still have a lower priority than bondholders.
- They can be perpetual (i.e., have no fixed maturity date), can pay dividends indefinitely, and can be callable or putable.

Preference shares can be classified into the following categories:

- **Cumulative:** Unpaid dividends on cumulative preference shares accrue over time and must be paid in full before dividends on common shares can be paid.
- **Noncumulative:** Unpaid dividends for one or more periods are forfeited permanently and are not accrued over time to be paid at a later date.
- **Participating:** These are entitled to preferred dividends plus additional dividends if the company's profits exceed a pre-specified level. Further, investors in participating preferred shares might be entitled to an additional distribution of the company's assets upon liquidation above the par value of the preference shares. Participating preference shares are more common in smaller, riskier companies in which investors are concerned about the company's possible future liquidation.
- **Nonparticipating:** These are only entitled to a fixed preferred dividend and the par value of shares in the event of liquidation.
- **Convertible:** These are convertible into a specified number of common shares based on a conversion ratio that is determined at issuance. They have the following advantages:
  - They allow investors to earn a higher dividend than if they had invested in the company's common shares.
  - They offer investors the opportunity to share the profits of the company.
  - They allow investors to benefit from a rise in the price of common shares through the conversion option.
  - Their price is less volatile than the underlying common shares because their dividend payments are known and more stable.

Convertible preference shares are becoming increasingly common in venture capital and private equity transactions.

LOS 48c: Distinguish between public and private equity securities.
Vol 5, pp 161–163

Equity securities can also be issued and traded in private equity markets. Such securities are issued primarily to institutional investors via nonpublic offerings, such as private placements, and have the following characteristics:

- There is no active secondary market for them as they are not listed on public exchanges. Therefore, they do not have market-determined quoted prices.
- They are highly illiquid, and require negotiations between investors in order to be traded.
- The issuing companies are not required by regulatory authorities to publish financial statements and other important information regarding the company, which makes it difficult to determine fair values.

Types of Private Equity Investments

- **Venture capital:** Venture capital funds invest in companies that are still in the early stages of development and require additional capital for expansion. These investments are usually made through limited partnerships, where managing partners actively participate in the management of the investee. These investments require a horizon of several years, as the securities are not traded publicly. Eventual exit is a very important consideration in such investments and available exit routes include buyouts and initial public offerings (IPOs).

In cases where the group of investors acquiring the company is primarily comprised of the company's existing management, the transaction is referred to a management buyout (MBO)

- **Leveraged buyout (LBO):** An LBO occurs when a group of investors uses debt financing to purchase all of the outstanding common shares of a publicly traded company. The company is then taken "private" and its shares cease to be traded publicly. Typically, companies with undervalued assets and/or assets that can generate high levels of cash flow are subjects of LBOs. Companies that are bought out in this manner are usually restructured and later taken public again by issuing new shares to the public in the primary market.

- **Private investment in public equity:** Sometimes private investors may invest in a public company that is in need of additional capital quickly in return for a significant ownership position (typically at a discount to the publicly quoted market price). Companies may require funds quickly to avail significant investment opportunities or to deal with high levels of debt.

Advantages of Private Companies

- The longer investment horizons allow investors to focus on long-term value creation and to address any underlying operational issues facing the company. As a result, private equity firms are increasingly issuing convertible preference shares to attract investors with their greater total return potential. Publicly traded companies feel pressured to focus on short-term performance (e.g., to meet market expectations regarding earnings, growth, etc.)
- Certain costs that public companies must bear, such as those incurred to meet regulatory and stock exchange filing requirements, are avoided by private companies.

Advantages of Public Companies

- Public equity markets are much larger than private equity networks. Therefore, they provide more opportunities to companies for raising capital cheaply.
- Publicly traded companies are encouraged to be open about their policies, which ensures that they act in shareholder interest.

LOS 48d: Describe methods for investing in nondomestic equity securities. Vol 5, pp 163–168

Technological advancements have led to the growth and integration of global capital markets. The ability to exchange information quickly through electronic networks has helped both companies and investors in the following ways:
- Companies are able to issue shares in international markets, making it easier and cheaper for them to raise capital and to expand their shareholder base beyond their local markets.
- Investors are able to invest in companies that are located abroad, which has enabled them to diversify their portfolios.

Studies have shown that reduced barriers to foreign ownership have led to improved equity market performance over the long term. As a result, more and more countries are becoming increasingly open to foreign investment. The following trends have emerged over the past two decades:

- An increasing number of companies have issued shares in markets outside of their home country.
- The number of companies whose shares are traded in markets outside of their home country has increased.
- An increasing number of companies are dual-listed (i.e., their shares are simultaneously issued and traded in two or more markets).

Listing a company on an international exchange has the following benefits:

- It improves awareness about the company's products and services.
- It enhances the liquidity of the company's shares.
- It increases corporate transparency due to the additional market exposure and the need to meet a greater number of filing requirements.

Methods for Investing in Nondomestic Equity Securities

Direct Investing

The most obvious way to invest in equity securities of foreign companies is to buy and sell securities directly in foreign markets. However, direct investing has the following implications:

- All transactions are in the company's, not the investor's domestic currency. Therefore, investors are also exposed to exchange rate risk.
- Investors must be familiar with the trading, clearing, and settlement regulations and procedures of the foreign market.
- Investing directly may lead to less transparency (due to the unavailability of audited financial statements on a regular basis) and increased volatility (due to limited liquidity).

Depository Receipts

A depository receipt (DR) is a security that trades like an ordinary share on a local exchange and represents an economic interest in a foreign company. It is created when a foreign company deposits its shares with a bank (the depository) in the country on whose exchange the shares will trade. The bank then issues a specific number of receipts representing the deposited shares based on a pre-determined ratio. Hence, one DR might represent one share, a number of shares, or a fractional share of the underlying stock.

The structure of the DR causes its price to be affected by the same factors that influence the price of the underlying shares, such as company fundamentals, market conditions, analysts' expectations, and so on. However, there might be short-term differences in the prices of the DR and the underlying stock giving rise to quick arbitrage opportunities.

A DR can be sponsored or unsponsored.

- A sponsored DR is when the foreign company that deposits its shares with the depository has a direct involvement in the issuance of receipts. Investors in sponsored DRs have the same rights as those enjoyed by direct owners of the company's common shares.
- In an unsponsored DR, the foreign company that deposits its shares with the depository has no involvement in the issuance of receipts. Therefore, it is the depository, not the investors, that enjoys rights as a direct owner of the company's common shares.

There are two types of depository receipts:

- *Global Depository Receipts (GDRs):* GDRs are issued by the depository bank outside of the company's home country and outside of the United States. Their main advantage is that they are not subject to foreign ownership and capital flow restrictions that may be imposed by the issuing company's home country, as they are sold outside of the home country.
- *American Depository Receipts (ADRs):* ADRs are denominated in U. S. dollars and trade like a common share on U. S. exchanges. They are basically GDRs that can be publicly traded in the United States. There are four primary types of ADRs, whose characteristics are listed in Table 1-1.

Table 1-1: Types of ADRs[1]

	Level I (Unlisted)	Level II (Listed)	Level III (Listed)	Rule 144A (Unlisted)
Objectives	Develop and broaden U.S. investor base with existing shares	Develop and broaden U.S. investor base with existing shares	Develop and broaden U.S. investor base with existing/ new shares	Access qualified institutional buyers (QIBs)
Raising capital on U.S. markets?	No	No	Yes, through public offerings	Yes, through private placements to QIBs
SEC registration	Form F-6	Form F-6	Forms F-1 and F-6	None
Trading	Over the counter (OTC)	NYSE, Nasdaq, or AMEX	NYSE, Nasdaq, or AMEX	Private offerings, resales, and trading through automated linkages such as PORTAL
Listing fees	Low	High	High	Low
Size and earnings requirements	None	Yes	Yes	None

[1] - Exhibit 16, Volume 5, CFA Program Curriculum 2014

Global Registered Shares (GRS)

A GRS is an ordinary share that is quoted and traded in different currencies on different stock exchanges around the world. GRSs offer more flexibility than DRs as the shares represent actual ownership in the issuing company, they can be traded anywhere, and currency conversions are not required to trade them.

Basket of Listed Depository Receipts (BLDR)

This is an exchange-traded fund (ETF) that represents a portfolio of DRs. Like all other ETFs, it trades throughout the day and can be bought, sold, or sold short just like an individual share. Further, it can be purchased on margin and used in hedging and arbitrage strategies.

LOS 48e: Compare the risk and return characteristics of types of equity securities. Vol 5, pp 169–171

Return Characteristics of Equity Securities

The two main sources of an equity security's total return are:
- Capital gains from price appreciation.
- Dividend income.

$$\text{Total Return, } R_t = (P_t - P_{t-1} + D_t) / P_{t-1}$$

where:
P_{t-1} = Purchase price at time $t - 1$
P_t = Selling price at time t
D_t = Dividends paid by the company during the period

The total return on nondividend paying stocks only consists of capital gains. Companies that are in the early stages of their life cycle generally do not pay any dividends, as they try to reinvest their profits to avail growth opportunities. On the other hand, companies that are in the mature stage may not have as many profitable growth opportunities to avail, so they distribute profits to investors in the form of dividends or through share repurchases.

Investors in depository receipts and foreign shares also incur foreign exchange gains (or losses). These arise due to changes in the exchange rate between the investor's domestic currency and the foreign currency over the investment horizon. Appreciation of the foreign currency (depreciation of the domestic currency) leads to foreign exchange gains, while depreciation of the foreign currency (appreciation of the domestic currency) leads to foreign exchange losses.

Another source of return arises from the compounding effects of reinvested dividends. Reinvested dividends are cash dividends that an investor uses to purchase additional shares in the company. Studies have shown that the compounding effects of reinvested dividends have significantly influenced long-run returns on equity securities.

The risk of an equity security refers to the uncertainty associated with its expected future cash flows or expected total return.

- Preference shares are less risky than common shares because:
    ○ Dividends on preference shares are known and fixed, reducing the uncertainty about future cash flows.
    ○ Preferred shareholders receive dividends and other distributions before common shareholders.
    ○ The amount that preference shareholders stand to receive if the company is liquidated is known and fixed as the par (or face) value of the shares. However, there is no guarantee that investors will receive this amount.

- Common shares are more risky because:
    ○ A relatively large proportion of their total return comes from capital gains and future dividends, which are unknown.
    ○ The amount that they receive if the company is liquidated depends on what is left over after all creditors and preferred shareholders have been paid off.

- Putable common shares are less risky than callable or noncallable common shares.
    ○ The option to sell the shares back to the issuer at a pre-determined price establishes the minimum expected return and reduces the uncertainty associated with future cash flows.

- Callable common and preference shares are more risky than their noncallable counterparts.
    ○ The option held by the issuer to buy back the shares at a pre-determined price limits the investors' potential total return.

- Cumulative preference shares are less risky than noncumulative preference shares as they accrue unpaid dividends.

LOS 48f: Explain the role of equity securities in the financing of a company's assets. Vol 5, pp 171–172

LOS 48g: Distinguish between the market value and book value of equity securities. Vol 5, p 176

Equity Securities and Company Value

A company may issue equity securities to raise capital, to acquire another company, provide stock option-based incentives to employees, acquire long-lived assets, invest in expansion projects, enter new markets, improve capital adequacy ratios, or to ensure that debt covenants are met.

The primary aim of management is to increase the book value and market value of the company. Book value (shareholders' equity on the company's balance sheet) is calculated as total assets less total liabilities. It reflects the historical operating and financing decisions made by the company. Management can directly influence book value (e.g., by retaining net income).

However, management can only indirectly influence a company's market value as it is primarily determined by investors' expectations about the amount, timing, and uncertainty of the company's future cash flows. A company may increase its book value by retaining net income, but it will only have a positive effect on the company's market value if investors expect the company to invest its retained earnings in profitable growth opportunities. If investors believe that the company has a significant number of cash flow generating investment opportunities coming through, the market value of the company's equity will exceed its book value.

A useful ratio to evaluate investor's expectations about a company is the price-to-book ratio (also known as the market-to-book) ratio.

- If a company has a price-to-book ratio that is greater than industry average, it suggests that investors believe that the company has more significant future growth opportunities than its industry peers.
- It may not be appropriate to compare price-to-book ratios of companies in different industries because the ratio also reflects investors' growth outlook for the industry itself. Companies in high growth industries (e.g., technology) will have a higher average price-to-book ratio than companies in mature industries (e.g., manufacturing heavy equipment).

An important measure used by investors to evaluate the effectiveness of management in increasing the company's book value is accounting return on equity.

LOS 48h: Compare a company's cost of equity, its (accounting) return on equity, and investors' required rates of return. **Vol 5, pp 172–177**

Accounting Return on Equity

The accounting return on equity (ROE) measures the rate of return earned by a company on its equity capital. It indicates how efficient a firm is in generating profits from every dollar of net assets. The ROE is computed as net income available to ordinary shareholders (after preference dividends have been paid) divided by the average total book value of equity.

$$\text{ROE}_t = \frac{\text{NI}_t}{\text{Average BVE}_t} = \frac{\text{NI}_t}{(\text{BVE}_t + \text{BVE}_{t-1})/2}$$

When using the ROE, analysts should bear in mind that net income and book value are directly affected by the management's choice of accounting methods (e.g., depreciation method and inventory cost flow assumption). These differences can make it difficult to compare the ROE across firms and to evaluate the ROE for the same firm over time (if accounting methods have changed).

In companies where book values are relatively stable, the beginning book value may be used in the denominator instead of the average book value. It is more appropriate to use average values for companies that experience more volatile year-end book values.

An increase in ROE might not always be a positive sign for the company.

- The increase in ROE may be the result of net income decreasing at a slower rate than shareholders' equity. A declining net income is a source of concern for investors.
- The increase in ROE may be the result of debt issuance proceeds being used to repurchase shares. This would increase the company's financial leverage (risk).

Therefore, investors should examine the sources of change in ROE. This can be done through DuPont decomposition, which has been discussed in Reading 28.

Book values and ROE do help analysts evaluate companies, but they cannot be used as the primary means to determine a company's intrinsic value. Intrinsic value refers to the present value of the company's expected future cash flows, and can only be estimated as it is impossible to accurately predict the amount and timing of a company's future cash flows. Astute investors aim to profit from differences between market prices and intrinsic values.

The Cost of Equity and Investors' Required Rates of Return

A company may raise capital by issuing debt or equity, both of which have associated costs.

- A company's cost of debt is easy to estimate, as it is reflected in the interest payments that the company is contractually obligated to make to debt holders.
- Estimating cost of equity is difficult because the company is not contractually obligated to make any payments to common shareholders.

Investors' minimum required rates of return refer to the return they require for providing funds to the company.

- For investors who provide debt capital to the company, their minimum required rate of return is the periodic interest rate they charge the company for using their funds. Further, all providers of debt capital receive the same interest rate. Therefore, the company's cost of debt and investors' minimum required rate of return on debt are the same.
- For investors who provide equity capital to the company, the future cash flows that they expect to receive are uncertain (in both timing and amount), so their minimum required rate of return must be estimated. Further, each investor may have different expectations regarding future cash flows. Therefore, the company's cost of equity may be different from investors' minimum required rate of return on equity.

You should think about the cost of equity as the minimum expected rate of return that a company must offer investors to purchase its shares in the primary market and to maintain its share price in the secondary market. If the required rate of return is not maintained, the price of the security in the secondary market will adjust to reflect the minimum rate of return required by investors.

- If investors require a higher return than the company's cost of equity, they will sell the company's shares and invest elsewhere, which would bring down the company's stock price. This decline in the stock price will lead to an increase in the company's cost of equity and bring it in line with the (higher) required rate of return.

Please note:

- The company's cost of equity can be estimated using the dividend discount model (DDM) and capital asset pricing model (CAPM), which are discussed in other readings.
- The costs of debt and equity are used to estimate a company's weighted average cost of capital (WACC), which represents the minimum required rate of return that the company must earn on its average investment. This measure is frequently used in capital budgeting process and is discussed in Reading 35.

READING 49: INTRODUCTION TO INDUSTRY AND COMPANY ANALYSIS

LESSON 1: INTRODUCTION TO INDUSTRY AND COMPANY ANALYSIS

LOS 49a: Explain the uses of industry analysis and the relation of industry analysis to company analysis. Vol 5, pp 188–189

Industry analysis has the following uses:

To understand a company's business and business environment. This is used in fundamental analysis, stock selection, and valuation as it provides insights into a company's growth opportunities, competitive dynamics, business risks, and credit risk.

To identify active equity investment opportunities. An analysis of industry fundamentals helps an analyst in forecasting the industry's growth and profitability. Analysts then decide the weights of different industries in their portfolios. Studies have shown that the industry factor is at least as important as the country factor in predicting stock returns. Industry analysis is also very important for industry and sector rotation strategies.

To attribute portfolio performance. Portfolio managers are evaluated on the relative performance of their sector and industry allocations. Industry classification plays an important role in performance attribution.

LOS 49b: Compare methods by which companies can be grouped, current industry classification systems, and classify a company, given a description of its activities and the classification system. Vol 5, pp 189–197

Industry classification divides companies into groups that have similar attributes. There are three major approaches to industry classification.

Products and/or Services Supplied

This classification scheme groups companies that make similar products and/or services. Companies are placed in industries based on their principal business activity (i.e., the source from which the company derives most of its revenues and/or earnings). Industries that are related to each other are grouped together to form a sector.

Business-Cycle Sensitivities

This approach groups companies based on their relative sensitivity to business cycles.

A cyclical company is one whose performance is positively correlated with the performance of the overall economy. Cyclical companies perform very well when the economy is booming, but perform relatively poorly during recessions. Cyclical companies typically have high operating leverage, which may be accompanied by high financial risk. Examples of cyclical industries include autos, industrialsm and technology.

A non-cyclical company is one whose performance is relatively independent of the business cycle. Demand for products made by non-cyclical companies remains relatively stable. Examples of non-cyclical industries include healthcare and utilities.

LOS 49c: Explain factors that affect the sensitivity of a company to the business cycle and the uses and limitations of industry and company descriptors such as "growth," "defensive," and "cyclical." **Vol 5, pp 189–197**

Analysts also often classify industries as defensive or growth industries. Defensive or stable industries are those whose profits are least affected by fluctuations in overall economic activity. Growth industries are industries whose specific demand dynamics override economic factors in determining their performance. These industries generate growth irrespective of overall economic conditions, though their growth rates may decline in recessions.

Limitations of these Classifications:

- The classification of companies as cyclical or non-cyclical is somewhat arbitrary. Economic downturns affect all companies, so cyclical and non-cyclical industries are better understood on a relative basis.
- At a given point in time different countries and regions may be undergoing different stages of the business cycle. Comparing companies in the same industry that are currently operating in very different economic conditions may help identify investment opportunities, but establishing industry benchmark values with the data would be misleading.

Statistical Similarities

Statistical approaches group companies on the basis of correlations of historical returns. For example, cluster analysis separates companies into groups such that companies within a group have a high correlation of returns, but correlations between groups are low. This approach has the following limitations:

- The composition of industry groups may vary significantly over time and across geographical regions.
- There is no guarantee that past correlations will continue to hold going forward.
- A relationship may arise by chance.
- A relationship that is actually economically significant may be excluded.

Industry Classification Systems

Industry classification systems help analysts in studying industry trends and valuing companies. They enable analysts to make global comparisons of companies in the same industry.

Commercial Industry Classification Systems

Major index providers around the world classify companies in their equity indices into industry groupings. These classification systems have multiple levels of classification. They include:

- *Global Industry Classification Standard (GICS)*, which classifies industries according to their principal business activity.
- *Russell Global Sectors (RGS)*, which classifies industries on the basis of goods and/or services produced.
- *Industry Classification Benchmark (ICB)*, which groups companies on the basis of primary revenue sources.

Table 1-1 lists the types of companies in each representative sector.

Table 1-1: Description of Representative Sectors

Broad Industry Classifications	Includes
Basic materials and processing	Companies that produce building materials
	Companies that produce chemicals
	Companies that produce paper and forest products
	Companies that produce containers and packaging
	Metal, mineral, and mining companies
Consumer discretionary (Demand for products and services offered by these companies exhibits a relatively high level of economic sensitivity).	Automotive, apparel, hotel and restaurant businesses
Consumer staples (Demand for products and services offered by these companies exhibits a relatively low level of economic sensitivity)	Manufacturers of food, beverage, tobacco, and personal care products
Energy	Energy exploration, refining, and production companies
	Companies that supply equipment to energy companies
Financial services	Banking companies
	Insurance companies
	Real estate companies
	Asset management companies
	Brokerage companies
Health care	Manufacturers of pharmaceutical and biotech products
	Manufacturers of medical devices
	Manufacturers of health care equipment
	Manufacturers of medical supplies
	Providers of health care services
Industrial/producer durables	Manufacturers of heavy machinery and equipment
	Aerospace and defense companies
	Transportation services
	Commercial services and supplies

(Table continued on next page...)

Table 1-1: (*continued*)

Broad Industry Classifications	Includes
Technology	Companies involved in the manufacture and sale of computers, software, semiconductors, and communications equipment Internet services Electronic entertainment Technology consulting
Telecommunications	Companies that provide fixed-line and wireless communication services
Utilities	Electric, gas, and water utilities Telecommunication companies are also sometimes included in this category

Governmental Industry Classification Systems

Various government agencies organize statistical data according to the type of industrial or economic activity to facilitate comparisons over time and across countries that use the same system. Governmental industry classification systems include:

- *International Standard Industrial Classification of All Economic Activities (ISIC)*, which classifies entities on the basis of their primary business activity. This system is currently being used by the UN and its specialized agencies, the International Monetary Fund, the World Bank, and other international bodies.
- *Statistical Classification of Economic Activities in the European Community (NACE)*, which uses a basis similar to that of ISIC.
- *Australian and New Zealand Standard Industrial Classification (ANZSIC)*
- *North American Industry Classification System (NAICS)*

Strengths and Weaknesses of Current Systems

Commercial classification systems generally have an advantage over government systems because of the following reasons:

- Most government systems do not disclose information about specific businesses or companies, so an analyst does not have access to the constituents of a particular category.
- Commercial classification systems are reviewed and updated more frequently than government classification systems.
- Government classification systems do not distinguish between small and large businesses, between for-profit and not-for-profit organizations, or between public and private companies. Commercial classification systems make distinctions between small and large companies automatically by virtue of the companies' association with a particular equity index. Further, commercial classification systems only include for-profit and publicly traded organizations.

LOS 49d: Explain the relation of "peer group," as used in equity valuation, to a company's industry classification. Vol 5, pp 198–202

The narrowest classification group assigned to a company by current classification systems generally cannot be assumed to be its peer group. A peer group is a group of companies engaged in similar business activities whose economics and valuation are influenced by closely related factors. Comparing a company to a well-defined peer group is very useful in evaluating company performance and in relative valuation.

Commercial classification systems do provide a starting point in the construction of a peer group, as they provide a list of companies operating in the same industry. Analysts can then filter this list to come up with a set of companies whose businesses are truly comparable with that of the company being studied.

Steps in constructing a preliminary list of peer companies:

- Examine commercial classification systems to identify companies operating in the same industry.
- Review the subject company's annual report to identify any mention of competitors.
- Review competitors' annual reports to identify other potential comparable companies.
- Review industry trade publications to identify comparable companies.
- Confirm that comparable companies have primary business activities that are similar to those of the subject company.

Companies with limited lines of business may easily be classified into a single peer group. However, companies with multiple divisions may be included in more than one category. Analysts should look to ensure that comparable companies have primary business activities and performance drivers similar to those of the subject company.

LOS 49e: Describe the elements that need to be covered in a thorough industry analysis. Vol 5, pp 202–203

Investment managers and analysts examine an industry's performance in relation to other industries to identify industries with superior returns. They also evaluate industries over time to determine how consistent and stable their returns are. LOS 59f, g, h, and i discuss the various elements of a thorough industry analysis in detail.

Figure 1-1 illustrates the macroeconomic, demographic, governmental, social, and technological factors that affect an industry at the macro level, and how an industry is affected by competitive forces, life cycle issues, business-cycle considerations, and its position on the experience curve.

Figure 1-1: A Framework for Industry Analysis[1]

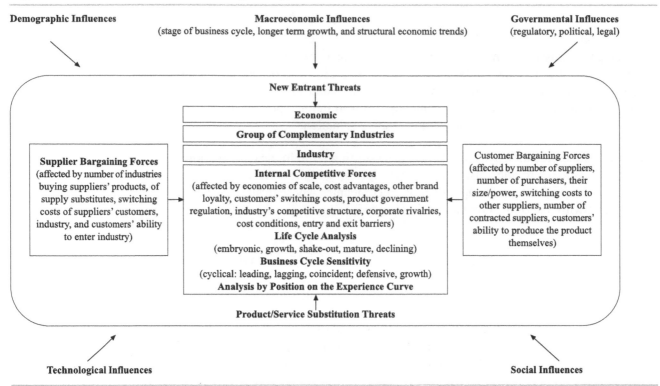

LOS 49f: Describe the principles of strategic analysis of an industry.
Vol 5, pp 204–205

When analyzing an industry, analysts need to understand the environment in which a company operates. Analysis of the industry with a view to examining the implications of the industrial environment on corporate strategy is known as strategic analysis.

Porter's Five Forces Framework

The starting point of strategic analysis is Michael Porter's "five forces" framework, which describes the following determinants of the intensity of competition in an industry.

- Threat of substitute products: If customers find products to substitute those produced by the company, demand for the company's products will decline.

- Bargaining power of customers: This refers to the leverage enjoyed by customers in their dealings with the company. If the company has a small number of customers, they can be tough negotiators when it comes to determining prices.

- Bargaining power of suppliers: This refers to the leverage enjoyed by suppliers in their dealings with the company. Suppliers of scarce or limited parts often have significant pricing power.

- Threat of new entrants: This depends on the strength of barriers to entry into an industry. Low barriers to entry imply a higher degree of competition within an industry.

1 - Exhibit 2, Volume 5, CFA Program Curriculum 2014

- **Intensity of rivalry**: This is dependent on the industry's competitive structure. Industries that exhibit the following characteristics experience relatively more intense rivalries:
  - There are many small competitors.
  - Fixed costs are relatively high.
  - The companies produce similar products.
  - There are high exit barriers.

Note that the last two forces merit further investigation because almost all companies have competitors and must be wary of new entrants to their industries. When studying these forces, analysts should bear in mind that:

- Higher/stronger barriers to entry reduce competition.
- Greater concentration (where a small number of firms control a large part of the market) implies lower competition, while market fragmentation (where a large number of firms each have a relatively small share in the market) implies higher competition.
- Unused capacity in an industry, especially over an extended period, results in intense price competition.
- Stable market shares for industry firms imply less competition.
- Greater price sensitivity in customer purchasing decisions results in greater competition.
- More mature industries tend to exhibit slower growth.

LOS 49g: Explain the effects of barriers to entry, industry concentration, industry capacity, and market share stability on pricing power and return on capital. Vol 5, pp 205–213

Barriers to Entry

Generally speaking:

- Low barriers to entry mean that new competitors can easily enter the industry, which makes the industry highly competitive. Companies in relatively competitive industries typically have little pricing power.
- High barriers to entry mean that existing companies are able to enjoy economic profits for a long period of time. These companies have greater pricing power.

However, bear in mind that the above mentioned characteristics of high and low barrier industries are not always observed. For instance, companies might have little pricing power in industries with high barriers to entry because of fierce competition among existing companies (e.g., autos and aircraft manufacturing). Further, it is important to note that:

- Barriers to entry should not be confused with barriers to success. Entering some industries may be easy, but that does not necessarily mean that new entrants will be successful.
- Barriers to entry can change over time.

Industry Concentration

Generally speaking:

- If an industry is relatively concentrated (i.e., a few large firms dominate the industry), there is relatively less price competition. This is because:
  - It is relatively easy for a few firms to coordinate their activities.

- ○ Larger firms have more to lose from destructive price behavior.
- ○ The fortunes of large firms are more tied to those of the industry as a whole, so they are more likely to be wary of the long-run impact of a price war on industry economics.

- If an industry is relatively fragmented (i.e., there is a large number of small firms in the industry), there is relatively high price competition. This is because of the following reasons:
  - ○ Firms are unable to monitor their competitors' actions, which makes coordination difficult.
  - ○ Each firm only has a small share of the market, so a small market share gain (through aggressive pricing) can make a large difference to each firm.
  - ○ Each firm is small relative to the overall market so it tends to think of itself individualistically, rather than as a member of a larger group.

Bear in mind that there are important exceptions to the rules defined above. For example, Boeing and Airbus dominate the aircraft manufacturing industry, but competition between the two remains fierce.

Industry Capacity

Generally speaking:

- Limited capacity gives companies more pricing power as demand exceeds supply.
- Excess capacity results in weak pricing power as excess supply chases demand.

In evaluating the future competitive environment in an industry, analysts should examine current capacity levels as well as how capacity levels are expected to change in the future. Further, it is important to keep in mind that:
- If new capacity is physical (e.g., manufacturing facilities) it will take longer for the new capacity to come online so tight supply conditions may linger for an extended period. Usually however, once physical capacity is added, supply may overshoot, outstrip demand, and result in weak pricing power for an extended period.
- If new capacity requires financial and human capital, companies can respond to tight supply conditions fairly quickly.

Market Share Stability

Generally speaking:

- Stable market shares indicate less competitive industries.
- Unstable market shares often indicate highly competitive industries with little pricing power.

Market shares are affected by the following factors:
- Barriers to entry: Other things remaining the same, high barriers to entry prevent new firms from entering the industry, resulting in stable market shares of existing companies.
- New products: Other things remaining the same, frequent introductions of new products in the market leads to significant variation in market shares of existing firms. Market shares change quickly if switching costs are low and there is a relatively high benefit from switching.

- Product differentiation: Other things remaining the same, firms that are able to effectively differentiate their products from those of competitors are able to increase their share in the market.

LOS 49h: Describe product and industry life cycle models, classify an industry as to life cycle phase (e.g., embryonic, growth, shakeout, maturity, and decline) based on a description of it, and describe the limitations of the life-cycle concept in forecasting industry performance. **Vol 5, pp 213–218**

Industry life-cycle analysis is an important part of strategic analysis of an industry. The sequential stages that an industry goes through are illustrated in Figure 1-2:

Figure 1-2: An Industry Life-Cycle Model[2]

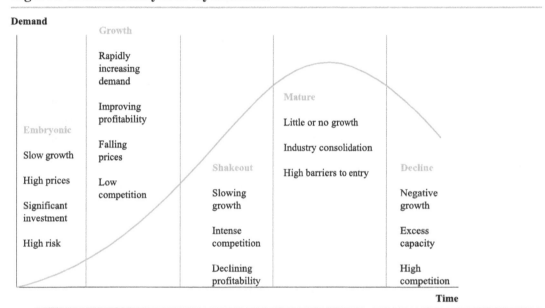

The different stages in an industry's life cycle are:

Embryonic: Industries in this stage are just beginning to develop. They are characterized by:
- Slow growth as customers are still unfamiliar with the product.
- High prices as volumes are too low to achieve significant economies of scale.
- Significant initial investment.
- High risk of failure.

Companies focus on raising product awareness and developing distribution channels during this stage.

Growth: Once the new product starts gaining acceptance in the market, the industry experiences rapid growth. The growth stage is characterized by:
- New customers entering the market, which increases demand.
- Improved profitability as sales grow rapidly.
- Lower prices as economies of scale are achieved.

---

2 - Exhibit 6, Volume 5, CFA Program Curriculum 2014

- Relatively low competition among companies in the industry as the overall market size is growing rapidly. Firms do not need to wrestle market share away from competitors to grow.
- High threat of new competitors entering the market due to low barriers to entry.

During this stage, companies focus on building customer loyalty and reinvest heavily in the business.

Shakeout: The period of rapid growth is followed by a period of slower growth. The shakeout stage is characterized by:
- Slower demand growth as fewer new customers are left to enter the industry.
- Intense competition as growth becomes dependent on market share growth.
- Excess industry capacity, while leads to price reductions and declining profitability.

During this stage, companies focus on reducing their costs and building brand loyalty. Some firms may fail or merge with others.

Mature: Eventually demand stops growing and the industry matures. Characteristics of this stage are:
- Little or no growth in demand as the market is completely saturated.
- Companies move toward consolidation. They recognize that they are interdependent so they stay away from price wars. However, price wars may occur during downturns.
- High barriers to entry in the form of brand loyalty and relatively efficient cost structures.

During this stage, companies are likely to be pursuing replacement demand rather than new buyers and should focus on extending successful product lines rather than introducing revolutionary new products. Companies have limited opportunities to reinvest and often have strong cash flows. As a result, they are more likely to pay dividends.

Decline: Technological substitution, social changes, or global competition may eventually cause an industry to decline. The decline stage is characterized by:
- Negative growth.
- Excess capacity due to diminishing demand.
- Price competition due to excess capacity.
- Weaker firms leaving the industry.

Limitations of Industry Life-Cycle Analysis

- The following factors may change the shape of the industry life cycle, cause some stages to be longer or shorter than expected, or even result in certain stages being skipped altogether.
  - Technological changes: An industry may go from growth to decline if a revolutionary product or distribution channel is introduced in the market.
  - Regulatory changes: Deregulation may suddenly increase competition in an industry.
  - Social changes: For example, the casual dining industry has prospered over the last few decades as a result of an increase in the number of dual-income families.
  - Demographics: For example, an aging population is likely to benefit the health care industry.

- Industry life-cycle analysis is most useful in analyzing industries during periods of relative stability. It is not as useful in analyzing industries experiencing rapid change.

- Not all companies in an industry display similar performance. For example, Nokia has consistently been able to earn above average returns in a fiercely competitive industry.

Price Competition

Generally speaking:

- Industries in which price is the most significant consideration in customers' purchase decisions tend to be highly competitive. A slight increase in price may cause customers to switch to substitute products if they are widely available.

- Price is not as important if companies in an industry are able to effectively differentiate their products in terms of quality and performance. Customers may not focus on price as much if product reliability is more important to them.

LOS 49i: Compare characteristics of representative industries from the various economic sectors. Vol 5, pp 219–221

Table 1-2: Elements of a Strategic Analysis for Three Industries[3]

	Branded Pharmaceuticals	Oil Services	Confections/Candy
Major companies	Pfizer, Novartis, Merck, GlaxoSmithKline	Schlumberger, Baker Hughes, Halliburton	Cadbury, Hershey, Mars/Wrigley, Nestle
Barriers to entry/success	*Very high:* substantial financial and intellectual capital required to compete effectively. A potential new entrant would need to create a sizable R&D operation, a global distribution network, and large scale manufacturing capacity.	*Medium:* Technological expertise is required, but high level of innovation allows niche companies to enter the industry and compete in specific areas.	*Very High:* Low finance or technological hurdles, but new players would lack the established brands that drive consumer purchase decisions.
Impact of industry capacity	*NA:* Pharmaceutical pricing is primarily determined by patent protection and regulatory issues, including government approval of drugs and of manufacturing facilities. Manufacturing capacity is of little importance.	*Medium/High:* Demand can fluctuate quickly depending on commodity prices, and industry players often find themselves with too few (or too many) employees on the payroll.	*NA:* Pricing is driven primarily by brand strength. Manufacturing capacity has little effect.

(continued)

---

3 - Exhibit 7, Volume 5, CFA Program Curriculum 2014

Table 1-2: Elements of a Strategic Analysis for Three Industries (*continued*)

	Branded Pharmaceuticals	Oil Services	Confections/Candy
Level of concentration	*Concentrated:* A small number of companies control the bulk of the global markets for the branded drugs. The recent mergers have increased level of concentration.	*Fragmented:* Although only a small number of companies provide a full range of services, many smaller players compete effectively in specific areas. Service arms of national oil companies may control significant market share in their own countries, and some product lines are concentrated in the mature U.S. market.	*Very Concentrated:* Top four companies have a large proportion of global market share. Recent mergers have increased level of concentration.
Industry stability	*Stable:* The branded pharmaceutical market is dominated by major companies and consolidation via mega-mergers. Market shares shift quickly, however, as new drugs are approved and gain acceptance or lose patent protection.	*Unstable:* Market shares may shift frequently depending on technology offerings and demand levels.	*Very Stable:* Market shares change glacially.
Life cycle	*Mature:* Overall demand does not change greatly from year to year.	*Mature:* Demand does not fluctuate with energy prices, but normalized revenue growth is only mid-single digits.	*Very Mature:* Growth is driven by population trends and pricing.
Price competition	*Low/Medium:* In the United States, price is a minimal factor because of consumer and provider driven, deregulated health care system. Price is a larger part of the decision process in single payer systems, where efficacy hurdles are higher.	*High:* Price is a major factor in purchaser decisions. Some companies have modest pricing power because of a wide range of services or best-in-class technology, but primary consumers (major oil companies) can usually substitute with in-house services if prices are too high. Also innovation tends to diffuse quickly throughout the industry.	*Low:* A lack of private level competition keeps pricing stable among established players, and brand/familiarity plays a much larger role in consumer purchase decisions than price.

Table 1-2: Elements of a Strategic Analysis for Three Industries (*continued*)

	Branded Pharmaceuticals	Oil Services	Confections/Candy
Demographic influences	*Positive:* Populations of developed markets are aging, which slightly increases demand.	*NA*	*NA*
Government and regulatory influences	*Very High:* All drugs must be approved for sale by national safety regulators. Patent regimes may differ among countries. Also, health care is heavily regulated in most countries.	*Medium:* Regulatory framework can affect energy demand at the margin. Also, government plays an important role in allocating exploration opportunities to E&P companies, which can indirectly affect the amount of work flowing down to service companies.	*Low:* Industry is not regulated, but childhood obesity concerns in developed markets are a low-level potential threat. Also, high growth emerging markets may block entry of established players into their markets, possibly limiting growth.
Social influences	*NA*	*NA*	*NA*
Technological influences	*Medium/High:* Biologic (large molecule) drugs are pushing new therapeutic boundaries, and many large pharmaceutical companies have a relatively small presence in biotech.	*Medium/High:* Industry is reasonably innovative, and players must reinvest in R&D to remain competitive. Temporary competitive advantages are possible via commercialization of new processes or exploitation of new accumulated expertise.	*Very Low:* Innovation does not play a major role in the industry.
Growth vs. Defensive vs. Cyclical	*Defensive:* Demand for most health care services does not fluctuate with the economic cycle, but demand is not strong enough to be considered "growth."	*Cyclical:* Demand is highly variable and depends on oil prices, exploration budget, and the economic cycle.	*Defensive:* Demand for candy and gum is extremely stable.

*Note: "NA" in this table stands for "not applicable."

Macroeconomic Influences

An industry's prospects are affected by overall economic activity. GDP, interest rates, availability of credit, and inflation all have an impact on the company's revenues, costs, and profits.

Technological Influences

Advancements in technology lead to new products being developed, which may replace older products. Further, these developments can sometimes change the way other industries that use these products conduct their operations.

Demographic Influences

Demography (population size, age distribution, and gender distribution) has important influences on economic growth and on the types of goods and services consumed. For example, an aging population has a negative effect on the economy as the size of the workforce declines. However, the healthcare industry benefits in the form of a larger customer base.

Governmental Influences

Government regulations have an impact on all sectors of the economy. Governments might exert their influence on an industry directly through taxes or subsidies, or indirectly by establishing regulatory bodies to govern the actions of an industry.

Social Influences

These influences refer to changes in how people work, spend their money, enjoy their leisure time, and conduct other aspects of their lives. Tobacco consumption has been on the decline as a result of increased social awareness regarding the harmful effects of smoking, and the perception that smoking in public is socially incorrect.

Company analysis includes an analysis of the company's financial position, products and/ or services, and competitive strategy. Porter identified two main competitive strategies:

Cost Leadership

Companies pursuing this strategy strive to cut down their costs to become the lowest cost producers in an industry so that they can gain market share by charging lower prices. Pricing may be defensive (to protect market positions when competition is low) or aggressive (to increase market share when competitive is intense).

Product/Service Differentiation

Companies pursuing this strategy strive to differentiate their products from those of competitors in terms of quality, type, or means of distribution. These companies are then able to charge a premium price for their products. This strategy is successful only if the price premium is greater than the cost of differentiation and the source of differentiation appeals to customers and is sustainable over time.

Elements that Should be Considered in a Company Analysis:

A thorough company analysis should:

- Provide an overview of the company
- Explain relevant industry characteristics
- Analyze the demand for the company's products and services
- Analyze the supply of products and services including an analysis of costs
- Explain the company's pricing environment
- Present and interpret relevant financial ratios, including comparisons over time and comparisons with competitors. See Exhibit 1-1.

Exhibit 1-1: A Checklist for Company Analysis[4]

Corporate Profile

- Identity of company's major products and services, current position in industry, and history
- Composition of sales
- Product life-cycle stages/experience curve effects
- Research and development activities
- Past and planned capital expenditures
- Board structure, composition, electoral system, anti-takeover provisions, and other corporate governance issues
- Management strengths, weaknesses, compensation, turnover, and corporate culture
- Benefits, retirement plans, and their influence on shareholder value
- Labor relations
- Insider ownership levels and changes
- Legal actions and the company's state of preparedness
- Other special strengths or weaknesses

(continued)

---

4 - Exhibit 8, Volume 5, CFA Program Curriculum 2014

Exhibit 1-1: (*continued*)

Industry Characteristics

- Stage in its life-cycle
- Business-cycle sensitivity or economic characteristics
- Typical product life-cycles in the industry (short and marked by technological obsolescence or long, such as pharmaceuticals protected by patents)
- Brand loyalty, customer switching costs, and intensity of competition
- Entry and exit barriers
- Industry supplier considerations (concentration of sources, ability to switch suppliers, or enter supplier's business)
- Number of companies in the business and whether it is, as determined by market shares, fragmented or concentrated
- Opportunity to differentiate product/service and related product/service, price, cost, and quality advantages/disadvantages
- Technologies used
- Government regulations
- State and history of labor relations
- Other industry problems/opportunities

Analysis of Demand for Product/Services

- Sources of demand
- Product differentiation
- Past records, sensitivities, and correlations with social, demographic, economic, and other variables
- Outlook—short, medium, and long term, including new product and business opportunities

Analysis of Supply of Products/Services

- Sources (concentration, competition, and substitutes)
- Industry capacity outlook—short, medium, and long term
- Company's capacity and cost structure
- Import/export considerations
- Proprietary products or trademarks

Analysis of Pricing

- Past relationships among demand, supply, and prices
- Significance of raw materials and labor costs and the outlook for their cost and availability
- Outlook for selling prices, demand, and profitability based on current and anticipated future trends

Financial Ratios and Measures
(In multi-year spreadsheets with historical and forecast data)

- Activity Ratios, measuring how efficiently a company performs such functions such as the collection of receivables and inventory management:
    - Days of sales outstanding (DSO)
    - Days of inventory on hand (DOH)
    - Days of payables outstanding (DPO)

- Liquidity Ratios, measuring a company's ability to meet its short-term obligations:

    - Current ratio
    - Quick ratio
    - Cash ratio
    - Cash conversion cycle (DOH + DSO – DPO)

- Solvency Ratios, measuring a company's ability to meet its obligations: (in the following, "net debt" is the amount of interest bearing liabilities after subtracting cash and cash equivalents)

    - Net debt to EBITDA (earnings before interest, taxes, depreciation, and amortization)
    - Net debt to capital
    - Debt to assets
    - Debt to capital (at book and market values)
    - Financial leverage ratios (Average total assets/Average total equity)
    - Cash flow to debt
    - Interest coverage ratio
    - Off-balance sheet liabilities and contingent liabilities
    - Non arm's-length financial dealings

- Profitability Ratios, measuring a company's ability to generate profitable sales from its resources (assets)

    - Gross profit margin
    - Operating profit margin
    - Pretax profit margin
    - Net profit margin
    - Return on investment capital or ROIC (Net operating profits after tax/ Average invested capital)
    - Return on assets or ROA (Net income/Average total assets)
    - Return on equity or ROE (Net income/Average total equity)

(continued)

Exhibit 1-1: (*continued*)

- Financial Statistics and Related Considerations, quantities, and facts about a company finances that an analyst should understand

  - Growth rate of net sales
  - Growth rate of profit
  - EBITDA
  - Net income
  - Operating cash flow
  - EPS
  - Operating cash flow per share
  - Operating cash flow in relation to maintenance and total capital expenditures
  - Expected rate of return on retained cash flow
  - Debt maturities and ability of company to refinance and/or repay debt
  - Dividend payout ratio (Common dividends/Net income available to common shareholders)
  - Off-balance sheet liabilities and contingent liabilities
  - Non-arm's length financial dealings

Spreadsheet Modeling

Spreadsheet modeling is an important tool available to analysts to evaluate the historical performance of companies and to forecast future performance. It is widely used to quantify the effects of changes in certain swing factors on the company's performance. However, such models can be quite complex and analysts should bear in mind that any conclusions drawn from the model are dependent on the assumptions that were made in developing it.

READING 50: EQUITY VALUATION: CONCEPTS AND BASIC TOOLS

LESSON 1: INTRODUCTION

LOS 50a: Evaluate whether a security, given its current market price and a value estimate, is overvalued, fairly valued, or undervalued by the market.
Vol 5, pp 244–246

The aim of equity analysis is to identify mispriced securities. Securities are mispriced or incorrectly priced by the market when their market prices are different from their intrinsic values. Intrinsic or fundamental value refers to a security's true value and is estimated by analysts using a variety of models/techniques.

- If the estimate for a security's intrinsic value is lower than the market price, the security is overvalued by market.
- If the estimate for a security's intrinsic value is greater than the market price, the security is undervalued by the market.
- If the estimate for a security's intrinsic value equals the market price, the security is fairly valued.

In practice however, the analysis is not so straightforward. There are several uncertainties regarding the intrinsic value estimate with respect to the appropriateness of the valuation method used and its underlying assumptions. The final conclusion also depends on the analyst's level of confidence in her estimate of intrinsic value. If she finds that her estimates of intrinsic value tend to fall short of market consensus and current market prices, she might want to revisit her valuation models and assumptions before acting on a conclusion of overvaluation.

LOS 50b: Describe major categories of equity valuation models.
Vol 5, pp 246–248

There are three major categories of equity valuation models:

- Present value models (also known as discounted cash flow models)
- Multiplier models
- Asset-based valuation models

Each of these categories is discussed in detail in the remaining LOS of this reading.

LOS 50c: Explain the rationale for using present value of cash flow models to value equity and describe the dividend discount and free-cash-flow-to-equity models. Vol 5, pp 248–251

LOS 50e: Calculate and interpret the intrinsic value of an equity security based on the Gordon (constant) growth dividend discount model or a two-stage dividend discount model, as appropriate. Vol 5, pp 254–258

LOS 50f: Identify companies for which the constant growth or a multistage dividend discount model is appropriate. Vol 5, pp 258–262

LOS 50k: Explain advantages and disadvantages of each category of valuation model. Vol 5, pp 254–262

Investors save money (defer consumption) in return for future benefits. Similarly, they make investments because they expect a return over the investment horizon. The value of an investment, therefore must equal the present value of its expected future cash flows. The simplest present value model for equity valuation is the dividend discount model (DDM):

The dividend discount model (DDM) values a share of common stock as the present value of its expected future cash flows (dividends).

$$Value = \frac{D_1}{(1+k_e)^1} + \frac{D_2}{(1+k_e)^2} + \ldots + \frac{D_\infty}{(1+k_e)^\infty}$$

$$Value = \sum_{t=1}^{n} \frac{D_t}{(1+k_e)^t}$$

Important:

- When an investor sells a share of common stock, the value that the purchaser will pay equals the present value of the future stream of cash flows (i.e., the remaining dividend stream). Therefore, the value of the stock at any point in time is still determined by its expected future dividends. When this value is discounted to the present, we are back at the original dividend discount model.

- If a company pays no dividends currently, it does not mean that its stock will be worthless. There is an expectation that after a certain period of time the firm will start making dividend payments. Currently, the company is reinvesting all its earnings in its business with the expectation that its earnings and dividends will be larger and will grow faster in the future. If the company does not make positive earnings going forward, there will still be an expectation of a liquidating dividend. The amount of this dividend will be discounted at the required rate of return to compute the stock's current price.

- The required rate of return on equity (k_e) is usually estimated using the capital asset pricing model (CAPM). Another approach for calculating the required return on equity simply adds a risk premium to the before-tax cost of debt of the company.

Examples of DDM in Valuing Common Stock

One-year holding period: If our holding period is just one year, the value that we will place on the stock today is the present value of the dividends that we will receive over the year plus the present value of the price that we expect to sell the stock for at the end of the holding period. See Example 2-1.

$$\text{Value} = \frac{\text{dividend to be received}}{(1+k_e)^1} + \frac{\text{year-end price}}{(1+k_e)^1}$$

Example 2-1: One Period DDM

An analyst gathered the following information about a company:
- Current dividend per share (D_0) of common stock = $4.00.
- Expected growth rate for the year (g) = 20%.
- Risk-free rate of return = 6%.
- Expected return on the market portfolio = 11%.
- Beta of the company's common stock = 1.2.

Given that the stock will sell for $15.40 at the end of the year and that it will make only one dividend payment over the holding period (at the end of the year), calculate the value of the company's common stock.

Solution

The next dividend is calculated by multiplying the current dividend by 1 plus the projected growth rate.

$$D_1 = D_0(1+g)$$
$$= 4(1+0.2)$$
$$= \$4.80$$

> The assumption here is that the stock only pays a dividend at the end of the year.

The required return on equity is estimated using the CAPM:

$$k_e = R_F + \beta(R_M - R_F)$$
$$= 0.06 + 1.2(0.11 - 0.06)$$
$$= 12.0\%$$

Finally, we compute the present value of the expected future dividend and the expected future selling price:

$$V = \frac{\$4.80}{(1+0.12)} + \frac{\$15.40}{(1+0.12)}$$
$$= \$4.29 + \$13.75$$
$$= \$18.04$$

The stock is worth $18.04 based on the analyst's expectations of dividend growth, beta, market risk premium, and future selling price. This may or may not be the price that the stock is currently trading at. If the price calculated by the analyst (intrinsic value) of the stock based on her assumptions is *greater* than the current market price, the analyst should *buy* the stock because she expects its return to be *higher* than the required return for the stock given its beta (systematic risk).

We apply the same discounting principles for valuing common stock over multiple holding periods. In order to estimate the intrinsic value of the stock, we first estimate the dividends that will be received every year that the stock is held and the price that the stock will sell for at the end of the holding period. Then we simply discount these expected cash flows at the cost of equity (required return). See Example 2-2.

$$V = \frac{D_1}{(1+k_e)^1} + \frac{D_2}{(1+k_e)^2} + \ldots + \frac{D_n + P_n}{(1+k_e)^n}$$

where:
P_n = Price at the end of n years.

If we assume that dividends are growing at a constant rate every year, then:

$$D_1 = D_0(1+g); \quad D_2 = D_0(1+g)^2 \text{ and } D_n = D_0(1+g)^n$$

Example 2-2: DDM for Multiple Holding Periods

Assume that a stock currently pays a dividend of $1.00, has an expected growth rate of 6%, and a required rate of return of 14.1%. Calculate the value of stock today if we expect to sell it for $15.30 in 2 years.

Solution

$$PV(D_1) = \frac{\$1.06}{1.141} = \$0.93$$

$$PV(D_2) = \frac{\$1.06(1.06)}{(1.141)^2} = \$0.86$$

PV of expected dividends over the holding period = $0.93 + $0.86 = $1.79

PV of the expected future selling price at the end of holding period = $\dfrac{\$15.30}{(1.141)^2}$ = $11.75

Value of stock = $1.79 + $11.75 = $13.54

The value of the stock based on the investor's expectations equals $13.54.

Infinite Period DDM (Gordon Growth Model)

The infinite period dividend discount model assumes that a company will continue to pay dividends for an infinite number of periods. It also assumes that the dividend stream will grow at a constant rate (g_c) over the infinite period. In this case, the intrinsic value of the stock is calculated as:

$$PV_0 = \frac{D_0(1+g_c)^1}{(1+k_e)^1} + \frac{D_0(1+g_c)^2}{(1+k_e)^2} + \frac{D_0(1+g_c)^3}{(1+k_e)^3} + \ldots + \frac{D_0(1+g_c)^\infty}{(1+k_e)^\infty}$$

This equation simplifies to:

$$PV = \frac{D_0(1+g_c)^1}{(k_e - g_c)^1} = \frac{D_1}{k_e - g_c}$$

The long-term (constant) growth rate is usually calculated as:

$$g_c = RR \times ROE$$

RR is the firm's earnings retention rate, which equals 1 minus the dividend payout ratio.

The Gordon growth model is highly appropriate for valuing dividend-paying stocks that are relatively immune to the business cycle and are relatively mature (e.g., utilities). It is also useful for valuing companies that have historically been raising their dividend at a stable rate.

Applying the DDM is relatively difficult if the company is not currently paying out a dividend. A company may not pay out a dividend because:
- It has a lot of lucrative investment opportunities available and it wants to retain profits to reinvest them in the business.
- It does not have sufficient excess cash flow to pay out a dividend.

Even though the Gordon growth model can be used for valuing such companies, the forecasts used are generally quite uncertain. Therefore, analysts use one of the other valuation models to value such companies and may use the DDM model as a supplement. The DDM can be extended to numerous stages. See Example 2-3. For example:
- A three-stage DDM is used to value fairly young companies that are just entering the growth phase. Their development falls into three stages—growth (with very high growth rates), transition (with decent growth rates), and maturity (with a lower growth into perpetuity).
- A two-stage DDM can be used to value a company currently undergoing moderate growth, but whose growth rate is expected to improve (rise) to its long-term growth rate.

Example 2-3: Applying the Gordon Growth Model

An analyst obtained the following information regarding Global Transporters Inc.:

Current share price = $28
Recent dividend per share = $1.95
Earnings per share = $4.25
Return on equity = 25%
Required rate of return = 20%

1. Use the Gordon growth model to estimate Global's intrinsic value.
2. How much does the dividend growth assumption add to the intrinsic value estimate?
3. Based on the intrinsic value estimate, is the company's share undervalued, fairly valued, or overvalued?
4. Calculate the intrinsic value if the growth rate estimate is lowered to 12%.
5. Calculate the intrinsic value if the growth rate estimate is lowered to 12% and the required rate of return estimate is increased to 22%.

Solution

1. Dividend payout ratio = 1.95 / 4.25 = 45.88%

   Therefore, earnings retention rate = 100% − 45.88% = 54.12%

   Dividend growth rate = Retention rate × ROE = 0.5412 × 0.25 = 13.53%

   $$\text{Intrinsic value} = \frac{1.95 \times (1 + 0.1353)}{(0.2 - 0.1353)} = \$34.21$$

2. Effect of the dividend growth assumption = 34.21 − (1.95 / 0.2) = $24.46

3. Global's current market price ($28) is lower than its intrinsic value ($34.21). Therefore, its stock is undervalued.

4. $$\text{Intrinsic value} = \frac{1.95 \times (1 + 0.12)}{(0.2 - 0.12)} = \$27.30$$

5. $$\text{Intrinsic value} = \frac{1.95 \times (1 + 0.12)}{(0.22 - 0.12)} = \$21.84$$

> If the growth rate were zero, the stock would be valued as a perpetuity and its intrinsic value would equal:
>
> $1.95/0.2 = $9.75

The relation between k_e and g_c is critical:
- As the difference between k_e and g_c *increases,* the intrinsic value of the stock *falls.*
- As the difference *narrows,* the intrinsic value of the stock *rises.*
- Small changes in either k_e or g_c can cause *large* changes in the value of the stock.

For the infinite-period DDM model to work, the following assumptions must hold:

- Dividends grow at a rate, g_c, which is not expected to change.
- k_e must be greater than g_c; otherwise, the model breaks down because of the denominator being negative.

Notice that the DDM formula on the previous page can be rearranged to make the required return, k_e, the subject:

$$k_e = \frac{D_1}{PV_0} + g_c$$

This expression for the cost of equity tells us that the return on an equity investment has two components:

- The dividend yield (D_1/P_0).
- Growth over time (g_c).

Valuation of Common Stock with Temporary Supernormal Growth

Growth companies are firms that are able to earn returns on investment that are consistently above their required rates of return. In order to take advantage of such opportunities, these companies tend to retain a very high proportion of their earnings and reinvest them in the business. These high retention rates translate into high growth rates (recall that a firm's sustainable growth rate equals its retention rate times its ROE). The assumptions of the infinite-period DDM do not hold for these growth companies because:

- They do not have constant dividend growth rates. The growth rate of dividends can be impressively high, but only for a temporary period. Eventually, competition catches up with these firms and their growth rate slows down.
- During periods when they experience extremely high growth rates, their growth rate can exceed the cost of equity (k_e).

The correct valuation model to value such "supernormal growth" companies is the multistage dividend discount model that combines the multi-period and infinite-period dividend discount models.

$$Value = \frac{D_1}{(1+k_e)^1} + \frac{D_2}{(1+k_e)^2} + ... + \frac{D_n}{(1+k_e)^n} + \frac{P_n}{(1+k_e)^n}$$

where:

$$P_n = \frac{D_{n+1}}{k_e - g_c}$$

D_n = Last dividend of the supernormal growth period
D_{n+1} = First dividend of the constant growth period

The following steps must be followed to value stocks of companies that experience temporary supernormal growth:

- Estimate the amount and duration of dividends during the supernormal growth phase.
- Forecast the normal, constant growth rate in dividends (g_c) that will occur once the supernormal growth period ends.
- Project the first dividend after the commencement of normal growth.
- Calculate the price of the stock at the end of the supernormal growth period using the infinite-period DDM. The first dividend after commencement of normal growth will be the numerator.
- Determine the cost of equity, k_e.
- Calculate the present value of supernormal growth-period dividends and the terminal stock price (the stock price at the end of supernormal growth).

If a company has two or three stages of supernormal growth, we must calculate the dividend for each year during supernormal growth separately. Once the growth rate stabilizes below the required rate of return, we can compute the terminal value of the firm by using the constant growth DDM. This method should become clear after going through Example 2-4.

Example 2-4: Valuation with Temporary Supernormal Growth

A company is expected to experience dividend growth rate of 20% for the next 3 years, 15% for the subsequent 2 years, and a constant growth rate of 6% thereafter. The last dividend paid out by the company was $1.50 per share and its cost of equity is 12%. Calculate the value of the company's stock.

Solution

First we calculate the dividends for each year during the supernormal growth phase:

$$D_1 = D_0\,(1+g_1)^1 = (1.50)(1.20)^1 = \$1.80$$
$$D_2 = D_0\,(1+g_1)^2 = (1.50)(1.20)^2 = \$2.16$$
$$D_3 = D_0\,(1+g_1)^3 = (1.50)(1.20)^3 = \$2.59$$
$$D_4 = D_3\,(1+g_2)^1 = (2.59)(1.15)^1 = \$2.98$$
$$D_5 = D_3\,(1+g_2)^2 = (2.59)(1.15)^2 = \$3.43$$

After Year 5, growth falls to a constant rate of 6%. The dividend for the 6TH year will be:

$$D_6 = 3.43(1.06) = \$3.63$$

We use D_6 to calculate the value of the stock as of the beginning of the constant, infinite-growth period (end of Year 5),

$$P_5 = \frac{D_6}{k_e - g_c} = \frac{\$3.63}{(0.12 - 0.06)} = \$60.56$$

This value (P_5) represents the present value of remaining (constant growth) dividends on the stock as of the end of Year 5. It is also called the terminal value of the stock.

Finally, we add the present values of the high growth-period dividends and the terminal value of the stock at end of Year 5 to determine the intrinsic value of the stock:

$$\text{Value} = \frac{1.80}{(1+0.12)} + \frac{2.16}{(1+0.12)^2} + \frac{2.59}{(1+0.12)^3} + \frac{2.98}{(1+0.12)^4} + \frac{3.43}{(1+0.12)^5} + \frac{60.56}{(1+0.12)^5}$$

$$\text{Value} = 1.61 + 1.72 + 1.84 + 1.89 + 1.95 + 34.36 = \$43.37$$

Another variant of the supernormal growth scenario is when a company does not pay out dividends in the high growth period because it chooses to reinvest all of its earnings in the business. The company then pays out a dividend at the beginning of the constant growth period, and maintains a stable dividend payout ratio thereafter. See Example 2-5.

Example 2-5: Delayed Dividend Payment

A firm is expected to have 3 years of extraordinary growth during which no dividends will be paid. Beginning in Year 4, earnings will stabilize and grow at sustainable 5% rate indefinitely, and the firm will pay out 45% of its earnings in dividends. Given that earnings in Year 4 (E_4) are expected to be $3.45 and the required return on equity is 10%, calculate value of this stock today.

Solution

$$D_4 = \text{(dividend pay out ratio)}(E_4) = (0.45)(3.45) = \$1.55$$

$$P_3 = \frac{D_4}{k_e - g_c} = \frac{\$1.55}{(0.1 - 0.05)} = \$31.05$$

The value of this stock today equals the present value of the terminal value (P_3), which equals $23.32

The Free-Cash-Flow-to-Equity (FCFE) Model

Many analysts assert that a company's dividend-paying capacity should be reflected in its cash flow estimates instead of estimated future dividends. FCFE is a measure of dividend paying capacity and can also be used to value companies that currently do not make any dividend payments. FCFE can be calculated as:

$$FCFE = CFO - FC\ Inv + Net\ borrowing$$

Analysts may calculate the intrinsic value of the company's stock by discounting their projections of future FCFE at the required rate of return on equity.

$$V_0 = \sum_{t=1}^{\infty} \frac{FCFE_t}{(1 + k_e)^t}$$

LOS 50d: Calculate the intrinsic value of a noncallable, nonconvertible preferred stock. Vol 5, pp 251–254

When preferred stock is noncallable, nonconvertible, has no maturity date, and pays dividends at a fixed rate, the value of the preferred stock can be calculated using the perpetuity formula:

$$V_0 = \frac{D_0}{r}$$

For a noncallable, nonconvertible preferred stock with maturity at time, n, the value of the stock can be calculated using the following formula:

$$V_0 = \sum_{t=1}^{n} \frac{D_t}{(1+r)^t} + \frac{F}{(1+r)^n}$$

where:
V_0 = value of preferred stock today (t = 0)
D_t = expected dividend in year t, assumed to be paid at the end of the year
r = required rate of return on the stock
F = par value of preferred stock

Preferred shares may also be callable or putable:

- A callable preferred stock grants the issuer the right to call the stock at some point prior to maturity at a price determined at inception. Such call options tend to reduce the value of the issue for investors, as they favor the issuer.
- A putable preferred stock grants the holder the right to sell the stock back to the issuer at some point prior to maturity at a price determined at inception. Put options increase the value of the issue for investors as they favor the holder. See Example 2-6.

Example 2-6: Preferred Share Valuation: Two Cases

Aramis International issued perpetual preferred shares with a par value of $20 and pays an annual dividend of $3.65. Given a required rate of return of 8%, answer the following questions:

1. Calculate the intrinsic value of the shares if they are noncallable and nonconvertible.
2. Calculate the intrinsic value of the shares if they are retracted at par value after 3 years.

Solution

1. Intrinsic value = Dividend / Required rate of return = 3.65 / 0.08 = $45.63

2. Retractable term preferred shares specify a retraction date, at which the preferred shareholders have the option to sell back the shares to the issuer at a predetermined price. The intrinsic value in such cases is calculated as follows:

   Intrinsic value = [(3.65 / 1.08) + (3.65 / 1.08^2) + (3.65 / 1.08^3) + (20 / 1.08^3)]
   = $25.28

LOS 50g: Explain the rationale for using price multiples to value equity and distinguish between multiples based on comparables versus multiples based on fundamentals. Vol 5, pp 263–271

Price multiples are ratios that compare the price of a stock to some sort of value. Price multiples allow an analyst to evaluate the relative worth of a company's stock. Popular multiples used in relative valuation include price-to-earnings, price-to-sales, price-to-book, and price-to-cash-flow.

A common criticism of price multiples is that they do not consider the future in that their values are calculated from trailing or current values of the divisor. For example a company's price to earnings ratio may be calculated by dividing the current market price by the company's earnings per share (EPS) over the most recent four quarters. To counter this criticism, analysts make forecasts of fundamental values (e.g., earnings) into the future and use forward-looking or leading multiples. For example, the leading P/E ratio may be calculated as the current stock price divided by expected EPS over the next four quarters.

Multiples Based on Fundamentals

A price multiple may be related to fundamentals through a dividend discount model such as the Gordon growth model. The expressions developed in such an exercise are interpreted as the justified (or based on fundamental) values for a multiple. Let's use the Gordon growth model to derive an expression for the justified P/E multiple for a stock.

Gordon growth DDM:

$$P_0 = \frac{D_1}{r-g}$$

Divide both sides of the equation by next year's earnings forecast, E_1.

$$\frac{P_0}{E_1} = \frac{D_1 / E_1}{r-g}$$

D_1/E_1 is known as the dividend payout ratio. It equals the proportion of its earnings that a company pays out as dividends.

Analysis of justified forward P/Es:

- The P/E ratio is inversely related to the required rate of return.
- The P/E ratio is positively related to the growth rate.
- The P/E ratio appears to be positively related to the dividend payout ratio. However, this relationship may not always hold because a higher dividend payout ratio implies that the company's earnings retention ratio is lower. A lower earnings retention ratio translates into a lower growth rate. This is known as the "dividend displacement" of earnings.

Justified forward P/E estimates are very sensitive to small changes in the assumptions used to compute them. Since the growth rate is calculated as ROE times the retention ratio, any changes in the dividend payout ratio also has an impact on the growth rate. Analysts usually carry out sensitivity analysis to study the impact of different assumptions on the justified ratio. See Example 3-1.

Example 3-1: Justified P/Es

Assume that a stock has an expected payout ratio of 40% and a required return on equity of 10%. With an expected growth rate of dividends of 8%, calculate the stock's justified P/E multiple.

Solution

$$\frac{P_0}{E_1} = \frac{D_1/E_1}{k_e - g_c} = \frac{0.40}{0.1 - 0.08} = 20$$

Multiples Based on Comparables

This method compares relative values estimated using multiples to determine whether an asset is undervalued, overvalued, or fairly valued. The benchmark multiple can be any of:

- A multiple of a closely matched individual stock.
- The average or median multiple of a peer group or the firm's industry.
- The average multiple derived from trend or time-series analysis.

Sometime analysts may face difficulties in finding a benchmark or "comparable" to evaluate a company's price multiple. For example, large companies have several different lines of business. Analysts should be careful to select only those companies that have similar size, product lines, and growth prospects to the company being valued as comparables.

LOS 50h: Calculate and interpret the following multiples: price to earnings, price to an estimate of operating cash flow, price to sales, and price to book value. Vol 5, p 263

Price to Earnings Ratio

Advantages

- Earnings are key drivers of stock value.
- The ratio is simple to calculate and widely used in the industry.
- According to empirical research, differences in P/E ratios are significantly related to long-term stock returns.

Disadvantages

- Companies that make losses have negative EPS and P/Es. Negative P/E ratios are useless as far as relative valuation is concerned.
- Earnings of some companies are very volatile, which makes the task of determining a fundamental stock value very challenging.
- Management can use different accounting assumptions to prepare their financial statements. This reduces the comparability of P/E ratios across companies.

Price to Cash Flow

See Example 3-2.

Advantages

- Cash flows are less prone to management manipulation than earnings.
- Price to cash flow is more stable than the P/E ratio.
- Using the price to cash flow ratio gets around the problem related to differences in accounting methods used by companies.
- Differences in price to cash flow ratio over time are related to differences in long term average returns on stocks.

Disadvantages

- When "EPS plus noncash charges" is used as the definition for cash flow, noncash revenue and changes in working capital items are ignored.
- Free cash flow is more appropriate for valuing a company than cash flow. However FCFE has the following drawbacks:
  - For many businesses, it is more volatile than CF.
  - It is more frequently negative than CF.

$$\text{Price to cash flow ratio} = \frac{\text{Market price of share}}{\text{Cash flow per share}}$$

Example 3-2: Calculating P/CF

ABC Company reported net income of $2.3 million for the year 2008. It recorded noncash charges of $0.4 million for the year, and has 2 million shares outstanding. The market price of the company's stock is currently $40. Compute its price to cash flow ratio.

Solution

Cash flow = $2,300,000 + $400,000 = $2,700,000
Cash flow per share = $2,700,000 / 2,000,000 = $1.35
Price to cash flow = $40 / $1.35 = 29.63

Price to Sales

Advantages

- Sales are less prone to manipulation by management than earnings and book values.
- Sales are positive even when EPS is negative.
- The P/S ratio is usually more stable than the P/E ratio.
- Price to sales is considered an appropriate measure for valuing mature, cyclical, and loss-making companies.
- Studies have shown that differences in price to sales ratios are related to differences in long-term average returns on stocks.

Disadvantages

- Using sales reveals no information about the operating profitability of a company. Ultimately, a company derives its value from its ability to generate profits.
- Using the P/S ratio does not reflect the differences in cost structure and operating efficiency between companies.
- Revenue recognition practices may allow management to distort revenue figures.

$$\text{Price to sales ratio} = \frac{\text{Market price per share}}{\text{Net sales per share}}$$

$$\text{Price to sales ratio} = \frac{\text{Market value of equity}}{\text{Total net sales}}$$

Net sales are calculated as gross sales less returns, customer discounts, and any dealer commissions. See Example 3-3.

Example 3-3: Calculating P/S

Krivya Chemicals reported net sales of $4,650,000 for the year ended 2008. It currently has 225,000 shares outstanding and its stock price is $14.35. Calculate Krivya's P/S ratio.

Solution

Sales per share = $4,650,000/225,000 = $20.67
Price to sales ratio = $14.35 / $20.67 − 0.69.

Price to Book Value

See Example 3-4.

Advantages

- Book value usually remains positive even when the company reports negative earnings.
- Book value is typically more stable over time compared to reported earnings.
- For financial sector companies that have significant holdings of liquid assets, P/BV is more meaningful, as book values reflect recent market values.
- P/BV is useful in valuing a company that is expected to go out of business.
- Studies suggest that differences in P/BV ratios over time are related to differences in long term average returns on stocks.

Disadvantages

- Book values ignore nonphysical assets such as the quality of a company's human capital and brand image.
- P/BV can lead to misleading valuations if significantly different levels of assets are being used by the companies being studied.
- Accounting differences can impair the comparability of P/BV ratios across companies. In most cases, book values of assets are based on historical cost adjusted for accumulated depreciation. However, over time, inflation and changes in technology may result in significant differences between accounting book values and actual values of a company's assets.

$$P/BV = \frac{\text{Current market price of share}}{\text{Book value per share}}$$

$$P/BV = \frac{\text{Market value of common shareholders' equity}}{\text{Book value of common shareholders' equity}}$$

where:

Book value of common shareholders' equity =

(Total assets − Total liabilities) − Preferred stock

Example 3-4: Calculating P/BV

The following table contains the equity portion of ADF Company's balance sheet:

	December 2006
Common stock (issued 20,000 common shares)	$200,000
Preferred stock (issued 1,000 preferred shares)	$25,000
Additional paid in capital	$1,000
Retained earnings	$43,875
Total shareholders' equity	$269,875

The current market price of ADF stock is $14.35. Calculate its P/BV ratio.

Solution

Common shareholders' equity = Total shareholders' equity − Total value of equity claims that are senior to common stock
= $269,875 − $25,000 = $244,875

Book value per share = $244,875/20,000 = $12.24

P/B = $14.35/$12.24 = $1.17

LOS 50i: Explain the use of enterprise value multiples in equity valuation and demonstrate the use of enterprise value multiples to estimate equity value. **Vol 5, pp 272–274**

Enterprise value (EV) is calculated as the market value of the company's common stock, plus the market value of outstanding preferred stock if any, plus the market value of debt, less cash and short term investments (cash equivalents). It can be thought of as the cost of taking over a company.

> EBITDA refers to earnings before interest, tax, depreciation, and amortization.

The most widely used EV multiple is the EV/EBITDA multiple. EBITDA is used as a proxy for operating cash flow, as it excludes noncash depreciation and amortization expenses. However, it may include other noncash expenses and revenues. The company pays out interest, dividends and taxes from its EBITDA. Therefore, EBITDA measures a company's income before payments to any providers of capital are made.

- The EV/EBITDA multiple is often used when comparing two companies with different capital structures.
- Loss-making companies usually have a positive EBITDA, which allows analysts to use the EV/EBITDA multiple to value them. The P/E ratio is meaningless (negative) for a loss-making company, as its earnings are negative.

Enterprise value may be difficult to calculate for companies whose debt is not publicly traded. Analysts may then use market prices of similar debt issues that are publicly traded as a proxy for the market value of the company's debt. Using book value as a proxy of market value will only provide a rough estimate, as book values do not incorporate changes in market interest rates and changes in the company's risk (as perceived by the market). See Example 3-5.

Example 3-5: EV/Operating Income

An analyst gathered the following information regarding five companies operating in the same industry:

Company	Enterprise Value ($)	Operating Income ($)
A	12,486,354	501,460
B	34,270,688	652,775
C	1,776,018	−306,210
D	6,688,225	210,985
E	3,206,250	427,500

1. Based on the information given, calculate each company's EV/OI.
2. Which company is the most undervalued?

Solution

1. The following table shows the EV/OI for each company:

Company	Enterprise Value ($)	Operating Income ($)	EV/OI
A	12,486,354	501,460	24.9
B	34,270,688	652,775	52.5
C	1,776,018	−306,210	−5.8
D	6,688,225	210,985	31.7
E	3,206,250	427,500	7.5

2. Company E has the lowest positive EV/OI ratio and therefore is the most undervalued or favorably priced stock. Note the negative EV/OI ratio of Company C. Negative EV/OI ratios are difficult to interpret and so the analyst must use some other means to evaluate such companies.

LOS 50j: Explain asset-based valuation models and demonstrate the use of asset-based models to calculate equity value. **Vol 5, pp 274-278**

Asset-based valuation uses market values of a company's assets and liabilities to determine the value of the company as a whole.

Asset-based valuation works well for:
- Companies that do not have a significant number of intangible or "off-the-book" assets, and have a higher proportion of current assets and liabilities.
- Private companies, especially if applied together with multiplier models.
- Financial companies, natural resource companies, and companies that are being liquidated.

Asset-based valuation may not be appropriate when:
- Market values of assets and liabilities cannot be easily determined.
- The company has a significant amount of intangible assets.
- Asset values are difficult to determine (e.g., n periods of very high inflation).
- Market values of assets and liabilities significantly differ from their carrying values.